LOSE IT *for* LIFE

DAY *by* DAY

SPIRITUAL MOTIVATION FOR
PERMANENT WEIGHT LOSS

LOSE IT *for* LIFE

DAY *by* DAY

Devotions for
Every Day of the Year

STEPHEN ARTERBURN, M.ED.
JANELLE PUFF
MISTY ARTERBURN

THOMAS NELSON
Since 1798

NASHVILLE   DALLAS   MEXICO CITY   RIO DE JANEIRO

Lose It For Life Day by Day

Published in Nashville, Tennessee by Thomas Nelson. Thomas Nelson is a registered trademark of Thomas Nelson, Inc.

Stephen Arterburn published in association with Alive Communications, 7680 Goddard Street, Suite 200, Colorado Springs, Colorado 80920.

Unless otherwise noted, Scripture quotations are taken from the Holy Bible, New International Version®. © 1973, 1978, 1984 by the International Bible Society. Used by permission of Zondervan. All rights reserved.

Scripture quotations designated MSG are taken from The Message by Eugene H. Peterson. © 1993, 1994, 1995, 1996, 2000, 2001, 2002. Used by permission of NavPress Publishing Group. All rights reserved.

Scripture quotations marked NASB are from the New American Standard Bible. © 1960, 1962, 1963, 1968, 1971, 1972, 1973, 1975, 1977 by the Lockman Foundation. Used by permission. All rights reserved.

Scripture quotations designated NLT are taken from The Holy Bible: New Living Translation. © 1986 by Tyndale House Publishers. Wheaton, Illinois, 60189. Used by permission. All rights reserved.

Scripture quotations designated TLB are taken from The Living Bible by Kenneth N. Taylor. © 1971. Tyndale House Publishers, Inc. Used by permission. All rights reserved.

Scripture quotations designated NKJV are taken from the Holy Bible, New King James Version. Thomas Nelson Publishers, Nashville, TN. © 1982. Used by permission. All rights reserved.

Scripture quotations designated AMP are taken from The Amplified Bible, Old Testament, © 1965, 1987 by the Zondervan Corporation and The Amplified Bible, New Testament, © 1958, 1987 by The Lockman Foundation. Used by permission. All rights reserved.

Scripture quotations designated KJV are taken from the Holy Bible, King James Version.

Cover design: Brand Navigation, LLC (Bill Chiaravalle, Terra Petersen); brandnavigation.com
Cover image: Steve Gardner, PixelWorks
Interior: Sharon Collins/Artichoke Design

ISBN 978-1-7852-9836-6

Printed in the United States of America
11 12 13 14 15 LSI 9 8 7 6 5 4 3 2 1

INTRODUCTION

To be a true "Loser For Life" does not mean losing weight, but losing our resistance to God's best for our life. We can begin to care for God's good creation in every part of us—spiritual, emotional, mental, and physical.

This devotional is designed to help you focus on spiritual solutions to physical problems that have emotional roots. The meditations have come from generations of people who have walked the road of surrender regarding food, health, and wholeness. Our prayer for you is that as you meditate on God's Word, His truths will penetrate your heart and heal you on all levels.

We are grateful for the courage of those who have shared their wisdom and resources and their insight and hope for new life.

May God richly bless the reading of His Word, and may you find freedom as He makes His message of hope known to you. He is with you!

The Authors

FOREWORD

For years I struggled with my weight, isolated and alone, with few tools other than the latest diet that was doomed to fail me. I was fat and ashamed and wanted to hide. I knew there had to be things within me that were driving me to eat—guilt, fear, and anger. But I didn't know how to get at those destructive emotions to resolve them. Food became my god because it controlled me and had so much influence over everything I experienced.

I don't want anyone to have to go through life the way I did. To that end, the Lose It For Life Institute was developed in 2002. Since then, we have witnessed hundreds of people make the choice to heal and keep off the weight for good. Now we are expanding the dream to equip fellow strugglers with tools that can not only help make the journey easier but also make it deeper, richer, and more authentic. This devotional has been specifically created to be one of those tools.

If you were to come to the Lose It For Life Institute, you would hear a lot about connection—how important it is, how we destroy it, and how we rebuild it. You would also hear talk of the soul and its longings that are never fulfilled by food.

This devotional has been written in a way that will help you discover what your soul really needs—that deeper connection with God and others. It is your tool for living a life no longer controlled by food. It is your pocket or purse companion to help nurture and inspire you. If you read it each day and focus your actions, thoughts, and prayers in the direction it points you, you will begin to reconcile some of

the unmet needs of your soul and find peace, fulfillment, and new insight.

My sincere thanks go to Misty Arterburn and Janelle
Puff, two fellow strugglers who have put their hearts
and souls into this devotional. They wrote this book
with you in mind and God in their hearts.

Steve Arterburn

JANUARY 1

Praise be to the God and Father of our Lord Jesus Christ! In his great mercy he has given us new birth into a living hope through the resurrection of Jesus Christ from the dead.

—1 PETER 1:3

Replacing Resolutions with Realism

In years past we've made many resolutions, plans, and new starts. We've bought the latest exercise equipment and joined the hottest exercise clubs. We were the first ones to catch on to the hippest fad diet or weight-loss program. We did carb counts before they were cool. But not anymore! This year, our resolution is to not make a new resolution! We've finally learned, through difficult experiences, that grand commitments to diets just don't work.

Through our program we are learning that we can start fresh any day, not just at the beginning of the year. We are learning to "lose it for life"—to make small, gradual changes that can be incorporated and continued throughout our lives. No longer do we hold stock in a big diet plan that makes sweeping promises; instead, we're relying on small but steady changes that add up to big results over time. Instead of all-inclusive resolutions, our commitment is focused on doing the next right thing for us, today. It's a plan that involves physical, emotional, and spiritual recovery, and this is simply yet another day on the path toward our ultimate goal. We can be encouraged by a resolve that seeks only to live the life God intended for us—one day at a time!

Today, Lord, I embrace the new year with commitment to my recovery plan, and I resolve to live the life You have for me, just for today.

JANUARY 2

There the angel of the Lord appeared to [Moses] in flames of fire from within a bush. Moses saw that though the bush was on fire it did not burn up. So Moses thought, 'I will go over and see this strange sight—why the bush does not burn up.' ...God called to him from within the bush, 'Moses! Moses!' And Moses said, 'Here I am.'...'I am sending you to Pharoah to bring my people the Israelites out of Egypt.' But Moses said to God, "Who am I, that I should go to Pharaoh and bring the Israelites out of Egypt?" And God said, "I will be with you."

—EXODUS 3:2-4,10-11

On Fire

When the Lord called to Moses out of the burning bush and declared His holy presence, Moses was commissioned with the call of a lifetime: Set the Israelites free from their slavery in Egypt!

Have you seen your "burning bush"? God is calling your name to come out of the desert and into a life of purpose and freedom. It's easy to hesitate, as Moses did, given the massive work ahead, the risks involved, and the vulnerability of coming out of obscurity. We are often comfortable in our little desert, existing in our routine life. But God called Moses on a deeper level. He spoke to his heart and soul.

That's what He is doing with us as we "lose it for life." He calls us into vibrant, passionate living that will touch and transform other lives. Just like Moses, the encounter with the burning bush turns our life from self-centeredness into dynamic self-lessness.

Today, Lord, I hear Your loving voice calling me out of my desert of self. Knowing You are with me, I can take steps toward a life of freedom.

"There's a young boy here with five barley loaves and two fish. But what good is that with this huge crowd?" . . . Jesus took the loaves, gave thanks to God, and passed them out to the people. Afterward he did the same with the fish. And they all ate until they were full. —JOHN 6:9-13

That's It?

Have you ever looked at a serving size and thought, *That's it? How could anyone fill up on this? This is nothing compared to my craving?* We may be so accustomed to eating without limits that we dismiss a smaller portion as insubstantial, considering only one way to fill our emptiness—with food. Lots of food.

The disciples had a similar problem as they spoke with Jesus. When they observed the multitudes of hungry people and the lack of available food, they dismissed the young boy with his small portion to share and asked Jesus the obvious question, "What are [these five loaves and two fish] among so many people?" In this great moment, imagine the twinkle in the eyes of Jesus, who already knew what He was planning to do.

The boy releases his food to Jesus to do with as He wills. And as it is given, Jesus is able to satisfy the crowd's immense hunger in a supernatural way. So, too, as we release our grip on our own portions, we can offer our food to Jesus, who is eager to fill us in a way we might never expect.

Today, Lord, may I eat servings that are healthy for my body and soul. As I offer You my food, may I participate in Your plan for how to fill my numerous cravings.

JANUARY 4

Just say a simple, "Yes, I will," or "No, I won't." Your word is enough. To strengthen your promise with a vow shows that something is wrong. —MATTHEW 5:37 NLT

No Need for Mind Games

When we are finally motivated to make changes in the way we live, we may be tempted to swear off our old habits and destructive patterns. In good faith, and energized with hope and impetus, we make declarations and promises—unrealistic vows for change that we truly intend to maintain forever. Quickly, however, the shock of our pledge overwhelms us, and we often give up before ever making the first step toward progress.

It is in this place of despair where Jesus' words can bring freedom. He encourages us to simplify. We can allow ourselves to make smaller, more manageable decisions throughout the course of one day. We can say no to what's unhealthy and yes to what is healthy—and follow through with it today. There is no need to muster up power for massive, life-changing vows that we will never keep. Rather than tackle the rest of life within a single moment, we can choose instead to tackle one small moment at a time. We have no need for mind games or radical promises when we simply allow our actions to flow from the life of truth to which we are called.

Today, Lord, I pray to live a simple life of truth.

JANUARY 5

More and more people are seeing this: they enter the mystery, abandoning themselves to God. Blessed are you who give yourselves over to God, turn your backs on the world's "sure thing," ignore what the world worships . . .

—PSALM 40:3B-4 MSG

Enter the Mystery

The process we are entering into may seem like just another weight-loss scheme to the outside world, another way to motivate people to lose weight. But we are actually turning our back on the world's "sure things." We are not being drawn into the newest fad diet plan; we are on the journey of losing it for life.

In this, we let go of what the world worships: oversized portions, trans fat-laden dishes, unstructured and unplanned eating, and all-you-can-eat buffets. Instead, we seek to worship God in even our food choices: accepting modest portions, choosing heart-healthy dishes, avoiding the sugar-coated enemies.

As others observe the spiritual and physical changes occurring in us, they enter into this miraculous mystery as well. For this is not just a food and exercise plan. It is the point at which we abandon ourselves to God in a deep and intimate way, right down to how, when, and what we eat. In doing so, we find the blessed, enriched, and abundant life we never dreamed possible.

Today, Lord, I abandon myself to You, entering into the mystery of recovery from this lifelong problem. I give myself over to You, worshiping Your majesty and grace.

"Do not lay a hand on the boy," he said. "Do not do anything to him. Now I know that you fear God, because you have not withheld from me your son, your only son." —GENESIS 22:12

Willing to Go to Any Lengths

This was quite a scene! Imagine Abraham holding the knife above his only, long-awaited son, Isaac, from whom the promise of a great nation was to come. Abraham had arrived at such a point of trust and obedience that he was willing to sacrifice that which he held most precious. We, also, must come to that place where we can lay down what we hold most dear, including certain foods and behaviors—putting everything on the altar.

God is looking for individuals who are willing to go to any lengths—to do whatever it takes—to honor Him. As God sees our obedient, surrendered hearts and actions, which display our complete trust, He provides His part—power to do what we could not do in times past. When our humility before God is apparent, His provision appears. We may not be able to eat whatever we want, but our obedience, shown in the willingness to refrain from overeating, brings us closer than ever to God.

Today, Lord, may I be willing to do whatever it takes to let go of extra food.

JANUARY 7

By faith Abraham, when called to go to a place he would later receive as his inheritance, obeyed and went, even though he did not know where he was going. —HEBREWS 11:8

Obey and Go

Just like Abraham, we have been called to leave our comfort zones and go to an unknown place. Living without the burden of extra weight and focus on food is an adventure most of us have only obtained in our imaginations. We may have been thin once or twice before, but maintaining that new shape has eluded us. Our obsession with food has always pulled us back to old eating habits, and the weight has returned.

Now, we are called to break free from on-the-diet/off-the-diet cycles that have left us with shame. Despite our past failures, we must envision the inheritance ahead. We must simply obey and go. We don't know what we will look like, how we will feel, what life will be like in "weightlessness"— when undefined by our weight. But by faith we must go. God is calling us out of life-as-we-know-it into a promised land where the "milk and honey" are spiritual food and rich relationships.

Today, Lord, may I envision the inheritance You have for me so that I take action, one more day, toward health and wellness.

*He has shown you, O man, what is good. And what does the
LORD require of you? To act justly and to love mercy and to
walk humbly with your God.* —MICAH 6:8

*True ambition is not what we thought it was. True ambition is
the deep desire to live usefully and walk humbly under the
grace of God.* —TWELVE STEPS AND TWELVE
TRADITIONS OF ALCOHOLICS ANONYMOUS

True Ambition

There are many markers of success in the Lose It
For Life program: physical weight loss; the admiration of others for our accomplishments; smaller,
more stylish clothing; a more active lifestyle; health
and wholeness. These can be motivators for following our program and food plan, but they are only
self-focused. They are benefits but not the goal.

By seeking spiritual markers for our program,
we learn that walking humbly with God means letting go of our will surrounding food, a little at a
time on a daily basis. We learn that when we are fair,
just, and merciful toward others, we experience fairness and mercy ourselves. As the qualities of
humility, mercy, and justice are developed in us, we
find that our life becomes useful to God's kingdom.
We find that we are living in a different realm with
a deep desire to please the Lord.

When this spiritual transformation occurs, we
receive results beyond mere weight loss. We gain
serenity over food and weight, and we develop a
deep desire to serve God and others instead of self.

*Today, Lord, I humbly seek to be useful to You by let-
ting go of my will over food. Help me to become more
useful in Your kingdom, every day.*

JANUARY 9

But we are not of those who shrink back and are destroyed,
but of those who believe and are saved. —HEBREWS 10:39

Nothing will ever be attempted if all possible objections must
first be overcome. —SAMUEL JOHNSON

Turning Objections into Actions

As we approach this task of losing weight for life, objections will inevitably attack our will to even try. All the failures of the past will march before our mind's eye, attempting to drain hope right from us. After trying so many other food plans, we may become overwhelmed with deciding on yet another food plan to follow. We may be daunted by our past resentments and painful memories. Who wants to deal with these roller coaster emotions? Who wants to go through this pain? Who wants to look at the past? How depressing!

But we must not shrink back in defeat! We must take action, even in the face of all our objections. We begin with the day we are facing. We don't have to wait for Monday, or after the holidays, or after the big event. We can begin *now*, which is all we have anyway. Despite all the objections, we can take courage to do what we can—just for *one* day. Repeated each day, with God's help, we find that we are able to do what we never before could do.

Today, Lord, I turn from my objections in order to take action (however small) for just one day.

JANUARY 10

"Behold, I send you out as sheep in the midst of wolves; so be shrewd as serpents and innocent as doves."

—MATTHEW 10:16 NASB

Being Nice

Many of us grew up with parents who emphasized being "nice." We learned that being nice was a way to fit in and be accepted. We may have even enjoyed the approval so much that we learned to act nice just to get people to like us.

The problem with being nice is that it can turn into people-pleasing, a practice that puts us at the mercy of others. As people-pleasers, we may find ourselves dissatisfied with who we are because our self-concept is based on whether others like us or not. If they don't, we try to be even nicer—to the point of squelching our opinions, feelings, and preferences. Who we really are is ultimately lost.

Jesus warned, and certainly modeled, that not everyone is going to like us. Our job is to own our feelings, thoughts, and desires—to deal with our own issues and concerns without the need for approval or permission from others. We do not do this harshly, but wisely, without harm to those around us.

There is power in just owning our part and sweeping our side of the street. Not only does God honor it, but by further establishing who we were meant to be, people respect us more as we're growing emotionally and spiritually.

Today, Lord, I pray to own my feelings, thoughts, and preferences. May I be wise enough to set limits and harmless enough to stay in relationship.

JANUARY 11

For everyone who asks receives; he who seeks finds; and to him who knocks, the door will be opened. —MATTHEW 7:8

Knock and the Door Will Open

Understanding that we have a problem with food is just the beginning. Having the faith to believe it is possible for us to overcome this problem is a tall hurdle indeed! In the past, defeat and failure to make lasting changes have led us into despair. But when we believe that a new life is possible, we knock on the door and ask for recovery. It takes willingness and belief to knock, request, and seek recovery. Yet that is all God needs to usher us through the door and into a fuller, richer life.

By God's grace we have a way out of the darkness, a road map to freedom and a better life. We can accept this gift with gratitude and do our part to stay on the path to physical, emotional, and spiritual health and wellness. We walk in the faith it takes to "lose it for life"!

Today, Lord, I am grateful for the opportunity to be on the journey of recovery from emotional eating and food obsessions.

JANUARY 12

Meanwhile his disciples urged him, "Rabbi, eat something."
But he said to them, "I have food to eat that you know nothing
about." Then his disciples said to each other, "Could someone
have brought him food?" "My food," said Jesus, "is to do the
will of him who sent me and to finish his work."

—JOHN 4:31-34

Fed by God

When struck with the kind of overwhelming
hunger that grabs all our attention, we may think
we'll simply die between meals. This unrealistic fear
puts us in danger of making a food choice that is
not in our plan or best interest. But there is a spiritual sustenance that will get us through this hunger
and fear.

We can ask God to "feed" us between meals.
Seeking the "bread" humans know nothing about is
the spiritual task. It means resting in the knowledge
that He is our true sustenance. It means resting in
faith that we will not die between meals; we are
merely uncomfortable. It means calming our spirit
by drawing closer to Him and humbly letting go of
our will when we're around food, even when others
urge us to eat. Like the disciples did to Jesus, those
around us may urge us to eat things that are not in
our plan, but we can remain steady and committed
by drawing on spiritual food.

Today, Lord, I ask You to feed me with Your presence
as I humbly let go of my hunger and fear between
meals.

*A man of many companions may come to ruin, but there is a
friend who sticks closer than a brother.* —PROVERBS 18:24

Closer Than a Brother

A teenager named Tommy had an autistic brother,
Jeremy. Jeremy had some annoying habits that
made him a target for bullies. It was embarrassing to
be related to Jeremy because others would pick on
him and then turn their comments on Tommy. Of
course, Jeremy couldn't understand that his own
behaviors had triggered the bullying.

One day Tommy overheard a boy planning to
jump Jeremy when they got off the bus. He couldn't
let this happen! Jeremy wouldn't know what to do,
nor would he understand. Tommy was determined
to stop it.

When Jeremy got off the bus, the bully followed, and Tommy followed the bully. As the bully
was just about to grab Jeremy, Tommy dove and
tackled the bully, pinning him to the ground.
Jeremy stood watching, not realizing he was in
danger. His brother told him to run home and not
to worry.

This is exactly what Jesus has done for us! We
don't understand it and will never truly comprehend it. But He tackled our enemies when our back
was turned the other way. He told us to run home
and not to worry. He said He would take care of
everything, and He has done and is doing just that.
When we need Jesus, He's there—closer than a
brother.

*Today, Lord, I thank You for loving me, even when I
am been unlovable. Thank You for taking care of me,
even when I don't know what's good for me.*

JANUARY 14

Cast your bread upon the waters, for after many days you will find it again. —ECCLESIASTES 11:1

The Truest Life

No, this verse is not urging us to jump on the low-carb bandwagon so we can pick up the bread again later!

Solomon, the writer of Ecclesiastes, encourages us to be generous—to let go of what we hold onto for life. The bread Solomon describes here is a symbol of what people of that time ate for survival. Yet he tells us to cast it into the water, making it inedible. But he also assures us that, even then, "life" will return to us.

We are in the process of letting go of the very thing that gives life—food, and specifically those foods which sabotage our vitality. In the past we have clung to junk food, fast food, and sweet and salty foods as if they were giving us life. Perhaps this made a pain-filled, emotionally starved existence bearable for us. But these foods will never bring us true life. Letting go of them and casting them back to the ocean of food choices, we are free to make healthy choices. Our very life can be found after many days.

Today, Lord, grant me the courage to cast away foods that have been holding me back from my truest life.

JANUARY 15

People were bringing little children to Jesus to have him touch them. . . . And he took the children in his arms, put his hands on them and blessed them. —MARK 10:13A, 16

Facing Childhood Wounds

Everyone has a painful childhood in some way—no one becomes an adult without some type of trauma. Childhood wounds often lead to compulsive behaviors, such as overeating, as a way to soothe the anxiety and anesthetize the pain. Growing up with this pattern and dysfunction over food in order to deal with feelings can lead to weight problems and, in turn, lessen our enjoyment and length of life.

Facing our childhood suffering can be frightening, but it can also be liberating. By asking Jesus for healing and blessing through the process, we find that we are not alone. We learn that all have suffered, so we can be more open and less ashamed about sharing our wounds. We find that others can relate to us, and it diminishes our loneliness.

Looking at memories of painful experiences and emotions with Jesus' supportive blessing, we are enabled to be less controlled by the cues to overeat. We become more present in life, able to enjoy God and His people more fully.

Today, Lord, may I face my painful childhood suffering with courage, find forgiveness, and put it to rest.

All a man's ways seem innocent to him, but motives are weighed by the LORD. Commit to the LORD whatever you do, and your plans will succeed. —PROVERBS 16:2-3

Commit Your Motives to God

We might be prompted to lose weight for our parents, our spouse, or our children. Perhaps we are motivated by wanting to impress someone of the opposite sex. We could be driven by several external circumstances: moving, going to school, summer beaches. But these reasons to lose weight never work for very long.

When we allow the Lord to weigh our motives, we might find that they are not "clean," or righteous, to Him. The only pure motive for losing weight and adopting a healthy lifestyle is for Him. But before we can actualize this, we must believe we are worth the effort—that God does care about us, right down to what and how we eat. When we commit everything to Him, our plans for weight loss and a vibrant, abundant life will be established.

Today, Lord, I let go of shortsighted motives for weight loss and commit my way to You, for Your glory.

JANUARY 17

On a Sabbath Jesus was teaching in one of the synagogues, and a woman was there who had been crippled by a spirit for eighteen years. She was bent over and could not straighten up at all.　　　　　—LUKE 13:10-11

Healing a Crippled Spirit

Imagine this woman's condition—the pain of being unable to live freely because of her twisted spine. Yet she was able to come to the synagogue on the Sabbath to worship God! Perhaps she had come for all those eighteen years. She probably wondered where God was in her suffering. And yet she still faithfully attended the synagogue for worship.

The conditions of obsessive control over food, compulsive eating, and being overweight are types of crippling spirits. We may have developed them from birth or acquired them in childhood from our family of origin. Regardless of where it originated, we have suffered for many years with our weight condition. It has cramped our full living experience and kept us from looking others straight in the eye. If our body has not been bent over, our spirit has been kept low, unable to stand tall from the weight of shame we've carried.

Following the example of this faithful woman, we can continue to bring ourselves to worship God, even in the midst of our suffering. Even when it seems it will take too long or that we have too much weight to lose before we'll see any difference, we can still worship God. As we do, we will be met by the Lord Himself.

Today, Lord, I worship Your wonderful name. I'm grateful for Your power and Your faithfulness to me.

JANUARY 18

When Jesus saw her, he called her over. "Woman, you're free!" He laid hands on her and suddenly she was standing straight and tall, giving glory to God. —LUKE 13:12-13 MSG

Miraculous Healing

Jesus sees us in our brokenness, unable to look up to His face from being so bent over. Yet He calls us to Himself, proclaiming our freedom! His touch is powerful, healing, strengthening. Miraculous! Glory to God!

As we faithfully come into the presence of the Lord, He is able to touch us and straighten us out. Standing tall, we can look Life in the eye and praise His name, for His wondrous works are evident in our life.

With food and weight problems, this is a one-day-at-a-time miracle. We present ourselves to Him for a new touch each day. Continually offering our brokenness to Jesus, we feel the power of His healing touch again and again. Recovery may not be as instantaneous as it was for the bent woman, but it is no less a strident example of His miraculous power to heal.

Today, I shout glory to Your name, Lord! Thank You for touching me anew.

Indignant because Jesus had healed on the Sabbath, the synagogue ruler said to the people, "There are six days for work. So come and be healed on those days, not on the Sabbath."

—LUKE 13:14

Letting Go of Legalism

This synagogue ruler was shocked and uncomfortable with Jesus' mercy to the afflicted woman. He was furious that the miracle occurred outside of the lawful six days for work. Jesus was not falling into the form he expected!

That we often attempt to control the Spirit of God seems to be human nature. When He doesn't fit into our prescribed mold or agenda, we become upset and begin telling Him what we feel needs to be done! Like the religious leader in this passage, it may be hard for us to recognize this within ourselves since we are trying so hard to be righteous. After all, how could we be wrong when we are so carefully following the rules and regulations of God and our food plan?

Being open to God's work in our life means being open to His love and His ways at a new level. We can allow ourselves grace for altering the specifics of today's food plan when it is warranted to do so. We can remain in view of the bigger picture, releasing control even in regard to our ideas about this program and the very freedom we are hoping to find. In this way we let go of rigidity; we let go of legalism—even as it pertains to our food.

Today, Lord, forgive me for trying to control Your work. I pray to be open to the freedom of Your Spirit.

But Jesus shot back, "You frauds! Each Sabbath every one of you regularly unties your cow or donkey from its stall, leads it out for water, and thinks nothing of it. So why isn't it all right for me to untie this daughter of Abraham and lead her from the stall where Satan has had her tied these eighteen years?"

—*LUKE 13:15-16* MSG

No More Excuses

Jesus was not acting within the prescribed form that the religious leaders wanted or expected. He goes right to the point, shaming them publicly for their lack of compassion and integrity: If we are able to have mercy on our beasts of burden and give them water on the Sabbath, then why refuse mercy to a child of God on the Sabbath?

The mercy and grace of God are quite surprising, especially when those qualities crowd in on our expectations of how we think He should behave. We may have to give up a cherished belief or practice if we want Jesus to be our Lord. If we have insisted that our food and weight problems are hopeless due to genetics, gender, food allergies, hormone imbalances, or age, then we have cut ourselves off from the power of God's healing grace. This is merely another form of attempting to control the Spirit of God.

Today, Lord, I confess the excuses I have used that have kept Your limitless power from being released in my life. I open myself to Your grace.

JANUARY 21

"Then should not this woman, a daughter of Abraham, whom Satan has kept bound for eighteen long years, be set free on the Sabbath day from what bound her?" When he said this, all his opponents were humiliated, but the people were delighted with all the wonderful things he was doing. —LUKE 13:16-17

Choose Freedom

Being set free from our bondage after so many long years is a miracle we must not miss! When the Lord has a decisive victory, opponents are silenced. There is a wonderful witness of His mercy, power, and grace.

After living with weight and food problems for many years, we are being set free from our bondage. By following our food plan and faithfully exercising, we become a witness of God's ability to do for us what we could not do for ourselves. Many will rejoice as we are transformed one day at a time. They will gain hope for God to work in their own lives.

As we choose freedom through surrender of our will toward food, we are then ready to allow God to do the rest!

Today, Lord, I choose freedom from bondage to food, weight, and diets, allowing You to transform me one day at a time.

JANUARY 22

I am the true vine, and my Father is the gardener. He cuts off every branch in me that bears no fruit, while every branch that does bear fruit he prunes so that it will be even more fruitful. You are already clean because of the word I have spoken to you.   —JOHN 15:1-3

A Process of Pruning

Our pruning began when we received the message of living free from overeating. We started to see greater results when we allowed God to prune those areas of our life that had the potential to bear sweeter fruit.

Yet there is another level of pruning that God wants to perform: The crop of resentments, hurts, and fears that has accumulated throughout our life must be cleared away. Its poisonous fruit will endanger the progress we make on the journey to wholeness and bearing fruit in the Spirit. How many times have we eaten over an old wound, a nurtured resentment, a harbored fear, or a shameful secret?

We must be willing to allow the Father's pruning. Inventories of our negative emotions, hurts, and secrets are great tools to begin the process. Clearing away the debris that litters our past and clutters the backyard of our heart frees us from the emotional weights that drag us into unhealthy patterns. Becoming fruitful in God's vineyard means allowing the deep pruning to take place that eventually produces a healthy harvest.

Today, Lord, as I let go of overeating, may I allow Your pruning to make me more fruitful.

Here is a simple, rule-of-thumb guide for behavior: Ask your-self what you want people to do for you, then grab the initiative and do it for them. Add up God's Law and Prophets and this is what you get. —MATTHEW 7:12 MSG

The Golden Rule of Self-Talk

Most of us know to treat others well—it's the golden rule. We get into trouble, however, when we treat others better than we do ourselves. We may say things to ourselves that we would never say aloud or to friends and family. We may even call ourselves names, cursing at our mistakes, holding onto shame and guilt over past events that showed our human-ness.

This negative self-talk is not allowing us to recover completely. We are talking ourselves into rationalizing extra portions of food, or too many desserts and sweets. We are punishing ourselves while trying to feel better emotionally, attempting to cover the negativity with food.

But we can lighten up on ourselves and instead be kind and gentle with our mistakes, allowing grace for our past. We can give ourselves the same allowances and understanding that we strive to offer to others.

Today, Lord, teach me to be gentle in my self-talk, and help me to be wise in my eating choices. I want to be graceful, gentle, and tolerant, with myself and with others.

I waited and waited and waited for GOD. At last he looked; finally he listened. He lifted me out of the ditch, pulled me from deep mud. He stood me up on a solid rock to make sure I wouldn't slip. —PSALM 40:1-2 MSG

Finding Your Balance

Remember when you were learning to ride a bike and your parents called out, "Find your balance!"? You had no idea what "balance" meant, but you knew you had to "find" it, and when you did, it would mean no more skinned knees! Maybe it took a few days of practice, but eventually you learned how to ride the bike. Balance was something that had to be developed with practice and experience.

This is very similar to recovering from food and weight issues. For most of us, learning to find balance and recovery is not easy, and it is not learned in a day. It may take a few tries. We sometimes fall and receive a scrape or bruise. You might say there is a balance—even an art—to it.

To take action even when it feels like we'll never "get it" requires practice and courage. But once we experience the sense of serenity, peace, and self-respect that comes with letting go of harmful eating habits, surrendering our will, and accepting the problem, we find a physical, emotional, and spiritual balance that we never knew existed.

Today, Lord, give me the courage to suffer the fall, the strength to get up again, and the tenacity to keep practicing recovery.

JANUARY 25

But the LORD said to Samuel, "Do not consider his appearance or his height, for I have rejected him. The LORD does not look at the things man looks at. Man looks at the outward appearance, but the LORD looks at the heart."   —1 SAMUEL 16:7

The True Definition of Beauty

It seems like the world rewards those who are thin, young, and beautiful. Our culture creates its own "in" crowd by defining beauty according to an unattainable standard. All others are marginalized and devalued.

Because we have a weight problem, we feel the scrutiny and the pressure to be thin as we attempt to fit into the world's definition of beauty. When we can't fit that mold, we have a tendency to give up, to hold a grudge, or to be resentful. We may have even said, "I'll just be fat. They can love me or leave me."

According to the Lord, outward appearance and height do not matter—but the quality of heart does. So why are we attempting this difficult journey? Good health, weight loss, and freedom from food obsession are surely secondary benefits. The true, richer goal is to develop a quality of heart that is deeper, more surrendered, and more completely His than ever! We can reject the world's definition of beauty and still moderate our consumption of food in pursuit of this good goal. We'll obtain a better outward appearance, but ultimately we obtain God's will for our body, mind, and heart.

Today, Lord, help me to let go of the world's definition of beauty, allowing You to live and work in my heart.

Look at the birds of the air; they do not sow or reap or store away in barns, and yet your heavenly Father feeds them. Are you not much more valuable than they? —MATTHEW 6:26

Eat Like a Bird

Jesus is urging us to live fully in the present and, like the birds, to leave all our worries to God. The birds do not sow, reap, or gather, yet they are fed and cared for by the Father. When we are willing to trust God's judgment regarding how and when we will be fed, we find His abundant provision; we are no longer controlled by food obsessions.

Living fully in the present means that although we make a plan each day for what we will eat, we can "let go" of food in our mind and tend to the next task at hand. We can "let go" of the constant obsessing and micromanaging over how much we can eat, how many calories we've had, and how much weight we must lose by a certain date.

When we make our plan and then surrender our choices to God, we are freed from obsession as well as compulsion. Like the birds, we can finally bask in the Father's present care of us.

Today, Father, You know what I need. Grant me the grace to live in the moment with You, eating healthfully and letting go of the micromanaging.

JANUARY 27

Light, space, zest—that's GOD! So, with him on my side I'm fearless, afraid of no one and nothing. . . . When besieged, I'm calm as a baby. When all hell breaks loose, I'm collected and cool.   —PSALM 27:1, 3 MSG

Calm and Cool

As we begin a plan of recovery from emotional eating, letting go of self-soothing with food, many new feelings arise. We begin to feel more than just anger, fear, and defeat. And circumstances can turn crazy, with all hell breaking loose around us.

Because we've eaten over feelings in the past, we may become distressed, certain we will be overwhelmed by the intensity of them and certain that they will never pass. Beware of this type of thinking! It can become an excuse to once again eat over our feelings just to take the edge off.

Instead, we can turn to the reality of God's presence: He is our light and our stronghold. We have nothing to fear from our feelings. When circumstances seem out of control, we can calm ourselves inside, becoming collected and cool because He will steady us and keep us on track.

Today, Lord, with You on my side, I am fearless about anything that comes my way. Even when everything seems out of control, I know it only appears that way. Help me to rest in You, calm and cool.

JANUARY 28

Celebrate God all day, every day. I mean, revel in him!

Celebration of Abundance

A grateful, celebrating heart will keep us from relapse! Celebrating God every day and reveling in Him keeps our spirits focused and light. We can enjoy our planned meals, the relationships around us, and our loving connection with God. There is no deprivation because we are filled with an awareness of the abundant grace of God.

We have the opportunity to live outside the prison of food and fat—to live free of the spiritual oppression this prison brings. We need only follow through on a plan of recovery: appropriate foods, adequate exercise, and spiritual devotion. Gratitude keeps us centered and humble, and there is no reason, then, to overeat.

Today, Lord, I celebrate You and Your grace toward me.

Jesus replied, "If anyone loves me, he will obey my teaching. My Father will love him, and we will come to him and make our home with him." —JOHN 14:23

The Abiding Place

What a beautiful picture of recovery, peace, and serenity! In love with the Lord, we keep His Word and follow His will, even when it comes to what we put in our mouth. In doing so, we are surrendered and display the spirit of humility that the Father loves. As the passage says, He comes to us and lives within our heart. He rests there and enjoys us, just as we enjoy His presence.

In this place of abiding, there is no compulsion; there is no struggle. We are no longer fighting to keep from overeating. We are calm and serene in our food choices and in following our plan. By staying in love with Jesus and keeping His Word, we can enjoy His presence. But even when we fall, He doesn't leave our side. The result of our devotion is serene recovery from compulsion and the accomplishment of our weight-loss goals.

Today, Lord, I seek to show my love for You by following Your will over food choices and portions. I rest and abide in Your presence.

JANUARY 30

I praise you because I am fearfully and wonderfully made . . .

—PSALM 139:14A

*Behold the duck. It does not cluck. A cluck it lacks. It quacks.
. . . Whenever it dines or sups, it bottoms ups.* — OGDEN NASH

Imperfect Uniqueness

Appreciating our uniqueness begins when we come to terms with those qualities, talents, and abilities which are *not* a part of us. If the duck would compare itself to a chicken, it would think it was lacking. And then it would miss the very component that makes it unique among fowl: the quack! In fact, every part of the duck—in terms of shape, size, feathers, and funny-looking webbed feet—contributes to its survival. If the duck spent time feeling disgruntled because of the "cluck it lacks," it would not perform its exact role in nature for which it was created.

We have spent precious hours in discontentment over what we think we lack. Focused on our imperfections, we have become unappreciative of the wonderful creation we are. This chronic discontentment has kept us from actualizing the life God intended for us. We can take time today to embrace the amazing love God has for us, along with the miracle of our uniqueness.

Today, Lord, I give You thanks, for "I am fearfully and wonderfully made"—even with all my seeming imperfections.

Thus says the LORD, "What injustice did your fathers find in Me, that they went far from Me and walked after emptiness and became empty?" —JEREMIAH 2:5 NASB

Walking Away from Emptiness

This rhetorical question from the Lord may strike remorse in our heart because we know there is no injustice in Him. Yet how is it that we have gone far from Him, walking after emptiness and finding ourselves empty? It is only explained by our human nature to want to make life work on our own.

Rugged individualism. Self-made men. A do-it-yourself mentality. Our culture values that kind of independence. It's no small wonder we approached adulthood with the attitude that we must not be vulnerable; we must not let anyone know we need anything. It's no wonder we learned to believe that food would always be there to comfort and soothe and to give us a type of companionship.

Only when we feel the extreme emptiness in our heart and soul do we begin to recognize that we have been walking *away* from God. We've relied upon food to anesthetize painful emotions, anxieties, fears, and resentments. Admitting this to Him is a first step toward freedom from this emptiness and toward the fullness of His healing love.

Today, Lord, I will take a step toward freedom by admitting that I have depended upon food more than I have depended upon You.

FEBRUARY 1

Watch out for the Esau syndrome: trading away God's lifelong gift in order to satisfy a short-term appetite. You well know how Esau later regretted that impulsive act and wanted God's blessing—but by then it was too late, tears or no tears.

—HEBREWS 12:16-17 MSG

Food Is Not the Answer

Esau was a short-term, concrete thinker. He was so focused on his present need and hunger that he was willing to sacrifice his future life and needs, unable to see the value of a lifelong gift because it was yet to be.

How many times have we done this with our dependence on food? We've reached for a bite in the moment, giving away our inheritance of a healthy, vital body in the future. We've impulsively consumed foods and quantities in the present that have significantly diminished our quality of life to come. We've put ourselves at risk of heart attack, stroke, diabetes, and joint replacements. The short-term fixes have overshadowed our long-term health and usefulness to God.

And afterward, we have all cried bitter tears, like Esau. Yet God's grace is abundant! We can start today, this afternoon, this evening! By focusing our eyes on the Lord and reaching out for help in times of temptation, we can be filled by Him and His people—even in our hungriest moments. Our future and hope is in Him.

Today, Lord, strengthen me in the intensely hungry moments when food looks like the answer. I entrust You with my future.

FEBRUARY 2

For momentary, light affliction is producing for us an eternal weight of glory far beyond all comparison, while we look not at the things which are seen, but at the things which are not seen; for the things which are seen are temporal, but the things which are not seen are eternal.

—2 CORINTHIANS 4:17-18 NASB

Eternal Weight

Our situation may seem chronic, arduous, and over-whelming right now—when we are constantly faced with food in restaurants, stores, and commercials. We may find it difficult to turn away consistently enough to make a difference in our weight. But someday we may see that this affliction was momentary and light!

When we meditate on this scripture, we can infuse our mind with an inspired image of this momentary, light affliction: It is producing an eternal weight of glory! Resting in this image of the present affliction as momentary and light, we raise our sights from the temporal to the eternal. Losing temporal weight, as hard as it seems to us right now, is producing eternal weight!

Let us be encouraged to look beyond the food we see and instead gaze upon things which are not seen—the extraordinary character developed in us by facing this affliction and our eternal relationship with God.

Today, Lord, may I gaze into Your face as You develop my character through this affliction.

The Serenity Prayer

God, grant me the serenity to accept the things I cannot change; the courage to change the things I can; and the wisdom to know the difference. Living one day at a time; enjoying one moment at a time; accepting hardship as the pathway to peace; taking, as He did, this sinful world as it is, not as I would have it; trusting that He will make all things right if I surrender to His will; that I may be reasonably happy in this life, and supremely happy with Him forever in the next.

—REINHOLD NEIBUHR

FEBRUARY 3

I am leaving you with a gift—peace of mind and heart.

"God, grant me the serenity..."

Serenity is a sign of recovery. It is the spiritual position of surrender and peace, marking our acceptance of reality. It represents our deep conviction of God's sovereignty and His boundless love for us. When we are serene, there is no more struggling to change our lives, limit our foods, lose weight, or be close to God. Rather, our hearts are at peace in the knowledge of God's presence in our lives.

When we do experience times of unease, however, we know we can always ask God to grant us peace. It is a gift that is given from Him who has all power. It is truly something that must be granted, something we could never achieve on our own. On our own, we could try to convince ourselves that we feel OK, but that sort of serenity is false and fleeting. In asking God for this gift instead of trying to create it ourselves, we acknowledge our surrender to His lordship, and thus to His will for our lives.

Today, Lord, wrap me in Your love and peace. Grant me nearness to You. Grant me serenity.

FEBRUARY 4

Where the Spirit of the Lord is, there is freedom.

" ...to accept the things
I cannot change ..."

Acceptance is a vital key to spiritual growth and recovery from compulsive eating. We must come to accept that for whatever reason—heredity, slow metabolism, body type, height—we cannot eat everything we want because of the weight consequences for us. It isn't easy, but in order to move forward, we must give up the excuses and face reality. No more saying, "It's not fair," or "Why me?"

There is freedom in accepting the reality of our condition today. Once we do, we can begin to attack the problem. We free ourselves to move on and say, "OK, now what am I going to do about it?" And in that acceptance, we can also begin seeking God's power rather than relying on our own. In this humble position, we can turn to Him for every answer.

Lord, may I accept the reality of my food and weight problems. May I live in reality and now seek for answers.

In the world you have tribulation, but take courage; I have overcome the world. —*JOHN 16.33B* NASB

"...the courage to change the things I can..."

Once we have acquired serenity and accepted reality, we can take action to change what's in our control. There are many things we have the power to improve with our food and weight management; yet because they go against our will, they have seemed impossible to us. Also, since improving our health and fitness can require massive life restructuring, we have often given up hope. We've succumbed to being overwhelmed with how difficult recovery might be. Yet it is in this defeated state where we find great hope in the words of Jesus. He tells us to take courage; He has overcome the world.

Jesus has declared His victory over every problem or situation we might face. Our food and weight issues are included in that. But it's up to us to confidently live in that reality, altering the things we can. We may not be able to change the fact that we struggle with food and weight, but we can change our behaviors involving food. We can take courage and adjust the variables of our eating and exercise for victory. These are the things we can change.

Today, Lord, may I take courage for action, knowing that You have overcome the world.

FEBRUARY 6

Who among you is wise and understanding? Let him show by his good behavior his deeds in the gentleness of wisdom.

—*JAMES 3:13* NASB

" ...and the wisdom to know the difference...."

Isn't it interesting that often we'd rather work to change everything and everyone around us instead of working to change ourselves? "If only I had a different job, a different boss, a different house, a different car . . . then I'd be happy." We convince ourselves that the solution to all our problems is based on yet another missing component. If such and such happened, then we'd eat better and lose weight!

In wisdom, however, we will first look at our own condition rather than at the conditions around us. We will realize that change is initiated from within, not without. We will also begin accepting the reality of that which is beyond our control. Wisdom brings a gentleness to our lives as we cease finger-pointing and blaming others for the choices we ourselves have made. By continuing to seek God, He grants us the wisdom we need for discernment in each new setting.

Today, Lord, please grant me wisdom for the challenges I face. May I stop blaming other people and things for my condition, and instead face up to reality.

FEBRUARY 7

So do not worry about tomorrow; for tomorrow will care for itself. Each day has enough trouble of its own.

—MATTHEW 6:34 NASB

"Living one day at a time ..."

Have you ever become so focused on what might happen in the future that you wasted time and energy that could have been used to get things done that day? When our eyes are continually on tomorrow's "what ifs," it's easy to end up feeling disheartened about what we didn't accomplish today. Focusing on one day at a time gives us the energy to take action on important things that bring recovery.

Granted, it's important to make plans for tomorrow, next week, or next year. But there is a difference between planning for tomorrow and living there, making so many plans in our heads that our focus remains in the future rather than the here and now.

To "lose it for life," we must focus on today and the tasks at hand while leaving the worries of what will happen tomorrow in God's hands. This includes our thoughts about food. When food is no longer the focal point of our lives, we have more energy and time to deal with today. And as we release tomorrow to God, we can enjoy today with peace, knowing He has given us everything we need to face the day.

Today, Lord, may I be focused on today, take action today, and leave tomorrow to You.

Be happy and rejoice and be glad-hearted continually; be unceasing in prayer; thank [God] in everything [no matter what the circumstances may be, be thankful and give thanks], for this is the will of God for you in Christ Jesus.

—1 THESSALONIANS 5:16-18 AMP

"...enjoying one moment at a time..."

We have been given a tremendous gift: recovery from compulsive eating. Compulsive eating has led us into dark places that have always before been a mystery. But now we can enjoy life! We can let go of concerns about our weight and appearance and just live today.

Having our flexible routine of recovery commitments (food plan, exercise plan, prayer, and buddy contact) allows us the freedom to let go each day and enjoy each moment. We can notice the sky, the flowers, the sunsets, the sunrises, the beauty of the earth, and the beauty of the people in our life. We can enjoy taking care of ourselves as we would a new friend. There is excitement in learning more, experiencing more, enjoying more.

Living in the gratitude of this recovery gift, we keep our spiritual condition refreshed and grounded, thus giving us the freedom to truly enjoy life.

Today, Lord, may I enjoy this day You've given me!

Consider it all joy, my brethren, when you encounter various trials, knowing that the testing of your faith produces endurance. And let endurance have its perfect result, so that you may be perfect and complete, lacking in nothing.

—JAMES 1: 2-4 NASB

"...accepting hardship as the pathway to peace..."

It's natural to want our lives to run smoothly—no disappointments, no heartaches, no rejections, and no hurt feelings. But that just isn't life! The verse doesn't say "if we encounter various trials," it says "when [we] encounter . . . trials"!

Both this scripture and the Serenity Prayer speak to accepting these trials and difficulties with joy—they are a means to becoming "perfect and complete." So accepting hardship is the "pathway to peace." The scripture even takes this one step further, saying that we are not only to accept hardship, but we are to "consider it all joy."

Our struggles with compulsive eating and weight problems may have made us very sensitive and easily hurt by the comments of others. Perhaps we have been teased mercilessly as children, shamed and ridiculed as adults. It is difficult to accept this type of hardship, let alone count it as "all joy."

But when we begin to have the "courage to change the things we can," we also start to accept the hardships. Neither acceptance nor joy means we have to like the hardships, but by accepting them we begin to grow in character and stamina, and that, in turn, leads us to peace.

Today, Lord, may I accept hardship as the pathway to peace.

When they got to the place called Skull Hill, they crucified him.
... Jesus prayed, "Father, forgive them; they don't know what
they're doing." —LUKE 23:33-34A MSG

"...taking, as He did, this sinful world as it is, not as I would have it ..."

For most people, Jesus' kind of humbleness is unfathomable. Here is God's Son, humiliated on a cross for something He didn't do. If we desire to be like Jesus, His simple yet profound prayer proves how essential complete humility is to a fulfilling spiritual life. Yet when we've resented people, situations, and institutions for their role in our current food struggles, "taking this sinful world as it is" is a huge attitude shift. For too long, we have turned to food to soothe our disappointment and anxiety.

To gain true serenity, we must accept what is happening outside of us, even when it is not as we would have it. Jesus' prayer testifies to this truth.

As we progress in Lose It For Life, we will learn the importance of surrendering our will and food to God. The same must be done regarding our will for the world and people around us. An attitude of forgiveness must replace the attitude of control and judgment. As we continue on this path, we find that the less resentment we hold, the fewer triggers to overeat we encounter.

Today, Lord, I trade in my resentment toward the outside world and replace it with Your ultimate humility. Help me surrender my will for those around me to You.

Trust in the LORD with all your heart, and do not lean on your own understanding. In all your ways acknowledge Him, and He will make your paths straight. —PROVERBS 3:5-6 NASB

"...trusting that He will make all things right if I surrender to His will..."

When we fully trust God we can surrender to His will, letting go of excess food and the need to control others. As we learn to do this each day, we begin to release control over many things in our lives. It is just another step toward the spiritual freedom of recovery from compulsive eating and weight issues.

Trust is the seed for surrender of excess food, our own will, and our life. Trusting God means surrendering to Him, even when we don't understand. Trust leads to surrender; surrender leads to humility; humility leads to greater peace.

Today, Lord, I will trust You with all things in my life.

Happy is the person who finds wisdom and gains under-standing. —*PROVERBS 3:13* NLT

Most folks are about as happy as they make up their minds to be. —*ABRAHAM LINCOLN*

"...that I may be reasonably happy in this life ..."

Our ability to be happy in this world is dependent on our ability to accept life as it is and to surrender to God's will for our life each day. The Serenity Prayer points to the value of giving up debate and criticism about how things are done at our church, our home, our job, and simply believing that God is at work in all our situations.

Our way is not necessarily God's way. If we are looking for what is wrong (in a person, organization, or ourselves), we'll find it! And then we'll become discouraged and disappointed. If we are recovering from compulsive eating and weight problems, this negative space is dangerous. In fact, it will kill our joy and make us vulnerable to slips and relapses.

Becoming "reasonably happy" is a choice! We must choose acceptance and surrender in order to clear our hearts and have a sense of happiness while we're living in this world.

Today, Lord, may I accept and surrender.

But we are citizens of heaven, where the Lord Jesus Christ lives. And we are eagerly waiting for him to return as our Savior. He will take these weak mortal bodies of ours and change them into glorious bodies like his own, using the same mighty power that he will use to conquer everything, everywhere. —PHILIPPIANS 3:20-21 NLT

"...and supremely happy with Him forever in the next [life]."

We are not losing our lives (and weight) for nothing! We have more to look forward to than just being healthy and trim; we are accepting life on God's terms and taking action to change the things we can because we are citizens of heaven. We have a future and a hope that is beyond this life, and we *can* have it all!

In the past, we may have thought that having great bodies would only happen in heaven. But now we have tools and skills and a new spiritual outlook that will help propel us toward our goals. Why wait for the Master to change our earthly bodies into heavenly ones when we can change our earthly bodies for our future on earth? We must humble ourselves and remember that we have been given the gift of eternal life, and in light of that good news, we are able to surrender our will to God in this life.

Today, Lord, help me to fearlessly surrender my will and lose my life to You.

FEBRUARY 14

A father to the fatherless, a defender of widows, is God in his holy dwelling. God sets the lonely in families, he leads forth the prisoners with singing; but the rebellious live in a sunscorched land. —PSALM 68:5-6

Our Loving Father

Many of us come from problematic families. Have you felt fatherless or motherless, with no emotional support from your natural parents? Have you tried to fill the painful void with food—either by overeating or undereating, or by sometimes controlling food and over-exercising?

Often we have run from the grief, thinking it will disappear if we don't look at it. We've used mindless activities and gadgets to distract us from the real pain. And we've found emotionally unavailable people who kept us in the same holding pattern of rejection we felt as a child. All of this has prevented true connections with people, thus making us vulnerable to emotional and compulsive eating.

But God is the Father to the orphan. He nurtures those who have had no substantial nurturing. He knows our losses and our grief from childhood and places us in new families of support. As we turn to these healthy relationships instead of food for our connection and comfort, He leads us out of the prison of food with joyful singing.

Today, Lord, I rest in Your loving arms and place all my pain and hurts in Your hands.

FEBRUARY 15

Submit therefore to God. Resist the devil and he will flee from you. Draw near to God and He will draw near to you.

—*JAMES 4:7-8* NASB

Food Thoughts

Obsession with food is the baffling nature of those with compulsive eating problems. Despite the relentless desire to lose weight, our thoughts may still be focused on food: how it smells, looks, tastes. By acting on these thoughts, we have allowed them to control us, hindering our efforts to reach a healthy body weight. Our feelings of failure may then pull us away from the people around us, and we are no closer to our goals.

In the midst of this demoralization, we must admit complete defeat over our own ability to control our eating habits, and "submit therefore to God." To resist and overcome the "evil" of food obsession, we need God's grace enfolded in the core of our life. We can phone a recovery buddy, go to a support meeting, talk to a counselor, listen to inspirational tapes and music, or read uplifting literature. Any time we reach outside of ourselves for true nourishment, we are submitting ourselves to God's will, opening ourselves to His grace, and resisting evil.

Today, Lord, I submit my food thoughts to You. May I reach out for grace today, resist evil, and draw closer to You.

But easy street is a dead-end street. Those who live there make their bellies their gods; belches are their praise; all they can think of is their appetites. But there's far more to life for us. We're citizens of high heaven! We're waiting the arrival of the Savior, the Master, Jesus Christ, who will transform our earthy bodies into glorious bodies like his own.

—PHILIPPIANS 3:19-21A MSG

Transforming Our Food Thoughts

Even with Christ in our hearts and a desire to live for God, there are still times when we are controlled by the powerful call of food. It's painful to admit we have bowed to our bellies and allowed appetite and obsessions over food to rule us. Despite our best efforts, we have felt ashamed of being part of this world and falling into its sinful traps.

The pain of it all has brought us to a new level of honesty and humility: We admit our powerlessness over unhealthy food thoughts and the compulsion to overeat. We now recognize that this is merely a part of our fallen nature as human beings.

Today, we can take hope in the fact that we are citizens of heaven. Food obsessions may be part of having an earthly body, but we have a choice over how long we'll allow them to control us. As we reach out for the grace of our Savior, our obsession is lifted. We do not have to overeat! Transformation occurs as we continually live by God's power and not the power of food. Day by day, we find there is more to life in store for us.

Today, Lord, I reach for You and not food. I need Your grace.

FEBRUARY 17

"Since I am telling you the truth, why don't you believe me?"

—JOHN 8:46B NLT

Liar, Liar, Pants On Fire

We may be good at asking for simple answers from God and from those around us, but often we are not good at receiving the truth. Crazy as it seems, we must consider the possibility that we have trained others to lie to us. How do we respond when receiving honest answers that we don't want to hear? Do we become defensive, making it unsafe for others to share truthfully? Do we resist what is said, writing it off as completely inaccurate, unwilling to consider any part of it?

It's not always easy to receive complete honesty from relatives and friends, but it is imperative that we at least listen and consider their thoughts. Openness is necessary for shedding light on our blindspots. We must ask ourselves, "Where is the truth in what this person is telling me?" Even if we can't accept the whole thing, we can strive to accept that it is this person's perception of the situation, and that does matter.

When we ask God for answers, however, there is no debate. He is always ready and willing to reveal His truths to us, and then we must ask, "Lord, how do You want me to apply what You're showing me?" This step involves the humility and willingness to listen to God and those around us for the sake of our recovery.

Today, Lord, I will listen to what others are telling me, even if I initially disagree. I will seek the truth in what they are saying. I ask for humility to heed what You are saying to me, too, directly and through others.

So put away all falsehood and "tell your neighbor the truth" because we belong to each other. —EPHESIANS 4:25 NLT

I Get By with a Little Help from My Friends

In the fellowship of recovery, we belong to one another, just as we do the entire body of Christ. We have a common bond through our shared challenges with food and weight problems, and in this we can find safety in sharing reality with one another. We are uncovering old wounds and mysteries from our childhood, and because we are in recovery together, we have no need for falsehood. Our commonality frees us to be authentic with each other and honest about all aspects of our lives.

Are you ready to be authentic? Are you willing to tell the truth? Are you willing to hear the truth? Dare to step into a world where truth opens the door to freedom.

Making ourselves so vulnerable involves risk and humility, but our success depends upon openly exchanging insight and truth. We find answers for today by reasoning things out together. We discover choices that we never knew were available to us. We build courage and laugh more.

Authentic fellowship opens up a new world of hope and possibility.

Today, Lord, may I walk in truth with the help of my friends.

FEBRUARY 19

Exercise daily in God—no spiritual flabbiness, please!
Workouts in the gymnasium are useful, but a disciplined life in
God is far more so, making you fit both today and forever.

—1 TIMOTHY 4:7-8 MSG

Exercise for Body and Spirit

Exercise is important for more reasons than just health of body. Thomas Jefferson said it also produces order for our life and a cheerful mind, making us "precious to our friends." It may also result in increased blessing to our children, spouse, or co-workers.

On the road to recovery from overeating and weight problems, we can heed this basic truth: Consuming fewer excessive junk foods, and combining them with exercise, can doubly expand our energy. Though it may feel like a chore initially, we find a healthier, more energetic and cheerful person inside as we apply ourselves in this area. This creates a greater capacity for us to be present in the meaningful relationships God has granted us.

Today, Lord, may I enjoy the blessing of my body through exercise, and may I offer blessing to my friends and family.

FEBRUARY 20

Expecting Too Much?

One of the triggers for compulsive and emotional eating is our expectation of perfection from others—or sometimes worse, from ourselves. When we forget that "all" have sinned, it becomes difficult to admit or recognize our own faults, or to show that we don't have it all together. We want to hide from others and place blame as a way of covering up our problems. This is when compulsive eating becomes a way of punishing ourselves, keeping us from feeling the freedom of Christ. We overeat as a way of expressing our self-hatred and belief that we're not measuring up to whatever standard we've held to or been taught for so long.

Now is the time to begin lowering our expectations to an acceptable, more appropriate level and allowing ourselves grace for today. Humans (including us) will always fall short of God's glory, so we must not punish ourselves with overeating, undereating, or bingeing. Yes, we must do our best to follow God's will, but we will always have failures and setbacks along the way. In recovery, we simply admit them, forgive ourselves for them, and add more grace (phone calls, reading, and fellowship) to keep us on track. All of this is building within us humility and character.

Today, Lord, I admit my imperfections to You and to others. I let go of the standard of perfection that has set me up to make poor choices.

FEBRUARY 21

Blessed is the man who perseveres under trial, because when he has stood the test, he will receive the crown of life that God has promised to those who love him. —JAMES 1:12

Avoiding Fast Results

In our "instant gratification" society, it's easy to expect fast results. Quick weight-loss schemes are on the cover of every magazine and late-night TV program. Unbelievable diet fads compete for popularity. If we become discouraged with our efforts to lose weight, we may be tempted to fall prey to one or more of them. We may even consider the myriad exercise machines that are promoted on infomercials. After all, they promise the fastest and most amazing muscles ever!

Yes, the message is out there: Lose weight *fast*. And we all want the pain and discomfort and shame of being overweight to end *fast*. But that's not God's plan.

By surrendering our will over food and eating more healthfully day by day, we will lose weight—but on God's timetable. It takes time to forge new habits, new ways of thinking, new ways of being, and new ways of connecting. Perseverance is necessary as God richly transforms our spiritual character—which is of utmost priority to Him—along with providing the benefits of weight loss, sanity, and serenity. We are making a shift from being "losers" to being "Losers For Life!" In doing so, we receive the "crown of life"—being able to live in richness with Him.

Today, Lord, may I persevere, letting go of the promise of quick results.

FEBRUARY 22

The conclusion, when all has been heard, is: fear God and keep His commandments, because this applies to every person. —ECCLESIASTES 12:13 NASB

Respecting God's Laws

Although at times fear can be very destructive, it also has the potential for motivating us to better ourselves. Looking ahead to the consequences of long-term overeating and weight gain, we may become afraid of what might happen to us if we fail to take action in recovery today. However, we don't want to be motivated by this type of fear alone.

There is a healthy fear—a fear of God—that is associated with respect, honor, and reverence of Him. Our motivation needs to spring from that place of honoring God's creation so deeply that we're compelled to respect our body, eating well and exercising adequately. In this position we reverence God's sovereign laws of the universe rather than pitying ourselves for having the wrong genetic makeup.

The laws of the universe are such that we must abide by them or suffer the consequences. Surrendering to them and believing that they apply, even to us, leads to the discovery of God's blessings on our efforts.

Today, Lord, may I be respectful of Your commandments, honor my body, and fear You.

There is no room in love for fear. Well-formed love banishes fear. Since fear is crippling, a fearful life—fear of death, fear of judgment—is one not yet fully formed in love.

—*1 JOHN 4:18* MSG

All of us are afraid sometimes, that's human. When our life is ruled by fear, that's addiction.

—*ANN WILSON SCHAEF*

No Room for Fear

Fear activates the dark side of our personality. When it takes hold, our emotions, behaviors, and attitudes are skewed: We relate less "person to person" and more "defense to defense"—each of us in protection mode, guarding ourselves, our image, perhaps our rights. Fear causes us to focus on what we may lose, or on what we may fail to attain when we think we deserve it. It is a type of self-based living that leads to unrest and frustration.

When we fear losing life as we want it, our own demands for satisfaction can put us in a continual state of dissatisfaction. Unmet demands drive us to excessive eating and unhealthy food choices.

Now we must move past this self-centered fear because we want to live free of the consequences of extra pounds. Turning our focus to the God of love, we let go of fear and grab on to faith, trusting that our needs and desires will be met as we do His will.

Today, Lord, may I focus on You and allow Your love to cast out my self-centered fear.

This resurrection life you received from God is not a timid, grave-tending life. It's adventurously expectant, greeting God with a childlike "What's next, Papa?" —ROMANS 8:15 MSG

From Fear to Gratitude

Fear can pop up to sabotage us even when we are losing weight and experiencing some physical success—fear of being noticed, of not being noticed, of being vulnerable if noticed; fear that we won't have a perfect body; fear of people expecting us to be more capable/responsible/active; fear of doing things that we've never done.

This is not the resurrection life God intends for us! We now must learn how to trust God as His child in all these new experiences of being thinner and healthier. This means allowing ourselves to be noticed and taking part in new activities, even when it's frightening. It means accepting our body as it is, not as we'd like it to be (like the magazine models).

Instead of receiving our excitement and pleasures from food, we learn to revel in being free from food obsessions and compulsions. We can develop humble gratitude for having infinitely more options for enjoying our time on earth.

Today, Lord, may I release the spirit of fear and live in humble gratitude for the changes in my body, mind, and heart.

When they had finished eating, Jesus said to Simon Peter,
"Simon son of John, do you truly love me more than these?"
"Yes, Lord," he said, "you know that I love you." Jesus said,
"Feed my lambs." —JOHN 21:15

Feed My Lambs

In this passage, Jesus reminds Peter he has greater purpose in the world than merely fishing to support himself. Jesus charges him with feeding His lambs and tending His sheep. It's a task Peter is to do out of his love for Jesus.

Jesus knows that fishing has been Peter's life and livelihood. For Peter, fishing is natural and even comforting to him. Yet there is a self-focus in it. Returning to life as a fisherman would keep Peter from moving into life with people, in community. "Feed my lambs," Jesus urges him.

There are people in this world who need us, and we need people. But we must let go of the familiar ways we turn to food and move out of our self-centered "fishing." Then we can be present to give and receive in connection, comfort, and community with others. In the process of turning to people, we begin to turn away from food as our safety.

Today, I will turn to You, Jesus, and then to people in order to turn away from destructive eating.

Don't become so well-adjusted to your culture that you fit into it without even thinking. Instead, fix your attention on God.

—ROMANS 12:2A MSG

The "More" Culture

The culture of "more" is all around us. Restaurants serve huge portions on oversized plates. We can "super-size" our fries and order "double the cheese" on our burgers. Buffets and family-style diners offering an overabundance of choices are given high ratings. This addiction to "more" is embedded in our culture of "more for the money." Most of us have adjusted to this so much that we are not even aware of its influence! But notice what happens when we attempt a food plan that offers simple, portion-controlled meals: Does it seem mundane and boring? Do you feel deprived?

The bottom line is this: Would you rather fit into the culture so well that you can't fit into your chair? The spiritual journey of recovery from the prison of food and weight requires that we operate in opposition to the culture of "more." We can learn to operate on "enough."

By fixing our attention on God, we can learn to enjoy simple foods that nourish and allow us to lose weight. "Enough" can be abundant when our attention is on spiritual sustenance.

Today, Lord, may I oppose the allure of "more" and simply remain content with enough.

Why spend money on what is not bread, and your labor on what does not satisfy? Listen, listen to me, and eat what is good, and your soul will delight in the richest of fare. Give ear and come to me; hear me, that your soul may live. I will make an everlasting covenant with you. —ISAIAH 55:2-3

Feasting on Fellowship

As compulsive and emotional overeaters, we have spent our time and money using food to deal with our feelings. We have thrilled our sweet tooth when we really needed the sweetness of love and connection with Christ and other people. We have even cocooned ourselves with high-fat foods when we really needed the protection and safety only God can offer. Sadly, we've never been satisfied because these are merely substitutes for real solutions!

But the Lord calls us to listen to Him. He wants us to eat what is good for us and delight ourselves in the abundance that He alone provides. This refers not only to actual, physical food (delighting ourselves in healthy meals and fresh produce) but also to God's spiritual provision.

Part of His provision for us includes a supportive fellowship that is able to meet our needs for love, connection, protection, and safety. There we find people who will listen when we're angry or afraid. We find arms that enfold us in times of despair or laughter. We learn to live fully, connected to God and His people.

Today, Lord, I admit I have spent my life seeking solace in food that does not satisfy. I turn to Your provision today to feast on perfect fellowship with You and Your people.

When a woman who had lived a sinful life in that town learned that Jesus was eating at the Pharisee's house, she brought an alabaster jar of perfume, and as she stood behind him at his feet weeping, she began to wet his feet with her tears. Then she wiped them with her hair, kissed them and poured perfume on them. . . . Jesus said to the woman, "Your faith has saved you; go in peace." —LUKE 7:37-38, 50

Total Brokenness

When was the last time you allowed yourself to be completely broken and humbled in worship?

The woman in this scripture wept over her sinful life—so much so that she soaked Jesus' feet with her tears. Wiping them with her hair was her way of showing complete surrender to His authority and majesty. The perfume she used to anoint His feet signified her reverence for the holiness of His lordship.

When we are at the end of our own resources to deal with our food addiction; when we have exhausted our lives with empty living; when our behaviors around food have become so shameful that we avoid people . . . then may we, too, come to Jesus in total brokenness.

Worshiping at His feet, we may shed tears of remorse and self-hate, yet we will find His loving acceptance for us and surely be moved to even greater devotion. The shame and guilt over what we have done to our body, mind, and spirit melt away at Jesus' feet. Our faith has saved us from this degradation. We can go in peace.

Today, Lord, I worship the beauty of Your holiness! Thank You for saving me daily.

MARCH 1

I'm running hard for the finish line. I'm giving it everything I've got. No sloppy living for me! I'm staying alert and in top condition.   —1 CORINTHIANS 9:26-27A MSG

The Finish Line

There is no finish line in our quest for better health. Embracing a lifelong process, performed daily with no arrival point, can be daunting. In our old life of dieting, we motivated ourselves into deprivation by focusing on the idea that it was only temporary; that when we reached our goal weight, we would be able to splurge again. We strove for that finish line—but it backfired on us. The deprivation dam broke when we allowed ourselves that splurge. And there we were, back to old eating habits and putting on pounds again.

In this verse Paul speaks about a finish line, but it's more like a rainbow—we run hard toward it, but we never fully arrive in this life. The rainbow is still out there ahead of us, so we learn to live well one day at a time. We let go of sloppy living by surrendering daily. We run this race with everything we've got—faithfully working our spiritual keys, diligently planning our food, energetically exercising our bodies. We stay alert and in top shape so that we feel enlivened, not beaten down by deprivation.

Today, Lord, I embrace this daily plan of living well, running the race with the willingness to stay in top condition.

MARCH 2

Then the king called in the man he had forgiven and said, "You evil servant! I forgave you that tremendous debt because you pleaded with me. Shouldn't you have mercy on your fellow servant, just as I had mercy on you?" Then the angry king sent the man to prison until he had paid every penny.

—MATTHEW 18:32-34 NLT

Weighted Down with Unforgiveness

Forgiveness is a vital component of spiritual progress. To truly recover from compulsive and addictive eating behaviors, we must forgive the many hurts and painful faults of the people in our lives. We may resist this and become defensive, not wanting to "let them off that easily"—much like the servant in this scripture.

A debtors' prison awaits not only the debtor himself, but also the one who does not forgive. The heaviness of resentment holds us back from the spiritual freedom and serenity we seek. This can also lead us to angrily consume foods that are not healthy. In this, we imprison ourselves with unforgiveness—eating up time that could be spent in positive endeavors instead of weighting ourselves down with extra pounds.

The only way out is for God to show us the way of mercy—remembering how much we have been forgiven by Him. Only then can we develop the humility to let go of resentment and forgive others.

Today, Father, I am awed by Your forgiveness toward me. May I have the same spirit of forgiveness for those who have hurt me.

But when the man left the king, he went to a fellow servant who owed him a few thousand dollars. He grabbed him by the throat and demanded instant payment. His fellow servant fell down before him and begged for a little more time. "Be patient and I will pay it," he pleaded. But his creditor wouldn't wait. He had the man arrested and jailed until the debt could be paid in full. —MATTHEW 18: 28-30 NLT

Consumed with Rage

When we experience relief from the constant pain of our compulsive and addictive eating and the pounds start to come off, we may have a reaction that is surprising to us. We may find ourselves consumed with rage! By not eating over our feelings in the present, memories from the past—which have been shoved down with food for years—may now begin to surface. Strong desire for vengeance and retribution may begin to grow within us. The intensity of these feelings then drives our craving toward the binge-evoking foods we know will soothe and calm our rage and humiliation.

This is when we need God's intervention; we cannot forgive by our own power. We need the Holy Spirit to infuse us. We must allow the waves of rage to release in tides of tears. Simply writing or journaling our feelings is one safe method of honesty, allowing us to be real before God's throne of grace. Then we can just wait upon His touch to free us from our debtors' prison of harbored resentments and unforgiveness.

Today, Father, I plead for a spirit of forgiveness to enfold me as I release all the rage and hurt of my past.

MARCH 4

If you forgive those who sin against you, your heavenly Father will forgive you. —MATTHEW 6:14 NLT

The forgiving state of mind is a magnetic power for attracting good. No good thing can be withheld from the forgiving state of mind. —CATHERINE PONDER

Releasing Moral Debt

On life's spiritual plane, having the quality of forgiveness in all our relationships, including with ourselves, is irresistible. Jesus teaches here that it is not in the asking to be forgiven that we are then forgiven. Our release from sin is found in the forgiveness we extend to those who have sinned against us. Forgiveness is a spiritual key that unlocks the door to a life of wonderful relationships, as well as freedom from self-hate and resentment.

As we paradoxically shift our focus from the rage and pain of being wronged, and move into a state of releasing the emotional and moral debt of our offender, we develop the humility necessary to forgive. We are opened to God's Spirit and grace at a deeper spiritual level than ever.

Once again, spiritual healing translates into physical and emotional health, relieving us from the unconscious triggers for compulsive eating.

Today, Lord, may I have grace to be in a forgiving state of mind, release the offenders in my life from their debts, and find Your forgiveness of my own sin.

MARCH 5

When an evil spirit comes out of a man, it goes through arid places seeking rest and does not find it. Then it says, "I will return to the house I left." When it arrives, it finds the house unoccupied, swept clean and put in order. Then it goes and takes with it seven other spirits more wicked than itself, and they go in and live there. And the final condition of that man is worse than the first. —MATTHEW 12:43-45A

Exorcising Evil Eating Patterns

There is an interesting parallel in this story for all of us who have dieted in the past. We exorcised our evil eating patterns in order to rigidly follow a diet. We may have even been successful at weight loss. But then, when we went off the diet, it seems that the evil bingeing spirit and all its buddies were unleashed upon us! Sooner or later we were struck with a compulsion to eat our way back up the scale, harming our bodies and shaming our souls once more. The end result was worse than when we started the diet! So, naturally, we concluded that dieting doesn't work, and we quit.

To "lose it for life," it's important to grasp the principle that "Nature abhors a vacuum." Recovery from the stronghold of food issues is not about a simple diet. It centers on putting a plan of recovery into place. In the absence of our comfort foods, it is imperative that we fill the void with new methods of feeling and dealing with our emotions. We must go deeper in our spiritual walk with God. In doing so, we are safeguarded from further evil returning to fill the places unoccupied with food.

Today, Lord, may I go deeper in my walk with You. Protect me from the evil one who seeks to destroy my progress.

Don't fret or worry. Instead of worrying, pray. Let petitions and praises shape your worries into prayers, letting God know your concerns. Before you know it, a sense of God's wholeness, everything coming together for good, will come and settle you down. It's wonderful what happens when Christ displaces worry at the center of your life.

—PHILIPPIANS 4:6-7 MSG

Shape Worries into Prayers

Aware of our tendency toward anxious, emotional eating, we must instead transform our worries into prayers. By turning to God with our fears and emotions, we let Him know our heart. It is then that He brings everything together for us. Our faith in His loving attention and protection is renewed. We are now able to settle down because we know Who is in control.

Our anxieties and worries are usually about things over which we want control but can't have it. Worries can be touched off by the fear that we will lose something we have—or that we won't get something we want. In the past, we have either eaten too much or avoided eating because it was something we felt we could control.

But fretting, worrying, and over/undereating do not accomplish much more than sheer harm to our overall wellness. When prayer and praise replace these behaviors and Christ is at center stage, a wonderful sense of peace and serenity flows.

Today, Lord, I turn over my worries and concerns to You, praising You for Your love and grace for my recovery.

MARCH 7

MARCH 7

A friend loves at all times, and a brother is born for adversity.

—*PROVERBS 17:17*

My best friend is the one who brings out the best in me.

—*HENRY FORD*

True Friend

Having food and weight problems is a good indicator that our relationship with food has gone beyond its intended purpose. We have turned to food as we would a friend—for comfort, soothing, recreation, and need. We have attempted to fill the empty space in our hearts by filling our bodies with food. By planning our binges, we have given more time and attention to food than to relationships. Even our relationship with God has not been tended to like our relationship with food.

But this friend turned on us! Food didn't enrich our life; it robbed us of it. It soothed us in the moment but later brought shame. It delighted us one moment but brought degradation in the next. This is not a friend that loves at all times, like the proverb describes.

When we transform our relationship with food to its proper place—nourishment—we can enjoy healthy foods and well-prepared, palatable meals. But we must remember that God is the one True Friend who brings out the best in us and loves us at all times. This is the relationship that soothes, comforts, and fills us.

Today, Lord, may I turn from my love-relationship with food in order to share true friendship with You.

For this reason I say to you, do not be anxious for your life, as to what you shall eat, or what you shall drink; nor for your body, as to what you shall put on. Is not life more than food, and the body than clothing? —MATTHEW 6:25 NASB

God Even Cares About Food

Sometimes it is difficult to believe that God would be interested in our struggles with food and weight. Isn't He more concerned with spiritual matters? Yet though our physical and emotional hunger receive much of our attention, we may be missing that these cravings often begin, and end, at the spiritual level.

When we become anxious about food, allowing thoughts of it to dominate our mind, then our trust in God is eclipsed. Think of how we have turned to food for comfort when we've been upset. Or the times we've hoarded food in the pantry in order to feel safe instead of trusting God for our needs. When food controls our lives, we allow our minds and hearts to be held captive to a substance that cannot meet our true needs. As a result, we are then burdened with the shame and loneliness of being overweight, and we are not present to enjoy life and people.

We've already missed out on real life for too long! Jesus calls us to see our lives as more than food. God does care about this area of struggle for us, and now is the time for us to take Him at His word, releasing ourselves from anxiety with food, detaching from its hold on us. Now is the time for us to really live in peace at all levels.

Today, Lord, I release my anxious food thoughts and focus myself on You.

"My people have exchanged their Glory for worthless idols."

—JEREMIAH 2:11B

Exchanging Our Idol

We have exchanged our glory for a worthless idol: food. In the past we've prized it, made time for it, prepared it, planned for it, looked forward to it, watched TV shows about it, and even driven in horrible conditions just to fill a hankering! Even when we were not actually eating food, we were thinking about it and romanticizing it. It became a god to which we gave too much of our lives.

When we get a glimpse of how we have replaced our divinely given glory with this worthless idol, we may feel a deep sense of shame over it. This only immobilizes us instead of motivating us. But we can make the exchange in reverse! We can let go of this worthless god by grabbing onto the glorious God of the universe, who sent His Son to rescue us from giving our lives to nothingness. Jesus has already made the greatest exchange of all time for our souls. Now we can exchange our food idol to truly live our lives for Him.

Today, Lord, I admit to You that I have spent too much of my life worshiping the idol of food. One moment at a time, I exchange it to spend more of my life with You.

MARCH 10

*When I was a child, I talked like a child, I thought like a child,
I reasoned like a child. When I became a man, I put childish
ways behind me.*   —1 CORINTHIANS 13:11

God Is Growing Us Up

God is growing us up! We are learning that it's not
the outside of us that must change but our inner
attitude. We are learning that our old childish
stance toward life—blaming people, situations, or
circumstances for our overeating—will not work if
we are to have lasting results physically.

It's not the world that must change in order for
us to eat healthfully. In taking care of ourselves
emotionally, spiritually, and physically, we're gaining
maturity for our food decisions, regardless of our
circumstances! We are then clear-headed enough to
handle whatever life situations arise.

This is another level of surrender and acceptance: Instead of forcing conditions to suit our will,
we learn to let God handle the conditions and then
conform our will to His. We are entering a deeper
level of spiritual maturity that displays responsibility and self-respect, as well as humility, before
God.

*Today, Lord, I thank You for growing me up and
teaching me to follow my plan of healthy eating, no
matter what the circumstances.*

Since, then, we do not have the excuse of ignorance, every-thing—and I do mean everything—connected with that old way of life has to go. It's rotten through and through. Get rid of it! And then take on an entirely new way of life—a God-fashioned life, a life renewed from the inside and working itself into your conduct as God accurately reproduces his character in you. —EPHESIANS 4:22-24 MSG

A New Way of Life, Fashioned by God

Everything about our old way of life has to go! To be "losers for life," we must change how we think, behave, and feel about food. We've been imprisoned too long in a rotten way to live, using food to reward ourselves, entertain us, fill time, cure anger, soothe loneliness, and calm anxiety.

We are now taking on an entirely new way of life, fashioned by God. He is renewing us from the inside out! By our surrender of old eating patterns, we find that food begins to take its proper place in our lives. It is now something that is nourishing, pleasing, and enjoyable, yet not relied upon for more than it can deliver. We find that we can now be present to experience our feelings, not run from them. We find that we are living free and enjoying life, even during painful times, because now we allow God to provide for our needs. He is the One who truly can do it!

Today, Lord, I disconnect from my old way of life around food and allow You to fashion a new life of recovery in me.

So Jacob was left alone, and a man wrestled with him till day-break. When the man saw that he could not overpower him, he touched the socket of Jacob's hip so that his hip was wrenched....Then the man said, "Let me go, for it is daybreak." But Jacob replied, "I will not let you go unless you bless me." The man asked him, "What is your name?" "Jacob," he answered. Then the man said, "Your name will no longer be Jacob, but Israel, because you have struggled with God and with men and have overcome." —GENESIS 32:24-28

Meeting God in the Struggle

We may think we are wrestling with food obsessions, weight issues, resentments, and hurts, but we are actually wrestling with the very essence of God! In this struggle we learn much about who God is, who we are, and what we are—and aren't—capable of. And as we overcome, we are transformed forever.

Jacob knew God already, but in the struggle he met God on a new, deeper level. His name was changed to mark the significance of this struggle. Jacob's hip was forever maimed also, altering the way he walked, which symbolized his changed life.

In dealing with food and weight issues, we once struggled against God in taking on this task to begin with; now we struggle with God in the midst of our pain and troubles around it. But there is a blessing here. We are now knowing God on a more intimate level, unlike before. We can face our past, our present, and even move forward in an uncertain future with courage and the sure hope that we'll be touched by Him.

Today, Lord, I am holding on to You in the midst of this struggle, asking for the blessing.

*In the distance, Jacob saw Esau coming with his four hundred
men. . . . Then Jacob went on ahead. As he approached his
brother, he bowed low seven times before him. Then Esau ran
to meet him and embraced him affectionately and kissed him.
. . . "And what were all the flocks and herds I met as I came?"
Esau asked. Jacob replied, "They are gifts, my lord, to ensure
your goodwill." "Brother, I have plenty," Esau answered. "Keep
what you have." "No, please accept them," Jacob said, "for
what a relief it is to see your friendly smile. It is like seeing the
smile of God!"* —GENESIS 33:1, 3-4, 8-10 NLT

Facing the Past, Making Amends

Jacob the trickster had been terrified to meet his
brother again. He was so frightened at what revenge
Esau might take that he sent gifts ahead to soften
his brother's heart. But over time, both men's hearts
were changed and prospered by God. Esau was as
full of forgiveness as Jacob was of repentance.

After wrestling with God and being touched in
a transforming moment, Jacob was ready to meet
his brother with humility and gifts of restitution.
The encouragement for those who struggle with
food and weight issues is in the spiritual character
gained. As we are touched and transformed by God
in the midst of our struggle, we are prepared to face
our past mistakes and begin healing. We find
humility and courage to make amends for wrongs
we have committed. We also have courage to face
another day—with all its anxieties, pain, and problems—with character and integrity.

*Today, Lord, I thank You for giving me Your strength
and encouragement to face my past and present with
a clear conscience.*

MARCH 14

You shall love the LORD your God with all your heart, and with all your soul, and with all your mind. —MATTHEW 22:37 NASB

Heart-Healthy Choices

We can choose to have wonderful heart-healthy foods today! We can enjoy the beauty of God's provision of nutritious vegetables, fruits, and meats that can support the physical health of our heart. We can revel in the awesome creation of foods that will nourish the first gift we received from God: our body and beating heart. In loving our body, we are loving God and thanking Him for His gifts.

As we do this, we are choosing to feed our spiritual "heart" as well, by surrendering to the will of God in our food choices. Our heart is content as we rest in His provision of nutrients and the spiritual sustenance of His Word. Without the interference of unhealthy food thoughts and compulsive eating behaviors, we are enabled to hear His voice with more clarity, acceptance, and joy.

Today, Lord, I will "lose" my life to You by choosing heart-healthy foods.

When I consider your heavens, the work of your fingers, the moon and the stars, which you have set in place, what is man that you are mindful of him, the son of man that you care for him? You made him a little lower than the heavenly beings and crowned him with glory and honor. —PSALM 8:3-5

When We Consider His Heavens

Do you feel dwarfed when you consider the expanse of the heavens, moon, and stars? Or when you watch a beautiful sunset? Or gaze out over the ocean and all its depths? To consider the vastness of creation gives us a glimpse of the majesty and power of the Creator! And like the psalmist, we often wonder, "Lord, how could You care about me and be so gracious as to keep me in Your thoughts?"

Yet God does care! And He has honored us by making us a little lower than the angels—to enjoy creation with Him. And we sense His loving care even more as we open our lives to Him, freeing ourselves from disabling food obsessions. As we let go of how weight has affected our lives, we experience a new realm, crowned with glory and honor.

Today, Lord, when I consider Your vast creation in the heavens, I marvel that You are concerned about me. I humbly accept Your work in my life as I live free of unhealthy food and weight obsessions.

Just then a woman who had hemorrhaged for twelve years slipped in from behind and lightly touched his robe. She was thinking to herself, "If I can just put a finger on his robe, I'll get well." Jesus turned—caught her at it. Then he reassured her: "Courage, daughter. You took a risk of faith, and now you're well." The woman was well from then on.

—MATTHEW 9:20-22 MSG

Hesitant yet Hopeful

As we begin our recovery process, we might feel like the timid woman in this scripture: barely believing that we are worth healing. She slipped through the crowd to touch Jesus' robe—lightly. Even that feeble yet faith-filled reach was felt by Jesus. He sensed her faith, her desperation—probably more than her actual touch—and He turned to see who it was. His reassuring words, "Courage, daughter... Now you're well," rang out and filled her soul.

Just like this woman, we have been drained of life for many years by our condition. We have felt depleted and hopeless, going to many doctors, trying everything we knew to get well. Now we have a glimmer of hope.

God senses our feeble, half-fearing/half-faithed attempt to reach for His power in our struggle with weight and food. Even our hesitant but hopeful stretch brings us face to face with God Himself. He is loving us and asking us what we need from Him to be healed. He then reassures us, encourages us, and heals us!

Today, Lord, may I have the faith to stretch out my hand for You.

MARCH 17

"These words I speak to you are not incidental additions to your life, homeowner improvements to your standard of living. They are foundational words, words to build a life on. If you work these words into your life, you are like a smart carpenter who built his house on solid rock." —MATTHEW 7:24 MSG

Moving to a New Foundation

If you've ever seen a house moved from its foundation, then you know it is a time-consuming and complicated procedure. First, all utilities (electrical, gas, sewage, and water lines) that connected the house to the earth must be detached. Then holes must be knocked into the foundation of the house in order to release the frame. Steel beams are placed through the foundation to lift the house, and wheels are added to roll it to its new location. The process is a messy and difficult struggle, but the owner perseveres because of the promise of a new location on a new foundation.

Recovery from food and weight problems is the same messy process as moving a house. We are letting go of our ties to a past that kept us down, mired in shame, demoralized, and stuck on a poor foundation. But the Lord is better than any crew of house movers! He provides our new foundation—if we will endure the struggle of getting free from the old one! When we are willing to go to any length for a new life of freedom, we are then set on a new foundation in a whole new neighborhood!

Today, Lord, I release my ties to the old life of food obsession and unhealthy choices in order to move to a new foundation built by You.

Humble yourselves in the presence of the Lord, and He will exalt you. —JAMES 4:10 NASB

Humility Not Humiliation

This verse commands us to "humble" ourselves— it's a verb that requires action! Even taking the smallest recovery step today is a way to do this. Choosing to limit our portions is an act of humility that brings us closer to God's will and presence. When we are hit with food obsession or are romanticizing food in our minds, the humble action of calling a support person breaks that negative power. Humility is required of us if we are to admit to another person that our craving is so severe we feel ready to abandon our goals and God's will just to eat!

As we make these choices continually, aspiring to move closer to God and His will, wholeness and serenity take hold in our minds and hearts. The compulsion to overeat is lifted. Rather than humiliation, in our humility God exalts us with weight loss, good health, and spiritual vitality.

Today, Lord, I humble myself by taking positive action to let go of unhealthy food obsession.

*You must clothe yourselves with tenderhearted mercy, kind-
ness, humility, gentleness, and patience.*

—COLOSSIANS 3:12

*Humility is perpetual quietness of heart. It is to have no
trouble. It is never to be fretted or vexed, irritable or sore; to
wonder at nothing that is done to me, to feel nothing done
against me. It is to be at rest when nobody praises me, and
when I am blamed or despised, it is to have a blessed home
in myself where I can go in and shut the door and pray to my
Father in secret and be at peace, as in a deep sea of calmness,
when all around and about is seeming trouble.*

—ANDREW MURRAY

Essential Humility

This meditation by Andrew Murray was found in
the office of Dr. Bob, one of the founders of
Alcoholics Anonymous. It is a summation of the
spiritual quality of humility that has proven to be
essential for an alcoholic's recovery. The premise is
that if an alcoholic is to live without his or her
obsession with alcohol and all its destructive consequences, he or she has to seek humility before God.

Our food addiction is no less obsessive and
destructive than alcoholism. And we need just as
much humility in order to recover. We need
humility in order to be teachable and able to let go
of our old ideas about ourselves, about God, and
about eating. When we kneel before our Father in
secret, we are then at peace about what we will eat
and how much we weigh.

*Today, Lord, I kneel before You to surrender all my
troubles and worries and to reach for humility.*

Jesus declared, "I am the bread of life. He who comes to me will never go hungry." —JOHN 6:35A

Hungry, I come to You, for I know You satisfy. . . . Broken, I run to You. . . . I know Your touch restores my life.
—KATHRYN SCOTT "HUNGRY" © 1999 VINEYARD SONGS (UK/EIRE)

Hungry

What a beautiful lyric of surrender and acceptance! We come to Jesus hungry, desiring more than mere food. What we need is His love to fill us, enfold us, and hold us when we're empty. Yet we must wait for Him—humbly, patiently, and surrendered to living on His terms.

Realizing our brokenness, our inability to continue our commitments on our own power, we must run to Him. We may become weary of our healthier food plan, but Jesus' touch restores our determination. In waiting for Him, we offer all of our lives, surrendering once again. Our will aligns with His, and we can live a new life, free of the food and weight obsessions.

Today, Lord, I wait for You. I am hungry for You. You are all this heart is living for.

*A good man leaves an inheritance for his children's children,
but a sinner's wealth is stored up for the righteous.*

—PROVERBS 13:22

Our Inheritance

What inheritance has your family left you regarding
attitudes about food and eating? We who are emotional eaters learned at an early age to regard food as
the salve, the balm, the bandage for feelings. Some
inherited messages were subtler, while others were
more blatant. Messages were conveyed not only in
words but in how meals, desserts, and snacks were
prepared and reverenced.

Now we must face these inherited messages and
how they have contributed to our difficulty with
weight. To learn to move past them, we can look at
how important food was in our family of origin.
Then we can evaluate those messages and values for
their validity and effectiveness. If food was used as
entertainment, does it really give us joy? If food was
a salve, does it really have healing properties? If food
was used as a pain, anxiety, or depression medica-
tion, does it really work for us in the long-term?

Our families did the best they could with the
knowledge they had at the time, and they only
passed on to us what they had inherited about food
and life from their own families. We can now accept
this and take responsibility for how it has affected
us. Then we can define our own values and make
life-enhancing changes that work for us.

*Today, Lord, as I look at my inherited messages about
food, may I have the courage to accept responsibility
for changing them into healthy ones.*

As iron sharpens iron, so one man sharpens another.

—*PROVERBS 27:17*

Solid and Sharp

People were not meant to deal with life alone. Likewise, God did not intend for us to find our way out of compulsive, emotional eating by ourselves. We need the interaction and fellowship of others to sharpen us into more useful tools for God. But we can only do this if we think of ourselves as equal to others. Remember, iron doesn't sharpen Swiss cheese! Iron sharpens iron!

We must be our true selves—the God-creation that does not see ourselves as less than, or better than, another person. When we are fearlessly and honestly ourselves, we are iron. We have a solidity that we can offer to others who are on the journey with us. When we are centered and grounded in the Lord, we are not arrogant or self-deprecating. We are able to reach out for help from others, and we are able to give help as well.

Today, Lord, I pray to be fearlessly myself and grounded in Your truth so that I may be useful like iron for others. Give me the strength to help others and the humility to accept help in return.

Who are you to judge someone else's servant? To his own master he stands or falls. And he will stand, for the Lord is able to make him stand. —ROMANS 14:4

Supporters, Not Judges

There is a fine line between helping others to follow the Lord's path and trying to control or push them into the way we believe is right. We may be tempted to tell everyone about our food plan because it works for us, and it seems like we should share it. But it may not work for everyone. They need to consult with their own doctor or nutritionist, who can guide them for the health of their bodies.

As godly supporters and encouragers for those on a like journey, we are not to evaluate whether they are "doing it right," or look down on them for making too many mistakes, or give them unsolicited advice. We can share our experience with what works for us and the success we have found when we take certain actions. This communicates hope to others, not judgment, and allows them to find their own path and accountability with the Lord. We are each His servant, and He is the One who is able to help each of us stand.

Today, Lord, help me to not judge others on this path. Help me to share my experience, strength, and hope in You.

MARCH 24

"The kingdom of God does not come with your careful obser-
vation, nor will people say, 'Here it is,' or 'There it is,' because
the kingdom of God is within you." —LUKE 17:20A-21

The Kingdom Is Now

Have you been searching for the kingdom of God
"here" and "there"? We've experienced just how hard
life can be: We have all been in the hell of compulsive eating and overweight, searching for the answer
to our problems from this theory or that diet. Our
pain has made us search "around," rather than focus
on, the kingdom of God that is within us.

Now we are finding a better way to live, facing
our challenges and feelings. We are learning to
relate to others and resolve broken relationships. All
this occurs by letting go of food each day and surrendering our will to God. Greatest of all, we have
a deeper faith and dependence on the Lord. We can
live in victory with Him now, in the present, not
waiting until heaven. The kingdom is within us,
because the King is within us!

Today, Lord, I surrender my will and my food to You,
to discover that Your kingdom is within me.

MARCH 25

But the Lᴏʀᴅ provided a great fish to swallow Jonah, and Jonah was inside the fish three days and three nights.... From inside the fish Jonah prayed to the Lᴏʀᴅ his God.

—JONAH 1:17, 2:1

A Raw Deal or God's Provision?

God does provide! Though His provision may not come in the form we'd prefer, it is always just what we need.

At the point in the story when he is swallowed by a fish, one might conclude that this is bad news for Jonah. Even Jonah saw it that way! Surely he initially assumed his life was over; no one would think being inside a fish was a good thing. Yet God, in His great provision, had a plan to reveal amid "disaster." And in truth, even though Jonah had caused his own trouble to begin with, the fish saved Jonah—an experience that provided the prophet with his own powerful call to repentance.

Some days we feel that our lives could not be in worse condition; that God has surely left us to die in our own trouble. We are swallowed in layers of fat that confine and steal away our life. We feel like a physical disaster. But God has a plan for us, too. As He provided an attention-getter for Jonah and good reason to pray, so He is providing for us. And now, just as with Jonah, God is calling us out of our despair and into victory by obeying and following Him. His ways are not always comfortable, but He knows exactly what we need. May we quickly get humble and be talking and listening to God, as Jonah did.

Today, Lord, I see that You may have provided this challenge for me. I am prompted to pray now and seek You.

*And the L*ORD *appointed a great fish to swallow Jonah, and Jonah was in the stomach of the fish three days and three nights.* —*J O N A H 1 : 1 7* NASB

Swallowed Up

It's easy for us to feel, like Jonah, that we've been swallowed by something bigger than ourselves. That's how it feels in the sea of overweight: It's full of shame due to food problems, emotional triggers, weight-loss schemes, exercise programs.

The issue is bigger, more profound, more overwhelming than just calories vs. exercise. The storm has been raging around us, we've been running from God's will, and we now find ourselves in the midst of chaos. God allows us to be held by this great "fish" of our own making: fat. There we must sit for the symbolic three days and three nights (which symbolizes death in this verse)—dying to self.

With nowhere else to go, Jonah had time to reflect on the mess he'd created and to remember Who controlled his life and his salvation. As we meditate on this while in the stomach of our great fish, may we come to that place of total surrender of "life as we know it" with food. May this internal work bring a new perspective on God's power.

Today, Lord, I surrender my will to You.

Then Jonah prayed to the Lᴏʀᴅ his God from the stomach of the fish, and he said, "I called out of my distress to the Lᴏʀᴅ, And He answered me. I cried for help from the depth of Sheol; You heard my voice. For You had cast me into the deep, into the heart of the seas, and the current engulfed me."

—*J O N A H   2 : 1 - 3   NASB*

Distressed but Alive

Jonah had been cast into the deep, but by the grace of God, he was kept alive! And even though he was held captive in the belly of a fish, he was grateful to have been rescued.

Living with a food obsession or an overweight condition may cause us to feel like we have been cast into the deep heart of the sea. We may feel engulfed in the undercurrent of endless diet fads, weight-loss schemes, and exercise infomercials. Having tried most of them with no long-term success, we may have lost all hope. Feeling empty and lonely, we cry for help from the depth of Sheol.

And God hears our cries. He is able to use our failings to bring us to surrender, where we reach out for His saving power. Despite our salvation and knowledge of God, we must come to know that He has power even in this facet of our lives. He will be Lord in this and in every other area.

Today, Lord, I cry to You in my distress and give up this fight with food and weight.

MARCH 28

"But I will sacrifice to You with the voice of thanksgiving; I will pay what I have vowed. Salvation is of the LORD." So the LORD spoke to the fish, and it vomited Jonah onto dry land.

—*JONAH 2:9-10* NKJV

Surrendering to God's Will

When we have tried and failed in every attempt to control our own lives, we are more willing to accept the spiritual help we need.

Jonah knew this was true as he turned to God after his own resources were exhausted. He admitted that his will—living his life his own way—had been a disaster. He brought his will into alignment with God's will and took the time to confess his faith in God's power to save him. As he committed to follow through with God's call on his life, God had the fish expel Jonah onto dry land.

This is what our own road to recovery will look like. We must admit that our efforts to control our food problems are useless. We have to concede that our physical, emotional, and spiritual selves are in critical condition and that only God's power can save us. Finally, we must commit to following through with a promise to do whatever it takes to recover, no matter what God requires of us.

At the moment of our surrender and acceptance, God is able to deliver us to dry land—a place where we can find sure footing and complete the journey of God's mission for our lives.

Today, Lord, I give up the fight and request Your saving grace. I am willing to do what it takes to fulfill Your will for my life.

A friend loves at all times. —*PROVERBS 17:17*

Friend to Self

We need the acceptance and love of dear friends who will support our mission to recover health and who will walk beside us through thick and thin (no pun intended). We need those into whom we can pour ourselves as well, and offer the same love and presence that is so important to us.

By being a friend who loves at all times, we find that we have something of value to offer. We can make a difference in the life of someone who will be blessed by our love.

Today, we have the perfect candidate to start blessing. This person desperately needs us to come through with consistent kindness. It is the person named "Myself." Just as we are friends with others, so we can be a friend to ourselves. Rather than condemn ourselves with cruelty we wouldn't give to a mangy dog, we can instead be gentle, acting from love at all times. We can support our own mission for healthy living and offer the same spirit of compassion that we so desperately need from others. We can receive and give love in friendship; we can be a friend to self.

Today, Lord, may I receive the love of my friends and offer that love to myself and to others.

"I'll make up for the years of the locust, the great locust dev-astation—locusts savage, locusts deadly, fierce locusts, locusts of doom, that great locust invasion I sent your way."

—JOEL 2:25 MSG

Restored

Locusts are the ultimate bingeing machines! They live by continuous eating, consuming everything in their path.

In this verse the prophet Joel is talking specifically about the destruction experienced by Israel during a locust invasion. But the damage could also be symbolic of what our compulsive eating has done to our lives over the years. Continuously eating unhealthy or even healthy foods has consumed our time day after day, making us unavailable for relationships and effective living. Bingeing has also had a devastating effect on our bodies and minds—we've become sluggish, physically and emotionally.

But through the prophet Joel, God is saying that He will make up for our devastation, even for that which was caused by our compulsive eating issues. With God, there are second and third and even fourth chances if we turn to Him! We can still live the life He intended as we surrender our food choices day by day.

Today, Lord, I thank You that even though many years have been eaten up by the locusts, I can still turn to You and live the life You intended for me.

"You will have plenty to eat, until you are full, and you will praise the name of the LORD your God, who has worked wonders for you; never again will my people be shamed."

—JOEL 2:26

The Promise of Plenty

Through the prophet Joel, the Lord promises abundance and provision following the destruction of the locusts. We may have felt shame once we began to comprehend what our emotional and compulsive eating habits have done to our lives. Up until now these problems have robbed us of experiencing the fullness of life, but the Lord God is working wonders within and through us!

By His power, we are able to put down the fork and spoon before we overeat. By His power, we can let go of certain trigger foods, one moment at a time. By His power, we are able to take loving care of our bodies with healthy foods and portions. We can praise the name of the Lord our God for these wonders! We no longer have to live with the shame of our food and weight problems. Praise God!

Today, Lord, I give praise to Your powerful name with deep gratitude for the wonders You are working in my life.

"The threshing floors will be filled with grain; the vats will over-flow with new wine and oil. . . . Then you will know that I am in Israel, that I am the Lord your God, and that there is no other; never again will my people be shamed." —JOEL 2:24, 27

A Prosperous Purpose

In this scripture the prophet Joel is painting a picture of Israel's prosperous future in order to instill hope to the devastated land. When we are at the end of our own resources and feeling empty and damaged, then we know our faith in God's presence is faltering.

Joel pictures the essence of prosperity, abundance, and happiness—threshing floors filled with grain as a symbol of life restored; new wine overflowing as a symbol of good times and celebration; oil as a sign of richness and the presence of the Spirit. The sorrow and pain of destructive emotional eating and weight problems are behind us. As we become healthier by eating nutritious foods and increasing exercise, even our internal knowledge of God's presence is restored. We know that He *is* Lord and that we no longer have to search for any other type of comfort.

As our faith is restored, our souls are filled with purpose, celebration, and the Spirit. Shame need never again be responsible for bringing darkness to our lives.

Today, Lord, as I come to the end of my own resources, I know I need You more than ever. Restore my faith and life.

A false balance is an abomination to the LORD, but a just weight is His delight. —PROVERBS 11:1 NASB

A Just Weight

We may have judged ourselves harshly by this verse in the past, cringing inwardly about not having a "just weight." It may have brought condemnation upon us, and perhaps it even made us feel like we were an "abomination"!

But we must take care to be gentle with ourselves, especially when we are working diligently toward that "just weight." We must be aware that God wants us to be healthy and take care of our body. Honestly and faithfully, we take the actions necessary to move toward our goal each day. In doing so, we can let go of any recriminating thoughts and feelings we may have toward ourselves.

Today, Lord, I accept the fact that I must take action each day to be a healthy and "just weight."

As Jesus continued on toward Jerusalem, he reached the border between Galilee and Samaria. As he entered a village there, ten lepers stood at a distance, crying out, "Jesus, Master, have mercy on us!" He looked at them and said, "Go show yourselves to the priests." And as they went, their leprosy disappeared. —LUKE 17:11-14 NLT

Modern-Day Leprosy

Being overweight in our modern culture can be a type of leprosy. No one wants to "catch" it. Just look at all the products on the market for weight loss programs, exercise equipment, low-fat foods, low-fat cookbooks, infomercials—the list seems endless! Magazines, movies, TV shows, and other media scream the message loud and clear: To be overweight is to be despised, ashamed, and marginalized! Despite how non-discriminatory we are told the workplace is, we know there are many places where a "weight barrier" exists.

The leprous men in these scriptures had faith and called upon Jesus from afar. They were not able to come close or touch Him, yet Jesus honored their pleas for healing and sent them to the priest for examination. By faith, they began the journey. As they took action, their healing was accomplished! Because they wanted more from life, and were bold enough to ask and then do, God's healing power was released.

Today, Lord, I call upon You for healing. No matter what my present condition is, I will begin the journey.

APRIL 4

One of them, when he saw that he was healed, came back to Jesus, shouting, "Praise God, I'm healed!" He fell face down on the ground at Jesus' feet, thanking him for what he had done. This man was a Samaritan. Jesus asked, "Didn't I heal ten men? Where are the other nine? Does only this foreigner return to give glory to God?" —LUKE 17:15-18 NLT

Gratitude for Healing

As we begin our journey of recovery—with new ways of thinking about and dealing with food—our lives reflect change physically, emotionally, spiritually. In our excitement, however, we can easily become complacent and even prideful. We can become so caught up in new freedoms, and even in receiving compliments, that we forget the source of our healing. It is only by God's grace that we have been set free from the constraints of our chronic condition.

To live truly liberated from food and weight problems, we must learn to live in gratitude—always aware of God's gift to us.

Today, Lord, I worship You with a thankful heart for healing me and allowing me the privilege of recovery.

Now one of them, when he saw that he had been healed, turned back, glorifying God with a loud voice, and he fell on his face at His feet, giving thanks to Him. And he was a Samaritan. Then Jesus answered and said, "Were there not ten cleansed? But the nine—where are they? Was no one found who returned to give glory to God, except this foreigner?"

—LUKE 17:15-18 NASB

Stranger in the Land

We have been, like this Samaritan, a foreigner in our culture—not able to be part of life in many ways. Marginalized and discounted, we have lived on the sidelines, full of shame, feeling "unclean." Due to our feelings about ourselves, we have "taught" others to treat us badly and/or ignore us.

As such, we can imagine the gratitude, the relief, the utter amazement of this Samaritan leper when he was healed from a condition that had so injured his quality of life. The chance for us to live free of the burden of weight-related problems— aching feet, shame to go out, being stared at or avoided— is also a wondrous gift.

While there are many who have gone on diets and lost weight successfully, God has given *us* the opportunity to live free of what has been, up to this point, a hopeless condition.

Today, Lord, I fall at Your feet in grateful amazement for Your mercy toward me. Thank You for the chance to live in "weightlessness."

APRIL 6

Then he said to him, "Rise and go; your faith has made you well."
—LUKE 17:19

Walking in Freedom

As we read Bible stories about lepers being healed, we may feel that our own healing from food and weight problems is much slower and much less dramatic. Yet one similarity lies in the miracle of our faith—we made a decision to take action toward recovery. Another similarity lies in Jesus' command. We are not just healed-and-then-it's-over; we now have a responsibility to walk in that freedom.

We must keep going on the path of recovery and get on with enjoying all parts of life. We are no longer stuck in the confines of our weight. We are now free to rise up and go our way. We can do what we couldn't do before—dance, chase our kids, climb hills, ride bikes. Go on and live!

Today, Lord, I will be responsible with the freedom You've given me to live and enjoy life.

APRIL 7

Thus says the LORD, "What injustice did your fathers find in Me, that they went far from Me and walked after emptiness and became empty? They did not say, 'Where is the LORD Who brought us up out of the land of Egypt? . . .'"

—JEREMIAH 2:5-6A NASB

Out of Emptiness into Power

When we tried to diet and exercise on our own power, not calling to the Lord for His, our "walk[ing] after emptiness" only continued. We thought we were taking action that would free us from the bondage of food, but it was just another type of bondage—to a rigid, restrictive diet that condemned us for "slipping" or eating something "illegal." The shame of losing and gaining weight left us hopeless, empty.

Once again we were trying to make life work by our own strength, not looking to the One who has all the strength to save us. We tried a Band-Aid, surface approach to a deep spiritual condition and came up empty.

The wonderful reality is that when we let go of our old ways, God's power rushes in for us. He fills us with life, not just food. We accept a food plan that meets our needs and still allows us freedom. Life can be experienced at a deeper and richer level than ever before because the Lord has delivered us from captivity.

Today, Lord, I walk away from my empty ways of using food and dieting to make my life work. May Your power flow through my life.

APRIL 8

And when [Jesus] had come out onto the land, He was met by a certain man from the city who was possessed with demons; and who had not put on any clothing for a long time, and was not living in a house, but in the tombs. And seeing Jesus, he cried out and fell before Him, and said in a loud voice, "What do I have to do with You, Jesus, Son of the Most High God? I beg You, do not torment me." For He had been commanding the unclean spirit to come out of the man. . . . And Jesus asked him, "What is your name?" And he said, "Legion"; for many demons had entered him. —LUKE 8:27-30 NLT

Spiritual Poverty

We who struggle with food and weight issues can identify with this man possessed by legions of demons. Because of our size, we may have given up on wearing stylish clothes and being part of society. We may have "lived in the tombs" by isolating ourselves from others. Having been ridiculed and teased, we may have believed all relationships were unsafe and untrustworthy, so we hid and ate. At times we have not even wanted Jesus to "torment" us! We may have felt so much shame, remorse, and bitterness that we have feared His call to live differently. Overeating kept us in pain, but we felt safe.

But as we can see, Jesus did not leave this man to live in his torturous situation. He took on the challenge of freeing this demon-possessed man. We must believe that because of His compassion for our torment, Jesus stays with us until we are made whole.

Today, Lord, may I see the spiritual poverty of staying in the torment of overeating. I allow You to draw close to me.

This spirit had often taken control of the man. Even when he was shackled with chains, he simply broke them and rushed out into the wilderness, completely under the demon's power. "What is your name?" Jesus asked. "Legion," he replied—for the man was filled with many demons.

—LUKE 8:29-30 NLT

Releasing the Demons

When we are filled with fear, resentment, hurt, anxiety, and rage, it's easy to think food will soothe and anesthetize. When times are particularly hard, it can feel like we are possessed by a legion of demons. Our internal emotional struggles can drive us toward self-destruction with food in hand.

We have made attempts to restrain our overeating by using outside measures to gain control—diets, shots, pills, doctors, exercise machines, health clubs, weigh-ins, pledges, promises, and resolutions. But these empty efforts proved to be outer constraints that only bound and imprisoned us further. The day always came when we broke the bonds and restrictions and were once again driven wildly to food by our obsession. The resulting weight gains were demoralizing, painful, and shameful for us—more demons!

But Jesus comes to cleanse and clear away those demons! The answer is not found in placing more outside restraints on our food behaviors. It is, rather, an internal, spiritual cleansing that brings peace.

Today, Lord, I release the demons of fear, resentment, and food obsession, allowing You to free me from my compulsions.

APRIL 10

The people went out to see what had happened; and they came to Jesus, and found the man from whom the demons had gone out, sitting down at the feet of Jesus, clothed and in his right mind; and they became frightened.

—LUKE 8:35 NASB

Focus on Fullness

The poor man in this scripture had been tormented and possessed by so many demons that he'd become a danger to himself and others. People could not believe his deliverance from such depravity, so they had to come and see for themselves. Seeing this man set free, clothed and returned to sanity, was so amazing that they were actually frightened!

We must be aware that some people will have doubts and may attempt to sabotage our progress in recovery, even when they are happy for us. They may say, "A little won't hurt!" or, "You can't have that *ever?*" This can be discouraging and throw us off track if we again focus our attention on deprivation rather than the fullness of life in God.

We must stay focused on how Jesus is restoring us to our "right mind." We have been given the opportunity to allow God to do the impossible through us. Sitting at the feet of Jesus—a surrendered position—we have become God-focused instead of food-focused. We begin to lose or maintain weight and grow spiritually. We are not bothered by the negative reactions of others.

Today, Lord Jesus, may I sit at Your feet and become restored to health, wholeness—to my "right mind."

Then those who had seen it happen told how the demoniac had been saved. Later, a great many people from the Gerasene countryside got together and asked Jesus to leave—too much change, too fast, and they were scared. So Jesus got back in the boat and set off. —LUKE 8:36-37 MSG

Fear of Change

Jesus broke onto the scene with a miraculous healing of a demon-possessed man, challenging the way people thought and felt about God. For those who witnessed it, the power that Jesus displayed meant that perhaps they would have to change as well. And change can be scary!

We are often afraid of change because it means giving up something we want or losing something we already have. We protect even the painful way things are because familiarity seems so much more comfortable and less scary. Like the Gerasene people, we may be so afraid of change that we are limiting God's ability to work and move us forward.

Changing how we deal with food—mentally, physically, and spiritually—is a huge shift that takes adjustment. Each time we make a healthy choice about food, we move further in recovery. The surrendering of the familiar allows God to make the internal changes necessary for our lasting success.

Today, Lord, I surrender my fear of change. Help me to make healthy alterations, day by day, in my thoughts and behaviors about food.

APRIL 12

The man whom [Jesus] had delivered from the demons asked to go with him, but he sent him back, saying, "Go home and tell everything God did in you." So he went back and preached all over town everything Jesus had done in him.

God's Power to Heal

We can become so overwhelmed with the miracle of our recovery that we become self-focused. There is a "honeymoon phase" when life seems to be opening up for the first time. Being free of food obsessions, losing weight, and living healthier, we become able to do things we weren't able to before. As exciting as this time is, we need to remember that there is a greater plan for our healing in God's realm.

Jesus tells the man in this passage to go back to his family and testify of God's work in his life. He speaks to us as well! We are to be a witness and spread the message of God's love and faithfulness— even about food and weight issues!

Because we were never before able to make a difference in the weight arena, we have a unique calling to attest to the power of God. Just like the healed man in this verse, our healing is not for us alone. There are thousands of people like us who have given up hope about their own weight issues. We can now share with them our firsthand account of Jesus' compassion and power to help and heal.

Today, Lord, may I be so full of serenity and gratitude that I am a testimony to Your power.

APRIL 13

Faith without works is dead.　　　　　—JAMES 2:26 NASB

Do or do not—there is no "try."　　　　—YODA, STAR WARS

I'm Trying!

If we only try, we may die! If we merely try to work the keys to our new eating program, yet only gain enough knowledge to understand them intellectually, then our problems with food and weight will continue. If we merely try to have a plan for our food, but not for any other aspect of our lives, we will bounce around between the myriad diets out there and never find solid, lasting recovery.

In the same way, having spiritual knowledge from studying the Bible accomplishes nothing if there is no action in our life to support it. As the Scripture says, "Faith without works is dead." No movement, no life! In fact, most of us have had exceptional faith and knowledge of the Word, but to bring that faith to life, we needed the ingredients of humility and surrender for taking action.

Action is the antidote to mere trying. There is action to be taken on each key component of our program. There is action to be taken each day to plan out our food and portions. There is action to be taken in our spiritual routines. Sometimes there is even opposite action to be taken when we are faced with certain foods that could trigger a binge! It is all movement toward recovery and toward God's will for our eating patterns.

Today, Lord, no matter how I feel, I seek to take action toward Your will over my food choices.

So the king gave the order, and they brought Daniel and threw him into the lions' den. The king said to Daniel, "May your God, whom you serve continually, rescue you!" —DANIEL 6:16

The Lions' Den

Compulsive eating can be like a lion seeking to devour our time and our lives from God's intentions. We may feel trapped in the den with this beast that could easily overtake us at any moment. It's a baffling condition because at times, we have been able to make progress with our weight and eating habits, taming this lion for a while. But the occasion always came for us to eat again.

Even when we felt like we were finally able to conquer our situation, we came to realize that the beast only sleeps for a time. Sometimes we did well and felt surrendered, serene. But other times, the lion of appetite attacked and we became overwhelmed, thrown back into the den of overeating. And although the lion may be sleeping now, we've lived in fear, knowing it could be triggered by the mere aroma of certain foods.

Today, our hope is in seeing how Daniel trusted God completely for deliverance from being consumed by the lions. God's ultimate purpose is for us to comprehend and accept our utter dependence on Him for survival. As we face our lion of appetite with God's protection, we don't need to fear! We are delivered!

Today, Lord, I surrender in trust. Tame this "lion" in me.

APRIL 15

"Are you listening to this? Really listening? Listen carefully to what I am saying—and be wary of the shrewd advice that tells you how to get ahead in the world on your own."

—MARK 4:23-24A MSG

Listening

Many voices in the world compete for our attention. Some voices lead us to recovery, and some lead us to bingeing. In this verse we are instructed to listen for God's voice in the everyday, for it is He who gives us good direction toward recovery.

While scads of other voices are also telling us how to diet and exercise, we must be discerning and listen for Jesus' voice of reason. We must allow Him to ground us in truth and help us remember: If it sounds too good to be true, it probably is! We know fad diets don't work; we have tried most of them. Instead, we must listen to His simple answer of letting go and focus on our spiritual condition.

In His truths we find we can surrender our food to Him and choose to eat more balanced, beneficial meals. We can add gentle exercise to affirm our physical being. We can find a healthy support system of other people who are walking the same path. These are decisions to which God will lead us—tools of truth and action that fill us with strength and grace for the life of recovery.

Today, Lord, may I hear Your voice above the clamor.

Therefore, I urge you, brothers, in view of God's mercy, to offer your bodies as living sacrifices, holy and pleasing to God— this is your spiritual act of worship. —ROMANS 12:1

Living Sacrifice

Highlighted in this verse is a common theme that runs throughout Scripture: In order to live a life truly pleasing to God, we must let go of our lives as we would have them. In this, the ordinary/everyday becomes an act of worship. Even our eating behaviors can reflect our worship of the One whose mercy saves us.

So "offering our body" is an act of surrender to God's rule. We "sacrifice"—or put to death—those desires for food that once controlled us. Where we have allowed food to overtake and rule us, we now allow the Spirit to enliven us. Sacrifice can be a painful process in the beginning, and it often feels overwhelming. But holiness is produced within us as we present ourselves to our Creator and Redeemer. This is our personal act of spiritual worship.

Today, Lord, I present my body and all my desires for food to be sacrificed for Your glory.

APRIL 17

"My people have committed two sins: They have forsaken me, the spring of living water, and have dug their own cisterns, broken cisterns that cannot hold water." —JEREMIAH 2:13

Living Springs

The spring of living water is a wonderful image of God, because a spring simply emerges from the ground; it does not flow from another source. It is also the sole provider of water for those who draw from it, giving nourishing hydration for their lives.

As the prophet Jeremiah laments, Israel had forsaken its "spring"—the Lord Himself! Digging their own cisterns to catch rainwater, the people had turned from Him. Yet the cisterns were broken and could not hold the water they were created to catch.

This is a relevant and timely message for our modern culture. In hundreds of forms, we have dug cisterns instead of trusting in the Spring of living water. We have sought in vain to catch life-support from water that is not even fresh. Money, sex, entertainment, sports, and yes, even food, are all broken cisterns that provide only enough water to whet our appetites for more. But all go dry eventually.

We must turn to the eternal Spring of living water—the Lord God Himself! In the dryness of our lives, He bubbles up and nourishes us with His life-giving power.

Today, Lord, I turn from the broken cisterns I have used as substitutes for You. I drink deeply from Your spring, living in trust.

APRIL 18

But Lot's wife looked back, and she became a pillar of salt.

—GENESIS 19:26

The "Good Old Days"?

While we are in the process of healing from our relationship with food, weight, resentments, and fears, we are still vulnerable to relapsing into our old eating patterns. As with Lot's wife, when we look back and long for certain things, all spiritual growth and movement abruptly stop. We may not become a pillar of salt, but we are no longer a vibrant vessel for God in this state, either.

Looking back at the good old days when we could eat whatever and whenever we wanted is dangerous. Some people are not able to return to recovery because of shame, guilt, and the sheer intimidation of the uphill climb ahead. Having a healthy respect for the possibility of relapse can motivate us to continue moving toward solid recovery. Accountability to a food buddy, prayerfully surrendering our food each day, journaling our consumption, growing in humility, acceptance, and gratitude—these are all ways we maintain our commitment to progress in recovery and leave the old life where it belongs: behind us.

Today, Lord, I continue my recovery plan, taking action and focusing on Your salvation instead of those not-so-good old days.

APRIL 19

Life Budding

We are ready for spring! The winter of weight loss is a time of harsh realities, accepting our problems, and deep grief over the pain in our life. It takes humility and endurance to survive the suffering of this season. However, after the winter comes the spring. Always the spring.

With the death of our old lifestyle, we can plant new seeds of hope for our future. As the Lord showers rain upon us, we can ask Him to use any storms for our benefit. Our new life buds, and then He makes our endeavors with weight loss and emotional health begin to bear fruit in this season of intense spiritual growth.

Today, Lord, I ask You for showers of rain in my life. May I see the hope of new life in the spring of my recovery.

Charm is deceitful and beauty is vain, but a woman who fears the LORD, she shall be praised. Give her the product of her hands, and let her works praise her in the gates.

—PROVERBS 31:30-31 NASB

Vanity or Sanity?

Some people may think that losing weight in order to be thin and attractive is a sign of vanity and goes against the rules of modesty and selflessness valued in Scripture. If the only reason we are losing weight is for beauty in and of itself, then it is vanity. But when we are surrendering our will to God and losing our self-focus, we are losing weight for His glory, not our own. Then our beauty becomes a witness to the power of God, for here He is doing for us and through us what we have not been able to do on our own. Our physical body then becomes tangible evidence of God's work in our lives. We not only become more physically attractive but emotionally and spiritually attractive as well.

Surrendered food choices bring health to our minds and emotions. Our minds become clearer, not weighed down with excess carbohydrates, fear, and shame; emotionally, we become more even-tempered, serene, and full of God's peace.

Today, Lord, may I lose weight, not for vanity but for sanity. May I attest to Your love and care for me.

APRIL 21

Listen and hear my voice; pay attention and hear what I say.

—ISAIAH 28:23

Whose Voice?

Do particular foods seem to call your name? For people with food and weight problems, it can feel like certain items are calling from television advertisements, magazine pages, the grocery store aisles, or restaurants.

Hearing God's voice above the clamor is a monumental challenge to our recovery. We need to be wary of the messages to which we give our time and attention. God's voice is a still, small voice that we can hear from within our heart. It can be a gentle nudge to eat smaller portions, a whisper of encouragement to forgo dessert, or even an exciting plan for activity and connection. God wants us to take care of ourselves around food so that it is no longer the center of our lives.

When we listen to that voice—the voice of God —food is then brought into proper perspective. With God in the center, we are more conscious of His presence, even in the clamor.

Today, Lord, I pray to truly hear Your voice above the clamor. Help me to take positive action.

The riff-raff among the people had a craving and soon they had the People of Israel whining, "Why can't we have meat? We ate fish in Egypt—and got it free!—to say nothing of the cucumbers and melons, the leeks and onions and garlic. But nothing tastes good out here; all we get is manna, manna, manna." —NUMBERS 11:5-6 MSG

Boredom Leads to Relapse

"I can't eat another vegetable!" There will be days like that—days when you won't want to wash another lettuce leaf or chop another carrot; when your healthy food plan begins to look bland and boring; when you'll want variety and exciting food. We all experience this type of boredom with our new food choices.

That's when the whining begins, and we look back to when we were eating whatever and whenever we wanted. But this is expecting food to be our excitement in life once more, rather than the heavenly delicacies of communion with God.

When this bored and whining attitude strikes, we need outside help. We must reach for our support people and be honest about what we are feeling—no matter how humbling it is for us! The complaining of the Israelites caused them to miss out on many blessings in the wilderness, but most of all, their ingratitude cost some of them their lives! We need not allow the whining and boredom to cost us our "lives" by dragging us into relapse.

Today, Lord, I turn to You with gratitude for the opportunity to recover from this condition. Pull me out of the wilderness of boredom and whining.

APRIL 23

"But now we have lost our appetite; we never see anything but this manna!" —NUMBERS 11:6

Whining: One More Day of Life, or Death?

It's overwhelming to think of eating only healthy foods for the rest of our life! *You mean I can never have _____ again?* It's easy to become weary of healthy food when we see new restaurants opening and it seems like everyone around us can eat whatever they want.

This train of thought can tempt us to give up on our goals because we've lost our appetite for nutritious food options and the promise of a healthier life. But beware! This is dangerous territory for your mind and heart. The Israelites knew such temptation when they wandered in the wilderness.

We may have allowed ourselves to be in a rut with our food choices. Eating the same thing every day can set us up for a sense of deprivation. For long-term success with our program, it's important to be creative with our food preparations while paradoxically not obsessing over them.

At this point, we truly need the grace of God. We can recharge our commitment to stay the course by listening to inspiring tapes, reading the Word, talking to a supportive friend, and praying. When times of discontent arise, we need grace from friends, too, to help steady us on our journey.

Today, Lord, I admit my dismay at having to eat healthy for "the rest of my life." I pray for the grace to eat healthy food for one more day.

APRIL 24

Give thanks in all circumstances, for this is God's will for you in Christ Jesus. —1 THESSALONIANS 5:18

Ungratefulness

The Israelites' biggest problem was their ungratefulness. They had been rescued from slavery in Egypt by God Himself. They had seen the miracles He performed in the wilderness, and they had been fed daily with God's provision of manna, a wafer-like substance that appeared each morning with the dew.

We, too, are being led away from all we've ever known—our whole way of life! At first, freedom can feel like a relief. But then we may begin to realize that our bondage had certain comforts and rewards that are no longer available. As slaves, the Israelites were confined in a foreign land, forced into dreadful work, and their lives were not their own—but at least they had decent food, a home, and some measure of predictability. Now in the wilderness, they had become aware of all the things they "loved" about slavery. So they ate the manna because that's all there was to eat, but they missed what a wonderful miracle God's provision of manna was for them.

For us, any day that we are not obsessing and overeating is a miracle. When we are tempted toward missing our slavery, we can instead be reminded of the miracle in God's provision for us today. Ingratitude robs us of the blessing and gift which He so lovingly grants us, a day at a time.

Today, Lord, I will just enjoy Your presence and miraculous provisions for me.

Then the LORD said to me . . . "These things won't happen right away. Slowly, steadily, surely, the time approaches when the vision will be fulfilled. If it seems slow, wait patiently, for it will surely take place. It will not be delayed."

—HABAKKUK 2:2-3 *TLB*

A Vision Worth Waiting For

We can't help but look for quick results. We want the weight to be gone—yesterday! If we see someone who is losing weight quickly on a particular food plan, we may think that is the answer to our problem. But in this verse, God is saying to Habakkuk that visions for our future take time. When we are more concerned with the results than the process, we're wanting relief without having to address the root of the problem—our emotional and compulsive eating and the reasons for it.

If we are steady in our adherence to our own sensible food plan, our vision of a slimmer body and healthier life will come to fruition. This vision is worth waiting for. And having peace and moderation around food while we serenely attend to our emotional and spiritual life will surely come true.

It is a vision of balance and health in our rhythm of life. It is one that takes patience to cultivate, and it will be fulfilled when we take actions toward that vision daily.

Today, Lord, I pray for the grace to steadily take action toward the vision of recovery. I wait patiently and trust in You.

My counsel is this: Live freely, animated and motivated by God's Spirit. Then you won't feed the compulsions of selfishness. —GALATIANS 5:16 MSG

Walk in the Spirit

When we consider the desires of the flesh, we can begin to grasp the condition of an emotional eater. The flesh has the desire for more than its share of food, money, love, or even sex. When we try to fulfill these desires, we become compulsive in our indulgences and "self" is placed on the throne.

We may have started out with a normal appetite for one or more of these desires, because they are natural human needs. It is the compulsion of selfishness, though, that leads us away from God and His gift of spiritual freedom.

The realm of the Spirit is where we find true life. By allowing our actions around food to be informed by His Spirit, we can live free from compulsions. As we listen to the Spirit, we are connected to the vast power and awesomeness of God, who then animates our entire life and motivates us to walk with Him. Connected at this Spirit level, our compulsion is quelled, and selfishness vanishes!

Today, Lord, I receive this counsel: to allow Your Spirit to guide my food choices and behavior, thereby fulfilling Your will for my health, not my compulsion for more selfish desires.

"Watch and pray so that you will not fall into temptation. The spirit is willing, but the body is weak." —MARK 14:38

Give Up the Fight—and Pray!

Thinking of our overweight condition as a champion prizefighter—always working out and planning his moves—we get a glimpse of what we're really up against. How many times have we gotten into the ring with this opponent, only to be beaten and bloodied, our self-esteem bruised and our spirit demoralized? Too many to count. Do we believe that we are going to take on this giant one more time with another diet, another weight-loss program, another piece of exercise equipment, another membership at another gym?

Recovery is about giving up the fight and refusing to even get into the ring. It is not declaring defeat, but becoming a spectator of God's power as we work the keys of surrender and acceptance from the sidelines. It is a letting go of our own feeble attempts at control and truly living by God's own power in the ring!

Now our energy goes into practicing ownership of our problem, following our plan of eating and exercise. But we are no longer fighting. There is no forced feeding of diet foods or deprivation in order to eat later. Our fight is over.

Today, Lord, I am watching and praying to do my part while You fight for me.

Jesus answered and said to her, "Everyone who drinks of this water will thirst again; but whoever drinks of the water that I will give him shall never thirst. . . ." —JOHN 4:13-14 NASB

Empty Wells

Placing unrealistic expectations on others is like going to an empty well that cannot give us what we need. This may be a familiar scenario for you when you think about your parents, spouse, employer, friends, or even your church. We all go back to these empty wells, demanding and pouting for them to give us what we want: attention, support, nurturing, acknowledgment, praise. When they can't deliver in the ways we expect, we may become more demanding, and even judgmental or indignant, about how they have failed us.

This feeling from being let down has been one of our invitations to fill the void with food, either by over-consuming or over-controlling it. We rationalize that because we have unmet needs, we deserve to treat ourselves with desserts, or a snack, or just large quantities of food. Then, disappointed in ourselves, we fall into discontent and shame.

It is actually our expectations that are off track. We need to look at all our empty wells with forgiveness, realizing that the people we love are doing the best they can with what they know. We must let go of our demands upon them to give us what they do not possess to give. Then we must turn to Jesus for our deeper spiritual thirst to be met.

Today, Lord, forgive me for going to empty wells and demanding that all my needs be met. I want to run to You and drink from the bottomless well of Your presence, love, and mercy.

A leper came to Him and bowed down before Him, and said, "LORD, if You are willing, You can make me clean." Jesus stretched out His hand and touched him, saying, "I am willing; be cleansed." And immediately his leprosy was cleansed.

—MATTHEW 8:2-3 NASB

God's "Will" Power

The will can be a powerful thing. The leper in this scripture recognized this when he approached Jesus and appealed to His will to make him clean. The focus of Jesus' will and the action of fearlessly touching the leper cleansed the man of leprosy.

We have berated ourselves for not having enough willpower to control our eating. We thought we needed more of it to be successful with weight loss. We thought willpower was the answer. And it has worked, for a while. We've had lots of willpower, for a while. But only for a while.

Many, many times we've restricted our food to lose weight—which took plenty of willpower. But eventually the times of restriction gave way to slips and then binges. Our weight went down, then up, and then we gained even more. On the way "up" we asked ourselves, "Where is that willpower I used to have?" Permanent weight loss eluded us.

We must have the same level of faith as the leper here—faith that Jesus has the power to heal us. We then must align our will with His and seek His power. Taking action is the final step.

Today, Lord, I approach You with my dreadful, life-stealing condition. I come to You with faith in Your power and willingness to heal me.

Everyone brings out the choice wine first and then the cheaper wine after the guests have had too much to drink; but you have saved the best till now. —JOHN 2:10

Transforming the Ordinary

To understand the significance of Jesus' first recorded miracle of changing water into wine, we must know that in the culture of that time, wine symbolized celebration of good things. The prophets used the image of full wine vats to indicate prosperity and abundance. Jesus turning water into wine points to how He takes our ordinary life and transforms it into celebration. There is a rich and abundant quality for us to enjoy. There is a fulfillment of purpose to be tasted.

We may not always experience times of celebration in our journey of recovery. In fact, there will be hard work, dying to self in our food choices, facing painful memories, handling intense emotions, and confronting difficult relationships. But the transforming power of Jesus in our life is cause for celebration! He brings a quality of elegance to our living that was not there before we set out on this road.

Today, Lord, I am awed and grateful for the miracle of transformation that You are creating in my life.

MAY 1

Joyful Laughter

Has the Lord made you laugh and shout with joy? Recovery brings back enjoyment to our lives so that even laughter is possible again. We've been shamed, saddened, depressed, and hopeless about our weight for long enough. We've been sobered and intensely regimented about calories, carbs, fats, and exercise. Finding joy, laughter, and humor in life has been difficult in the midst of all that seriousness!

But now God has prepared a path of recovering for our lives—a path lined with fullness and abundance. We have the opportunity to be transformed spiritually, emotionally, and physically. This is a miracle! In gratitude, let's savor the day-by-day healing until joy bubbles up into laughter and shouting. The Lord will fill our mouth with laughter.

Today, Lord, may I be so aware of the miracle of recovery that I am filled with joy.

MAY 2

The LORD is my shepherd, I shall not be in want. —PSALM 23:1

Whose Flock?

If only someone could ease our pain, make us feel better about ourselves, and solve our problems— especially our weight problems. There are many famous people who have written books about how they keep slim, their personal diet plan, their personal chef's recipes for low-fat meals, or even about how their trainer keeps them fit! These books appeal to a part of us that wants someone to tell us how to lose weight, what to eat, and the most efficient exercises to perform. Each celebrity, author, or fitness expert grabs the attention of their own flock. But all they really have to share is what worked for them. We can appreciate their knowledge and be happy about their success, but we must ask if they are the right shepherds for us.

For solid recovery, we must banish the fantasy that there is one person, one book, or one method that can "fix" us. The reality is that only God can shepherd us on this winding, sometimes rocky, journey toward better health. Only the Lord can fill the emptiness that we have tried so hard to sate with food. With this in mind, we can receive information from books and other media as helpful and yet not be deterred from our one true Shepherd. Jesus is the only One who can fill our deep longings, ease our pain, and lead us toward wholeness.

Today, Lord, and every day, You are the true Shepherd. You fill my wants, my needs, and my hurting heart. In Your flock I lack nothing.

MAY 3

I was pushed back and about to fall, but the LORD helped me. The LORD is my strength and my song; he has become my salvation. —PSALM 118:13-14

A Slip or a Relapse?

In recovery, we must be prepared for the possibility of slips to happen or even full relapse to occur. A slip can be as simple as adding to our menu an item that is not on our plan. If we continually make these kinds of exceptions, our spiritual focus can become blurred and the occasional exception become more of the rule. Soon we may find ourselves in full relapse, losing our overall values and boundaries around food.

Recovery from compulsive and emotional eating is like trying to go up the down escalator. If we stand still and don't take daily steps to grow spiritually, we can slowly slip backward. Yet even when we are experiencing frequent slips or we're about to fall into relapse, God as our Helper comes through for us. By stepping back into sync with Him at the spiritual level, we find Him as our strength and our song, our salvation from the despair of unhealthy living. He helps us get back on course in recovery.

Today, Lord, I will reach for You when I am about to fall.

A farmer went out to sow his seed. As he was scattering the seed, some fell along the path, and the birds came and ate it up. Some fell on rocky places, where it did not have much soil. It sprang up quickly, because the soil was shallow. . . . Still other seed fell on good soil, where it produced a crop—a hundred, sixty or thirty times what was sown. He who has ears, let him hear. —MATTHEW 13:3-5, 8-9

The Beaten Path

As we meditate on this parable, there are many spiritual lessons to reap from the images. The good news of the gospel is that our lives can be fully transformed into growing agents of God. This is the message of recovery from compulsive and emotional eating as well. As we examine the role of the soil, we see that Jesus is illuminating His people's responses to the seed of good news.

Sometimes the seed (typically the gospel, but here we apply it to the message of recovery) falls on soil as hard as a beaten path. Some people are so resistant to change that no matter how much excess food issues affect their lives, they are unable to receive the potential of this recovery message. They remain on their beaten path with food, and the seed of recovery goes unnoticed and disappears.

We don't have to live in that defeated place! In this process, and on our path of recovery, every day that passes can change us into more fertile soil for receiving the good news.

Today, Lord, I recognize the potential for healing and growth contained in the seed of recovery.

As he was scattering the seed, some . . . fell on rocky places, where it did not have much soil. It sprang up quickly, because the soil was shallow. But when the sun came up, the plants were scorched, and they withered because they had no root.

—MATTHEW 13:4-6

No Roots

This parable addresses a message (for us, a seed of recovery) that falls on rocky places where soil is shallow. Some people receive this message with great excitement in the beginning—they lose weight and may even be doing it perfectly. Yet the pressure of food thoughts, the temptation when desserts are served, or the going out to restaurants that serve unhealthy foods can quickly turn seemingly good soil into rocky terrain. These people shrink from the goal because they have nowhere to go for spiritual and emotional support to help them with their temptations.

We who have struggled for years know this cycle all too well. We have started strong in the new year; then, within a few weeks or months, we were withered and scorched and had given up on yet another attempt at permanent weight loss. But now we can know that we have victory in Christ and that He will grow and strengthen our roots toward health and wholeness. Then we will be healthy and ready to serve Him with our improving body.

Today, Lord, may my roots grow deeper as I trust in You for my lasting recovery.

MAY 6

A farmer went out to sow his seed. As he was scattering the seed, some . . . fell among thorns, which grew up and choked the plants. Still other seed fell on good soil, where it produced a crop—a hundred, sixty or thirty times what was sown.

—MATTHEW 13:3-4, 7-8

The Trouble with Thorns

The trouble with thorns is that, although the plants get a good start, the thorns grow faster and overtake them. This is how the cares, concerns, and worries of our lives distract us from the priority of our new attitudes around food, too.

"Thorns" can take the shape of many things: money, family, housekeeping, jobs, hobbies, and interests. While these may be important parts of our life, they can also serve as distractions and excuses that keep us from doing what is necessary in the recovery process.

We must tend our soil so we don't get too busy to ask God for help with our food plan. Also, we must get up and exercise, go to the grocery store and purchase healthy food choices, and take the time to prepare nutritious meals and snacks.

The trouble with thorns is that they are sneaky, devious, and persistent. But we have made recovery a priority in our lives, so we have nothing to fear!

Today, Lord, I will be wary of thorns that try to choke my relationship with You and distract me from my recovery.

A farmer went out to sow his seed. As he was scattering the seed, some fell along the path, and the birds came and ate it up. Some fell on rocky places, where it did not have much soil. It sprang up quickly, because the soil was shallow. But when the sun came up, the plants were scorched, and they withered because they had no root. Other seed fell among thorns, which grew up and choked the plants. Still other seed fell on good soil, where it produced a crop. . . . He who has ears, let him hear. —MATTHEW 13:3-9

The Soil of Growth

In this parable we learn that good soil produces a crop that multiplies far beyond what a few seeds can do! But what does it take to be good soil?

First, good soil must be soft, rich, and pliable for planting. It must have space for the seed. And it must have depth so the roots can reach for nutrients and water.

For us to hear the message and make lasting progress in our recovery, we must be this kind of soil. We must remain teachable, humble, and open to surrendering a little more each day. We must enrich ourselves with the fertile Word of God. We must have the water of fellowship with others in order to encourage our growth. Then God is able to work miraculous healing in our lives!

We may never know the extent of the crop in our recovery. But, one day at a time, we learn that this has been God's intention all along: for us to be good soil that supports new life.

Today, Lord, may I be good soil for Your message of recovery.

Anyone who listens to the word but does not do what it says is like a man who looks at his face in a mirror and, after looking at himself, goes away and immediately forgets what he looks like. —JAMES 1:23-24

True Beauty

Although one benefit of Lose It For Life is enhancement of our physical attractiveness, we must remember that true beauty can't be seen in our physical attributes. In fact, it's not the amount of time we spend in front of a mirror that brings out beauty; it's the amount of time we spend looking into the Word of God. Gazing into the mirror of God's Word, we see the true picture of our spiritual condition, and that allows us to be transformed into God's image. The rough edges are smoothed; the harshness is softened.

True beauty of spirit is developed and polished as we become ready to do the will of God.

Today, Lord, I will gaze into Your Word and allow You to create my beautiful character.

MAY 9

Our people must learn to devote themselves to doing what is good, in order that they may provide for daily necessities and not live unproductive lives.   —TITUS 3:14

Direction, Not Location

We have dreams of experiencing radical transformation in life with our weight, appearance, and overall well-being. In our deep desire for healing and wholeness, we are faced with the task of actually carrying our load in the endeavor. Yearning to get from point A to point B, we may immediately be overwhelmed by how far we have to go. Discouragement may stop us dead in our tracks. We may freeze—a deer in the headlights, immobilized by fear—and never even start the transformation process.

Here Paul suggests a better way—one that keeps us from becoming overwhelmed. It's what people in recovery call doing the next right thing. Instead of looking at tomorrow, next week, or next month, we must devote ourselves to what's good and right to care for our needs today.

As we simply do the next right thing, we find that we are less overwhelmed with the future and better able to move in the direction of radical transformation. We can allow ourselves the grace of today's position and remember that location is not as important as direction!

Today, Lord, may I practice doing the next right thing. May I rejoice in where I am headed.

MAY 10

But they that wait upon the LORD shall renew their strength; they shall mount up with wings as eagles; they shall run, and not be weary; and they shall walk, and not faint.

—ISAIAH 40:31 KJV

Great Expectation

Waiting upon the Lord is not a matter of sitting still, twiddling our thumbs, or tapping a foot until something happens. It is not mindless whistling, wandering around aimlessly, or watching the pot for some boiling action. No, waiting on the Lord is an entirely different ballgame. Waiting on God means looking to Him with great expectation, trusting in Him to deliver on the goods He has promised!

With our eyes on God and the hope of His plans, our strength is renewed. We begin to fly, in the same manner as an eagle. Consider it—the wings of an eagle are broad and strong and lift the amazing creature into flight by sure and powerful motion. Its wings do not flap and flutter as the littler birds, but rather, mount up in great strength and soar. In waiting on God, we also mount up for flight. As we expect great things from Him, He renews our strength, restores our energy, and we gain motivation for the tasks at hand.

Today, Lord, I wait upon You in great expectation. Fill me with Your life and energy! May I move and exercise by Your power. May I soar like an eagle, renewed in Your strength.

Finally, brothers, whatever is true, whatever is noble, whatever is right, whatever is pure, whatever is lovely, whatever is admirable—if anything is excellent or praiseworthy—think about such things. —PHILIPPIANS 4:8

What Will Be Prominent?

Have you ever noticed that the more you focus on something, the larger it becomes in your life? Likewise, the less you think about something, the less prominent it becomes in your life.

Obviously, when it comes to our weight, this concept isn't so easily applied. We can't just think (or unthink) the pounds off! However, there is an invaluable lesson in understanding the importance of what consumes our mental energy. When we stare only at our problems, we end up having neither the time nor energy for finding solutions—and certainly not for finding joy.

An integral part of our healing with food and weight issues is just what we will do with our mind. It's not about ignoring our sometimes dismal reality; it's about not getting stuck in it to the point where our entire focus is set on what's wrong. We must turn our gaze toward what is true, right, and pure if we are to make any progress. As we do, our praise to God and His solutions for the day become the most prominent things in our life. Our hope increases and our energy rises when we take care to de-emphasize misery and fix our eyes on what is excellent and praiseworthy.

Today, Lord, I will spend more time thinking on what is right and true than on the lies I've been told.

MAY 12

We demolish arguments and every pretension that sets itself up against the knowledge of God, and we take captive every thought to make it obedient to Christ. —2 CORINTHIANS 10:5

We Need Not Be Frail

Regardless of what we may know about God's love for us, His will for us, or His desire to fill us with His abundant riches, our negative thinking and critical voices can quickly drown out the truth we've found in Christ. Our minds will run with harmful background noise from our past, too, if we don't put a stop to it. Fortunately, God is more powerful than whatever tricks our minds can play, so we need not be mentally frail.

When discouragement or hopelessness sets in, when the voices of our past begin shouting lies to distract us from healing, then we can remember that we have authority in Christ to shut them down. We can quickly say no to lies and remind our thoughts that they are slaves to Jesus. This slavery does not confine us, but rather, it sets us free by demolishing all arguments and pretension that would seek to derail our progress toward health and wholeness. This is not merely positive thinking; it is the surrender of our sometimes-deceptive mind and its susceptibility to lies.

Jesus has given us power and authority over every thought, and that is reason for courage.

Today, Lord, when a critical voice in my head tries to discourage me, I will take it captive to the obedience of Christ.

There is a time for everything, and a season for every activity under heaven. —ECCLESIASTES 3:1

I'll Have an Order of Dramatic Weight Loss with a Side of Transformation—On the Fly!

At times we are tempted to judge God based on how quickly He moves in accordance with our own personal agenda. We can be so certain we know the answers for our problems that we just "place an order" with the sovereign God of the universe. After all, we know what we need and how that need should be filled!

Yet very often God declines to give us everything we want. He doesn't operate on our time frame, or even in our realm of understanding. His ways are not our ways. While we're busy living by clocks, calendars, and schedules, disgruntled by the pace of God, we may be missing the very lessons and beauty in life He would grant us.

When we choose to slow down, however, we allow God's process of growth to carry us, all in His time. There's no need to rush, for God is rarely early. But He is never late. And He will accomplish all that He desires and wills for us, in His own time.

Today, Lord, may I trust in Your timing for all my needs. May I embrace this season of life as You teach me Your path for healthy living.

MAY 14

And working together with Him, we also urge you not to receive the grace of God in vain—for He says, At the acceptable time I listened to you, and on the day of salvation I helped you; behold, now is the acceptable time, behold, now is the day of salvation. —2 CORINTHIANS 6:1-2 NASB

State of Grace

Living a life of recovery and health is a state of grace—God's grace. And He offers that grace in the form of new, healthy lives for us. By working together with God to make small but consistent changes, His grace creates huge benefits over time.

We must not receive this grace in vain or take it for granted, though. We must take action today, because today is the day of salvation—not only from sin, but also from our condition, which has robbed us of the life God intended for us. It's time for us to fully experience the joy of relationships and love, of acceptance as valuable creations of God, and the intimacy with God that was once hidden because of our shame.

Behold, now is the acceptable time! We receive God's grace right now to eat healthier, even if it means saying no to that particular food item that we love and need so much. We receive His grace every time we exercise for just fifteen minutes instead of giving in to the part of us that wants to relax. We receive His grace each time we reach out to connect with a supportive person instead of reaching for food. And as we do our part, God's grace flows freely!

Today, Lord, I receive Your grace and trust in Your salvation from my previously hopeless condition.

"But God did say, 'You must not eat fruit from the tree that is in the middle of the garden, and you must not touch it, or you will die.'" —GENESIS 3:3

One Bite

For some of us in the Lose It For Life program, we can have a portion of our favorite food or treat occasionally. It may not bother us to have a taste of ice cream or cake, or a bite of a dessert shared with others. We may find relief in those moments, feeling less deprivation and more hope for staying on the long-term path of healthy living.

But there are others of us for whom one bite may be too many. Just one bite can set up a craving for more that leads to a binge—and when does that stop? One bite can become life threatening. It can lead to demoralization, guilt, and shame; it can keep us from spiritual growth, closeness with the Lord, and weight loss.

As in the Garden, where Eve was tempted by Satan to try just one bite of the food that would surely bring her death, so we must consider the cost of taking the bite. We must know ourselves and respect that knowledge as we answer the question, "Is this bite worth the pain that may follow?" We might be giving up our progress and boundaries—and risk losing the great life that God has for us in the process—if we succumb to the craving for just one nibble.

Today, Lord, may I give up "one bite" of the food that triggers binges.

MAY 16

"Then you will know the truth, and the truth will set you free."

—JOHN 8:32

Head and Heart Knowledge

We have been trapped in lies for years—lies which tell us that we don't matter . . . we don't belong . . . it's better to hide . . . no one really cares . . . we'll always be heavy . . . we don't deserve God's help . . . and much more. Believing these falsehoods has kept us locked in the heaviness that comes when we've given up hope for our body and for energetic, vivacious, connected living.

Truth does exist, but it has been obscured by our belief in the lies. We may have never truly understood the important realities of Jesus that can free us from captivity. Many of us have plenty of head knowledge of God's love for us, His plans for us, our worth in Christ Jesus, that our sins are washed away, that He gives abundant life to His people, and so on. But these truths have yet to penetrate our hearts and be made manifest in our lives.

Our task is not only to seek truth in Jesus but also to open our hearts and try to believe it. We need the voices of those who will speak God's love to us. We need people to pour His grace and compassion over our wounds. We need the truth of Jesus, who sets us free.

Today, Lord, I pray to know the truth. I pray to know You, the ultimate Truth, deep in my heart.

But Uriah wouldn't go home. He stayed that night at the palace entrance with some of the king's other servants. When David heard what Uriah had done, he summoned him and asked, "What's the matter with you? Why didn't you go home last night after being away for so long?" Uriah replied, "The Ark and the armies of Israel and Judah are living in tents, and Joab and his officers are camping in the open fields. How could I go home to wine and dine and sleep with my wife? I swear that I will never be guilty of acting like that." —2 SAMUEL 11:9-11 NLT

Loyal to the Fellowship

Uriah had been off at war, away from his wife and home for an extended period of time. Upon returning briefly to speak with King David, he was urged to return home to eat, relax, and sleep with his wife for an evening. Yet Uriah's loyalty and strong character wouldn't let him indulge himself while the rest of the troops were without such comforts. He denied himself and chose to identify with the men on the frontlines instead.

When we are encouraged by others to indulge in the many comforts of food and leisure, we, too, can identify ourselves with an army—a fellowship of men and women around the world fighting for freedom from food. Through loyalty to this clan, we gain self-control and the encouragement of knowing that we are not alone; we are together in this battle against unhealthy eating.

Today, Lord, may I find strength through the fellowship of others in this battle.

MAY 18

For every child of God defeats this evil world by trusting Christ to give the victory. —1 JOHN 5:4 NLT

In the Heat of Battle

The idea of trusting Christ to give the victory sounds simple enough. Yet how many times have we binged on sugar foods without reaching for help from Christ and His followers? How many times have we felt completely defeated after falling prey again to comfort foods? How many times have we stayed on the couch rather than exercising the body we've been given?

Defeating this "evil world" of cravings for unhealthy foods and our lack of enthusiasm about physical activity was never a task we were meant to accomplish on our own. By the power of Jesus and what He has already done for us, we are not helpless in our stand for health and wholeness. Our challenges may be the worst imaginable, but we need not despair. No matter what our difficulty, we know that Christ will give us the victory as we trust Him.

As we do our part to put our faith in Him, whatever that requires—praying, joining a support group, etc.—He will always come through for us. The next time we're tempted, we have the battleground choice of reaching for excess food or reaching out to Christ for the victory.

Today, Lord, may I reach for You in the heat of the battle.

MAY 19

For the vision is yet for the appointed time; it hastens toward the goal and it will not fail. Though it tarries, wait for it; for it will certainly come, it will not delay. —HABAKKUK 2:3 NASB

Right in Time

God is moving—in perfect time. When we catch a vision for what God has in store for us personally, we may be so excited for the hope in our future that we burn with urgency to see it fulfilled and are tempted to reject the notion that healing is a process. We want to be well today!

God is no stranger to human impatience. For centuries upon centuries, people have doubted His wisdom, questioned His purposes, and scoffed at His timing. Yet He has a plan, and He is right on schedule.

Much of our healing and recovery from food and weight issues will be a slow and steady process of gradual change—we can count on that. But in our yearning and eagerness, God brings us such hope: "Wait patiently," He says, "for it will surely take place. It will not be delayed."

We can rest, knowing that He is sovereign over all, and that all He's planned will take place, right in time.

Today, Lord, may I trust in Your timing and find peace in Your words of assurance. Help me to be steady and patient in my path of recovery, and to rejoice as Your plans are fulfilled.

But if we walk in the light, as he is in the light, we have fellowship with one another, and the blood of Jesus, his Son, purifies us from all sin. —1 JOHN 1:7

Walking Together in Light

Hiding our problems and embarrassment is a lifestyle of darkness in which we isolate and disconnect from God and His people. Yet it is in connection that we find the very grace and love of God that we need. So we must get out of the dark and into the light.

When we walk in the light, where Jesus is, then we can enjoy fellowship with Him and His people. There is no hiding when we are in relationship with Him; He sees everything. The darkness is banished and shame is lifted when we also share our vulnerabilities with others who have their own vulnerabilities. We discover we are all more similar than we realized: We all struggle; we all feel shame at times; we all need a Savior . . . and we have one.

The blood of Jesus purifies all of the reasons we're hiding. We can get through our challenges when we walk through them with each other—and with Him.

Today, Lord, may I call on a friend and discuss my shame at overeating. I pray that as I walk in the light, I will find great fellowship with You and with a friend who understands this journey.

MAY 21

My brothers, if one of you should wander from the truth and someone should bring him back, remember this: Whoever turns a sinner from the error of his way will save him from death and cover over a multitude of sins. —JAMES 5:19-20

Blessed by Accountability

Remember this song? "They call me the Wanderer. . . . I roam aroun' aroun' aroun' aroun' around . . ." That's who we are! Wanderers, all of us.

No matter how much we love God or how dedicated we are to Him, we human beings tend to wander. We may even have a deep, powerful relationship with God—rich in knowledge of His Word and principles—and yet, as sinners, we still get distracted. Our struggle with food and weight is a blatant example of this. Though many of us know the power of prayer and the benefits of healthy eating and exercise, on our own we recline in our chair, watch television, and eat junk foods.

Our goal, however, is not to wander around aimlessly, but to live each day deliberately and in truth. This demands accountability to one another. We need the encouragement of friends so we do not despair, and others need that encouragement from us as well. The commonality of fellow strugglers brings not only insight and guidance but deep connection and often great joy amid the challenge.

Today, Lord, when I find myself straying from Your path with food, may I call on a friend for help and guidance back into truth.

MAY 22

"How long, O Lᴏʀᴅ, must I call for help? But you do not listen!"
The Lᴏʀᴅ replied," . . . Watch and be astounded at what I will
do! For I am doing something in your own day, something you
wouldn't believe even if someone told you about it."

—HABAKKUK 1:2, 5 *(Habakkuk's complaint)*

Hellooooo! Anybody Home??

When our hearts are discouraged, we can feel very
alone. There are days, sometimes years, when we
feel completely abandoned by God in our struggle.
Exhausted from calling to Him in despair, we complain, "You're not even listening!" Even worse, we
look to His Word and see the history of His many
miracles and wonders, yet we're unable to see Him
moving so profoundly in our own life today.

In truth, we are sometimes too simple-minded.
God says to us, "You just watch what I've got
planned for *you*!"

What reassurance this is when we're feeling
abandoned! God is always, always up to something.
He has not left us or forgotten us. He really does
hear our prayers. He sees our limited perspective
and beyond, into eternity—He knows what He's
doing.

While it's very tempting for us to whine in our
suffering, it is much more exciting to hope on His
promised plans for our good. Even if He told us
what He has in store for us, most likely we wouldn't
believe it.

Today, Lord, may I live in the excitement of knowing
You. I believe in Your plans for me. I eagerly expect
great things from You!

MAY 23

"Watch and pray so that you will not fall into temptation. The spirit is willing, but the body is weak." —MATTHEW 26:41

An Ounce of Prevention, a Pound of Cure

"The spirit is willing, but the body is weak." How true this is! While we may have the desire for all-around wellness, our bodies are weak with cravings, emptiness, and easy access to short-lived solutions for pain. We may even know more spiritually than we can apply physically. So we must be alert to this reality.

Being proactive will go a long way in our recovery from food and weight issues. We must be on guard, watching for temptations and praying for God's guidance and strength in each new situation. If we walk about unaware, we will easily fall into serving our flesh—giving into the temporary gratification of bingeing. But as we instead live aware of our surroundings, predictable traps, and our own weaknesses, we can then walk in the spirit and provision that comes from God. In this way, we guard our progress in losing it for life.

Today, Lord, I watch and pray to avoid the temptations of my old lifestyle.

If I go up to the heavens, you are there; if I make my bed in the depths, you are there. —PSALM 139:8

God Is with Us

Even in the midst of our compulsive, emotional eating, God has been with us. Despite our obsessive food thoughts, God has been with us. If we decide to make our bed in the depths of this condition and allow it to overtake our lives, He will still be there with us. If we choose the upward, heavenly path of recovery and let go of emotional eating, He will be with us then, too.

God does not judge us if we shy away from the overwhelming task of recovery from our food and weight problems—it is our own shame and guilt that condemn us. We must reach out in faith, even when we are at the bottom, and take comfort in His presence, in His unfailing love.

Today, Lord, I confess that even I have been running from Your will for me with eating, but I cannot escape Your presence. Help me turn to Your Spirit for strength to face this problem.

MAY 25

Where can I go from your Spirit? Where can I flee from your presence? —PSALM 139:7

God Will Not Leave Us

Whether we perceive this verse as good news or bad news, here is the reality: We can try to flee from God and His will for us with food, but He will not leave us. We may have tried to avoid what God has been nudging us toward for many years, but our attempts have been futile; we didn't "lose" Him by running away.

No matter where we are in the continuum of the struggle, God's Spirit is here; He is with us. Can you feel His presence? Will you embrace His mercy? Are you ready to enjoy His love?

When we obsess over food—whether controlling it, eating it, or thinking about it—it's difficult for us to be in touch with His Spirit. Because of that obsession, it's even harder to believe in His love for us enough to be motivated toward self-care around food. But with the comfort and strengthening of God's presence in this huge task, we can make a beginning toward that self-care, for just one day. Maybe just for one meal.

As we practice new behaviors and new attitudes with God's Spirit supporting us, we take on new life. We are moving toward the fullness and purpose that He intends for us.

Today, Lord, I confess that I have tried to flee from Your will. I ask to be strengthened in faith to take action on new behaviors.

And we are eagerly waiting for him to return as our Savior. He will take these weak mortal bodies of ours and change them into glorious bodies like his own, using the same mighty power that he will use to conquer everything, everywhere.

—PHILIPPIANS 3:20-21 *NLT*

Give Me That Glorious Body

Oh, how we can get stuck just dreaming of that day! We are so aware of the less-than-ideal state of our body. And though we are probably not at the point of wanting to leave this earth just yet, the mere thought of exchanging this weak, overweight, mortal shell for a body described as "glorious" can be very tantalizing!

We eagerly await that day. However, for now, our body has been given to us as a gift from God to host His Holy Spirit. When we accept His lordship in our life, we admit that our body is not our own. We simply reside in this vehicle for fulfilling His purposes in us here on earth.

To eagerly await does not mean to give up until Jesus comes back. Rather, as we anticipate Christ's return, we are called to strengthen His creation—today. Our current body is weak compared to what's coming, but it can be improved and empowered for use here on earth. We must resist the urge to be passive and instead remain active—participating in the life God has for us now.

Today, Lord, I will not be stuck waiting passively. Help me to engage in life on earth and to care for my mortal body.

Cast your cares on the LORD and he will sustain you; he will never let the righteous fall. —PSALM 55:22

He Will Sustain You

Remember the Weebles? They wobble but they won't fall down. They're the toys that always get back up again.

It may seem simplistic, but that kind of fortitude is just what God helps us have. We experience deep and painful emotion on the road to recovery. We are often troubled by the load before us— having to stick with healthy eating and exercise while facing the harsh realities of life—and our legs may begin to buckle beneath the burden of our task.

These "weights" are heavy. But instead of collapsing under them, we can cast our cares on the Lord and let Him sustain us. This does not mean we don't care anymore; it means we entrust these concerns to the One who keeps us from falling under them.

It's quite a deal! The Lord upholds and steadies us as we trust Him. He is gentle, caring, and always there. Though we may wobble at times, unsure of our footing and unsure of His plan, He guides us, and we progress in recovery with His support.

Today, Lord, I may wobble, but I trust You to steady me.

MAY 28

When David and his men saw the ruins and realized what had happened to their families, they wept until they could weep no more. —1 SAMUEL 30:3-4 NLT

Let Sorrow Run Its Course

In healing and growing through our food and weight challenges, at some point we must journey into our family history. We gain insight for today by examining our past.

Sadly, realizing the truth of our lives as children, the dysfunction of our families, and the ways we've suffered from the effects of others can be very painful. Owning the poor choices we've made as adults and accepting that we have harmed others can be just as devastating.

There is a time for coming to grips with reality. When we see the ruins and realize what has happened, we may need to let sorrow run its course. We may need to weep until we can weep no more. In doing so, we may find new freedom from our past that will allow us to take action today.

Today, Lord, please help me to see the reality of my life. Help me to grieve and feel sorrow as long as I need to.

"Don't you see that nothing that enters a man from the outside can make him 'unclean'? . . . What comes out of a man is what makes him 'unclean.' . . . For from within, out of men's hearts, come evil thoughts, sexual immorality, theft, murder, adultery, greed, malice, deceit, lewdness, envy, slander, arrogance and folly. All these evils come from inside and make a man 'unclean.'" —MARK 7:18, 20-23

What Makes You Unclean?

You are to be commended for making strides toward a better life! The danger comes when we use our performance with food to determine our level of wellness today.

Avoiding what's "bad" can evoke a sense of pride for our "clean" behavior. Conversely, eating something harmful may evoke a sense of shame. In this, we are once again giving food more power than it deserves and allowing our behaviors to define us.

Jesus explained this mystery to His disciples to free them from ritualistic ideas, not only about food but about God's definition of cleanliness. He explained that when our attention is on our eating habits and activities and not who we are inside, then our focus is off. It is more important to tend to matters of the heart than to ceremonies and rituals.

For determining well-being, we must shift the emphasis away from performance. This is not a license to throw away our devotion to eating excellence. Instead, it refines our purpose and improves our character so that our eating can follow suit.

Today, Lord, I will examine my heart for impurities and remove any false rituals of cleanliness.

MAY 30

When tempted, no one should say, "God is tempting me." For God cannot be tempted by evil, nor does he tempt anyone; but each one is tempted when, by his own evil desire, he is dragged away and enticed. Then, after desire has conceived, it gives birth to sin; and sin, when it is full-grown, gives birth to death.   —JAMES 1:13-15

Who's Doing What?

How many times have we blamed God for something that, in hindsight, we know we ultimately caused? Often our gut reaction is to get angry with God, certain that He is teasing us with food and waiting for the opportunity to pounce on us at the moment of our failure. It's frustrating to us that the very thing He created to be good is one of our biggest problems in life! But we also conveniently disregard that we are the ones who have misused food. God is not to blame, and He is not tempting us toward sin.

When we decide to take ownership of our own responsibilities, then we come closer to being able to change our behavior. This is not about shaming ourselves; it's about the appropriate designation of who's doing what. By acknowledging our desires that lead us away from God's good plan for us, we are no longer the helpless victim without any choices. Instead, we are more aware of reality and better able to participate in the healing process.

Today, Lord, I will walk in reality and be responsible for my choices.

The word of the LORD came to me, saying, "Before I formed you in the womb I knew you, before you were born I set you apart; I appointed you as a prophet to the nations."

—JEREMIAH 1:4-5

Who Are You?

Sometimes we can feel lost inside, like we've been disguised by our excess pounds. Who would we be if we weren't overweight or defined by our appearance? What would we do if we didn't obsess over food or fret about wearing a bathing suit? Apart from the distractions of our body, who would we really be?

We may have no idea who we are apart from our struggles with food and weight, but God does. He knows every ounce of our being today, and He has known every bit since before we ever came to exist. He knows His creative purpose in us. He is aware of every trial, tear, and joy we've experienced thus far. He has not lost us.

This is not merely comforting; it is our hope. As we move along each day in recovery, we can invite God to show us who we really are. He is not only all-knowing but tender and intimate, concerned and ready to provide for our every need.

Today, Lord, may I learn from Your knowledge of me. Reveal to me more of who I was created to be.

JUNE 1

"Come to Me, all who are weary and heavy-laden, and I will give you rest. Take My yoke upon you and learn from Me, for I am gentle and humble in heart, and you will find rest for your souls. For My yoke is easy and My burden is light."

—MATTHEW 11:28-30 NASB

The Easier Yoke

Jesus calls to us when we are so discouraged that we feel like quitting. In this passage, He paints for us the word picture of the yoke, a two-animal piece of equipment used for heavy, sweaty work. Jesus says that His yoke is easy, and the load is light. The translation of this imagery indicates that He will take on our hard work so that our soul can rest. But first we must surrender to His yoke.

This is a great concept! The diet mentality is a heavy burden of deprivation, self-loathing, and "white-knuckling" willpower. Putting on Jesus' yoke —a plan for our food, exercise, and spiritual work —is light and easy by comparison. When we yield to His will and take on His yoke, we find rest instead of heavy work. We find success instead of defeat. We find gentleness, humility, and acceptance instead of judgment.

In assuming Jesus' yoke and surrendering our will over food, we learn what life is really about.

Today, Lord, I completely surrender in humility to Your yoke and will follow my plan for recovery.

JUNE 2

Hey there! All who are thirsty, come to the water! Are you penniless? Come anyway—buy and eat! Come, buy your drinks, buy wine and milk. Buy without money—everything's free! Why do you spend your money on junk food, your hard-earned cash on cotton candy? Listen to me, listen well: Eat only the best, fill yourself with only the finest. Pay attention, come close now, listen carefully to my life-giving, life-nourishing words. I'm making a lasting covenant commitment with you, the same that I made with David: sure, solid, enduring love.   —ISAIAH 55:1-3 MSG

The Spiritual Realm of My Need

Often we spend our energy and resources for food that does not give us strength. We pay dearly for it even though it does us no good, and it affects us at all levels—physically, mentally, and spiritually. Yet we keep devouring what does not fill and searching for more, always more.

God sees our struggle and uses the pangs of hunger to show us our deeper spiritual need—for salvation and the abundance of life. We've attempted to fill our spiritual craving in the physical realm, and God is calling us to come, listen, and take the food that is good for our soul. He has more for us than a life of scavenging for meaningless, unsatisfying fill. We can allow our obsessions with food to point us to our deeper need for God's provision of what's good and healthy for the whole of our being.

Today, Lord, when my cravings roar, may I enter the spiritual realm of my need.

JUNE 3

When I think of the wisdom and scope of God's plan, I fall to my knees and pray to the Father, the Creator of everything in heaven and on earth. I pray that from his glorious, unlimited resources he will give you mighty inner strength through his Holy Spirit. —EPHESIANS 3:14-16 NLT

His Sheer Magnitude

Today we have the opportunity to think on God's vast, infinite wisdom and the scope of His plan. Instead of being swallowed up in the pain that can result from releasing our will around food, we can step out of our world for a few moments and open ourselves to the grander scheme. This is always a good exercise—one that gives us a more grounded perspective on our current challenges.

By availing ourselves to God's sovereignty and the magnitude of His plans—not only for all creation but for us individually and personally as well—we can better rely upon Him for our needs. Trusting in God's supremacy, we can talk with Him about our situation and know that He will provide for us by His wisdom. His resources are limitless, and we can rest in the assurance that He loves us. In facing temptation, we can call upon Him to give us self-control and strength through His Holy Spirit, who dwells within us.

Today, Lord, I know You are sovereign and limitless in resources, power, and love. Thank You for the wisdom and scope of Your plan. I pray to receive Your strength for letting go of my excess food and staying positive in the challenges of this day.

JUNE 4

And a certain man was there, who had been thirty-eight years in his sickness. When Jesus saw him lying there and knew that he had already been a long time in that condition, He said to him, "Do you wish to get well?" The sick man answered Him, "Sir, I have no man to put me into the pool when the water is stirred up, but while I am coming, another steps down before me." Jesus said to him, "Arise, take up your pallet, and walk." —JOHN 5:5-8 NASB

Roadblocks to Recovery

On the journey of recovery from weight issues, we must define the things in our lives that hold us back. In what ways do we sabotage our progress? Are we full of excuses for not taking action, like the man in this passage? Are we protesting and declaring, "It's not fair"?

Jesus came upon this paralyzed man and saw right past his reasons, his avoidance, his fear. The Savior must have had love and compassion in His eyes as He said to him, "Arise, take up your pallet, and walk." Amazingly, there was no more rebuttal—no more excuses, no more complaints. The man must have internally let go of all his reasons and excuses in a single moment. And then, he simply stood up and took action.

It takes but a single moment to decide on a change that will improve our lives forever. If we are stuck in rebuttal, then now is the time for us to discover what excuses we're using to keep from seizing our God-given moment.

Today, Lord, as I journal, please show me one area where I sabotage progress. With new information, may I seize my moments and move forward in recovery.

JUNE 5

The woman named Folly is loud and brash. . . . To those without good judgment, she says, "Stolen water is refreshing; food eaten in secret tastes the best!"

—PROVERBS 9:13, 16B-17 NLT

The Woman Named Folly

Do you hear the voice of Folly? Is she saying these things to you? Beware! She does not address us while at our strongest, but instead calls to us when we're lacking in judgment and most vulnerable to her trickery. She is persistent, persuasive, and when she speaks, she deceives.

When we are without the support of friends or disconnected from God, we are susceptible to foolishness. In these times we can easily be tempted back into bondage with food. We may then steal away from our program, savoring moments of rebellion and apparent control in which we eat what we want, when we want. Yet in the end, we are still enslaved to the grip of our addiction.

Wisdom will quiet the voice of Folly. To walk in recovery from food and weight issues, we must saturate ourselves in wisdom and in truth. By protecting our quiet time with God, staying connected to a mentor, and sharing the journey with fellow strugglers, we nurture ourselves and quiet the voice of Folly today.

Today, Lord, may I be saturated in Your truth.

JUNE 6

Jesus told them this story: "A man had two sons. The younger son told his father, 'I want my share of your estate now, instead of waiting until you die.' So his father agreed to divide his wealth between his sons. A few days later this younger son packed all his belongings and took a trip to a distant land, and there he wasted all his money on wild living. . . ."

—LUKE 15:11-13 NLT

Wanting It All Right Now

It takes courage to view ourselves as the son who asked for "his share" before his father was dead. In ancient culture, it was the height of rebellion and effrontery to make such a request of one's father. But for anyone who struggles with overeating tendencies, we know we have asked for—and eaten— more than our share of desserts, snacks, helpings, and rich foods. We have binged because we wanted more than our share. We have searched out the newest flavors and restaurants, always seeking satisfaction in quantity. Like the son prematurely requesting his share, we have asked for our inheritance—a whole lifetime of food—instead of waiting for a normal portion at the right time.

The realm of food is where we've rebelled against the goodness of God. We've wasted time, energy, and resources on indulgent eating.

Today, Lord, I humbly acknowledge that I have had my portion, my share of Your wealth of sweet, salty, and rich foods. Father, forgive me for wanting it all right now.

JUNE 7

"About the time his money ran out, a great famine swept over the land, and he began to starve. He persuaded a local farmer to hire him to feed his pigs. The boy became so hungry that even the pods he was feeding the pigs looked good to him. But no one gave him anything." —LUKE 15:14-16 NLT

Consequences Set In

At this point in the story, reality is beginning to sink in for the rebellious son. The excitement is gone, the fun has run out along with the money, and he's empty. He has to lower himself to not only become a hired man but to feed pigs. And then, revealing his pitiful state, he begins to desire what they are eating!

There comes a point when we realize we are in trouble with our weight, yet we just continue to grope for some sort of answer. We don't want to do what it takes to truly recover—it's too much work. So we lower our standards, attempt another quick-loss diet, join one more exercise club, or buy the latest cardio machine.

Although we may be hurting, our denial of our overconsumption problem pushes us to blend in when everyone else is having desserts or going to the buffet. We want to eat like everyone else, even though it is damaging to our body and spirit. Thus we remain in denial of our problem and thereby defile ourselves with unhealthy foods or quantities that are beyond moderate.

Today, Lord, may I be willing to turn away from unhealthy quantities of food.

JUNE 8

"When he finally came to his senses, he said to himself, 'At home even the hired men have food enough to spare, and here I am dying of hunger.'" —*LUKE 15:17* NLT

Out of Denial

Now the prodigal is beginning to see the total reality of his situation—he's coming out of denial. He finds himself in a place he never dreamed he'd be—slopping pigs, with no money, no food. All this, despite the early receipt of his inheritance.

The son begins to realize that his father was not as cruel as he'd thought. Even his father's hired hands were better off than those he saw around him. His father may have had rules and standards, but there was also abundance.

In the same way, we've had many plans for our lives and undoubtedly made great efforts to carry those out. Yet we never imagined we'd find ourselves 20, 50, or even 100 pounds overweight. If we want to change our lives for good, then we must step out of denial and realize: Our old ways have not been working. We must stop looking at diets as restriction and deprivation, and instead accept that a food plan actually brings freedom. It may require letting go of certain items, but there is an abundance of what really nourishes. As the prodigal son began to realize, a life based on self-gratification can never really satisfy.

Today, Lord, may I have the humility to accept the reality of the place where I now find myself, letting go of my own will regarding food.

JUNE 9

"I will get up and go to my father, and will say to him, 'Father, I have sinned against heaven, and in your sight; I am no longer worthy to be called your son; make me as one of your hired men,'"　—LUKE 15:18-19 NASB

Devise a Plan

The prodigal son was helpless and hopeless until he became proactive and devised a plan of action. But first he developed the necessary humility—being able to look at his behaviors and admit his failings to himself. He had learned through painful experience that when he indulged himself, he ended up empty. He was full but not satisfied. The result was the building of his character—he became open to honest work, and even grateful to serve as hired help in his father's house.

Without a plan of action, we are just as helpless and hopeless as the prodigal. We, too, must develop the humility to admit that we have indulged ourselves and ended up wanting. Though we might have been full from bingeing or continual snacking, if we are honest with ourselves, we can admit that we were never truly satisfied. The food could never fill the emptiness in our souls.

Structuring our meals—having a plan of action—allows us to be open to honest work in our Father's house. We are then open to hearing His will for our lives. This is a plan worth making.

Today, Lord, I confess my shortcomings to You, and I admit that my self-indulgence has left me empty. May I hear Your will for me.

"So he returned home to his father. And while he was still a long distance away, his father saw him coming. Filled with compassion, he ran to his son, embraced him, and kissed him. His son said to him, 'Father, I have sinned against both heaven and you, and I am no longer worthy of being called your son.'"

—*LUKE 15:20-21* NLT

Push Past the Shame

A sense of unworthiness could have caused this young man's downfall in the end, but it didn't! The forces of evil sought to keep him from his purpose in God, to keep him in the shame and degradation of his poor choices. But the desperation of the prodigal allowed him to push past the shame of what he had done to himself, thereby enabling him to face his father again. By developing humility and willingness, he could openly acknowledge to his father the extent of his selfishness. The son had finally grasped that his father was his source of safety, healing, and provision.

We can always return to the Father—no matter how many pounds we have to lose, no matter how many slips we've had, no matter how imperfectly we deal with our food issues, no matter how slowly the pounds come off. He is always waiting and ready for our return.

Today, Father, as I push past the sense of shame about my food and weight problems, may I feel Your compassion and embrace.

JUNE 11

Celebrate Recovery

The father doesn't really listen to his son's proposal of being a hired hand—he only celebrates the transformation of his son from death to life, from being lost to being found! The father is joyful, generous, and overwhelmingly gracious!

This is recovery! We make a small step in the arena of humility and willingness to let go of excess food—and we receive our very life, full of richness we never dreamed possible. We are truly satisfied with good, simple, nourishing food. Weight begins to drop off, and we find that life opens up with relationships and activities we could never before enjoy. We can revel in being God's child and embrace life!

Today, Lord, may I celebrate recovery with You by embracing all of life.

JUNE 12

"The older brother was angry and would not go in. . . . His father said to him, 'Look, dear son, you and I are very close, and everything I have is yours. We had to celebrate this happy day. For your brother was dead and has come back to life! He was lost, but now he is found.'" —LUKE 15:28A, 31, 32 NLT

From Separation to Communion

This is a classic tale of sibling rivalry. The older son was angry because he saw his father indulging the younger son once again. The father is quick to point out that it is not indulgent to celebrate when someone "comes back to life," rejoining the family.

The prodigal was isolated from genuine relationships through his self-indulgence. By leaving home, he had cut himself off from his father's household. Though our isolation may not be so blatant, we also cut ourselves off from others through compulsive and emotional eating. Most damaging, we've cut ourselves off from God in our guilt and shame. We've likely suffered from a lack of intimacy and avoided being truly known.

Here the father explains the cause for celebration—the younger son had been dead but was now alive; lost, but now found. The father cannot contain his joy. When we return to God in humility, He is always ready and waiting for open communion with us. We can return home, confident in His rejoicing love for us.

Today, Lord, may I have humility to stop indulging myself with food, and may I hunger for communion with You.

JUNE 13

Let the word of Christ dwell in you richly as you teach and admonish one another with all wisdom, and as you sing psalms, hymns and spiritual songs with gratitude in your hearts to God. —COLOSSIANS 3:16

We Go Together . . .

We need each other for the fulfillment of God's plan in each of us. Life is not an individual project; neither is the journey of weight loss. When we are tempted to isolate and tackle life with God by ourselves, then we immediately oppose His inspired Word to us. It is His plan for us to live in community and mutual encouragement.

As we "lose it for life," we can learn by the wise teaching and admonishment of one another. We can gather together for worship with gratitude for God's goodness and all that He is doing. We can rejoice with one another in triumph and encourage each other through sorrow. As we live out God's principles in the blessing of fellowship, we allow His Word to dwell richly within us.

Today, Lord, I will reach out to share life with friends.

JUNE 14

The sleep of a laborer is sweet, whether he eats little or much... —ECCLESIASTES 5:12A

Let's Get Physical

This one line of scripture is overflowing with truth and guidance for us! Here hard work and sleep are prized above the volume of food we consume.

Yet we know that food affects our energy levels, too. We can feel tired from overeating, or tired from undereating—and still need nourishment. With varying blood sugar levels and a lack of self-discipline, it's no wonder that many of us with eating problems also have sleeping problems.

The observation Solomon makes here about how our bodies operate can be helpful to those of us who need a good starting place. In an effort to reorient our bodies, we can begin by engaging in physical activity today. We can move and sweat for even just fifteen minutes. This may sound insignificant, but even a small step like this can trigger a chain reaction toward health and wholeness. Among the load of benefits that this exercise of our will and body can bring, it sets up our need for rest at the end of the day and improves our quality of sleep. When we rest well, we awake with renewed energy and hope for the new day.

Today, Lord, I want volume of food to be a non-issue with me. May I move and sweat today and sleep well tonight!

*But let the godly rejoice. Let them be glad in God's presence.
Let them be filled with joy. Sing praises to God and to his
name! Sing loud praises to him who rides the clouds. His name
is the Lord—rejoice in his presence! Father to the fatherless,
defender of widows—this is God, whose dwelling is holy. God
places the lonely in families; he sets the prisoners free and
gives them joy.* —PSALM 68:3-6 NLT

Every Reason to Celebrate

Such praise and rejoicing as this comes from a heart
that has tasted the goodness of God firsthand. It
comes from a heart loaded, overflowing with sheer
gratitude and love.

Despite our many trials, we, too, have every
reason to celebrate. In the face of all we endure on
a daily basis, it can feel unnatural to celebrate. But
praising God and rejoicing in His goodness is likely
the best thing we could do today. When we are
focused on Him and who He is, then the burden of
all our troubles is momentarily lifted. Suddenly we
find reasons to praise Him—not only for His character but also for the blessings He's granted us, for
the people we love, for the fact that we exercised this
morning, for the celery we chose over the potato
chips, for the beauty of the sunset this evening . . .
the list is never-ending.

When we spend more of our time celebrating
what's right, we have less time to pour tears over
what's wrong.

*Today, Lord, You give me every reason to celebrate. I
worship You for all that You are.*

JUNE 16

And then God answered: "Write this. Write what you see. Write it out in big block letters so that it can be read on the run."

—HABAKKUK 2:2 MSG

Write What You See

Write it down. As we overcome our challenges with weight, it is invaluable to record the Lord's answers to our prayers and His guiding hand in our life. At any given moment we usually have many questions we want Him to answer, many feelings to explore, many thoughts and helpful reminders we'd like to access along the way. God is speaking to us through His Word, through His people, and straight to our hearts. He is teaching us how to get well, step by step, and sometimes we are missing it.

Taking fifteen minutes a day to journal our experiences may help us to capture the lessons and solidify them in our hearts. In print, ideas are no longer swirling around and confusing our minds; they are instead laid to rest, in ink, for safe-keeping—and even for reference tomorrow.

As we look back at the record of our journey, we will not only see our own progress with time, but we may even notice that God has been speaking more than we thought He was. In hindsight, we'll realize we were learning more than we thought we were, too.

Today, Lord, I will listen for You to bring insight for my challenges with food. I will write down Your answers and pass them along.

JUNE 17

But God demonstrates his own love for us in this: While we were still sinners, Christ died for us. —ROMANS 5:8

He Loves You, Like It or Not

On days when we feel wholly undeserving of God's help with our weight loss, when we feel completely hopeless and ashamed, we can think upon this reality: Long before we were ever even aware of our need for a Savior, God loved us beyond measure. His greatest act of love was already completed before we ever came to exist. He knew we were sinners, and He loved us anyway.

What makes us think we could possibly be horrible enough to diminish God's love? He didn't wait around for us to earn it; it was already infinite and unstoppable before we ever had the chance to be good—or bad. His love has nothing to do with our performance; it has everything to do with who He is. And He is the definition of love.

If God loved us enough to help us then, in our total inability, then He will help us today, in our current challenges. His love is unending. He sees our current helplessness and provides for us, regardless of whether we deserve it or not. In His love we have great hope!

Today, Lord, I will simply accept the love You have for me. I will never deserve it, but I am so grateful for it.

JUNE 18

He entered a village; and a woman named Martha welcomed Him into her home. She had a sister called Mary, who was seated at the Lord's feet, listening to His word. But Martha was distracted with all her preparations; and she came up to Him and said, "Lord, do You not care that my sister has left me to do all the serving alone? Then tell her to help me." But the Lord answered and said to her, "Martha, Martha, you are worried and bothered about so many things; but only one thing is necessary, for Mary has chosen the good part, which shall not be taken away from her." —LUKE 10:38-42 NASB

The Good Part

Martha thought she was serving Jesus by working, but actually, Jesus told her that all her busywork was unnecessary for eternal living. In fact, it was keeping her from "the good part"!

It's easy to become so busy that we don't take time to plan our meals, fit in exercise, or go to the store so we'll have all we need to eat healthfully. If we're not making time for these things, then we're setting ourselves up to make poor eating choices and sabotage our progress. When we are too busy to take care of our needs, we miss "the good part"— being with Jesus.

When we sit at Jesus' feet and rest in our relationship with Him, we gain the strength to face the day with His power. Our anxieties about the day's tasks diminish. We are taking care of ourselves spiritually, and then our emotional and physical well-being follow.

Today, Lord, no matter how full my day looks, I commit to sit at Your feet, to listen and to rest.

JUNE 19

See to it that no one takes you captive through hollow and deceptive philosophy, which depends on human tradition and the basic principles of this world rather than on Christ.

—COLOSSIANS 2:8

Human Tradition

We might believe we're not captive to hollow and deceptive philosophy, but we must ask ourselves: How much do I base my ideas about food on what my parents taught me? It's natural for us to develop the same eating behaviors, attitudes, and values as our family of origin. But is it healthy?

A woman once spoke of how emotional eating began in her family: "My mother told me how her mother would always say, 'Eat something, Elizabeth; you'll feel better!' So what did my mother model for me? The same thing—that eating was a way of feeling better, of soothing oneself. And that is the point at which food and feelings collided for both myself and my sister."

Food can easily become a balm, a Band-Aid for our feelings. Any one of us could point to a family situation similar to this woman's. Whatever attitudes, habits, or values we were taught involving food (clean your plate, dessert at every meal, etc.), it is time to let go of them if we are to "lose it for life." They have kept us captive long enough—we can now claim our freedom in Christ.

Today, Lord, I let go of the attitudes and traditions involving food that may have kept me captive to destructive eating. I cling to the freedom I've found in Christ.

"Can a mother forget the baby at her breast and have no compassion on the child she has borne? Though she may forget, I will not forget you! See, I have engraved you on the palms of my hands." —ISAIAH 49:15-16A

Perfect Parent

If we have an unresolved, strained relationship with our mother, these words can be so comforting and healing to receive. We may have begun our emotional eating at a very young age because of insufficient nurturing and comforting—we ate to fill the loneliness. Or perhaps our mother only nurtured by feeding us. Many mothers prepare food as a way to connect with and give attention to their children. As we grow up, these early experiences become a way of life that is then deeply ingrained and mostly habitual within us.

In these verses the Lord reminds us of His devotion to our deepest needs. The implication here is that a mother cannot forget a baby at the breast— she will always have compassion on the child she has borne. But even if that baby was forgotten, the point is what the Lord will do: He will never forget us! In fact, we are engraved on the palms of His hands. Here God is underscoring the fact that it's impossible for Him to be non-nurturing or uncompassionate toward us. We have His word that He is always tenderly feeding and nurturing us. He is the only Perfect Parent.

Today, Lord, I rest in Your tender nurture and compassion, for I am Your child.

JUNE 21

You can't worship two gods at once. Loving one god, you'll end up hating the other. Adoration of one feeds contempt for the other. —MATTHEW 6:24 MSG

Food Is Not Your God

Focusing on food—whether by thinking about it, obsessing over it, preparing it, or constantly eating it—can usurp our commitment to God. When we turn to food to feel soothed, comforted, cheered up, or calmed down, that's an indication that it has become a very powerful substance in our lives. We can be committed to the Lord in every way but still struggle to loose the grip of food on us. It is certainly painful when we recognize that we have edged God out with food.

But surrendering our food to God leads to amazing freedom! By planning our healthy meals for the day and then following through with the plan, we become less aware of food and more aware of God. As we let go of our need for food to support us, we become more available to the nurturing of His presence. In time, we forget food and instead focus on life.

Letting go of food a day at a time amounts to worshiping Him with our very lives. Forgetting ourselves, we find our true life and true worship of God.

Today, Lord, may I worship You by letting go of food so I can serve You more completely.

For we do not have a high priest who cannot sympathize with our weaknesses, but One who has been tempted in all things as we are, yet without sin. Therefore let us draw near with confidence to the throne of grace, so that we may receive mercy and find grace to help in time of need.

—HEBREWS 4:16 NASB

Needing God

If we could will ourselves to be thin, we would have been a size 8 a long time ago! If diets worked— meaning we could stay on them perfectly, lose weight, and keep it off—we would have retired from them by now. If just praying to eat right and have the pounds disappear was the answer, we would likely be a prayer expert. But our struggle with food is obviously bigger and more complicated than just diet, calories, and exercise. In fact, it is bigger than us.

We are faced with the question: Am I ready to make lasting changes, or do I only want to be free of the consequences of my overeating? If we are ready to move forward in recovery, then we enter into this process with our High Priest. He deeply and profoundly understands our weaknesses and pain. He strengthens us for life with mercy and grace, and without the need to overeat or control our food. By accepting that this problem is bigger than we are, that we are at the end of our power, we surrender—and God's power is unleashed.

Today, Lord, I accept my condition of being over-weight and, more importantly, my need for Your help.

JUNE 23

Come, let us sing for joy to the LORD. . . . For the LORD is the great God, the great King above all gods. . . . The sea is his, for he made it, and his hands formed the dry land.

—PSALM 95:1A,3,5

Swimming in the Ocean

There is an art to swimming in the ocean. If we wade into the waves but stay where it's shallow, then the breakers crash in on us, roaring with foam and vengeance. Their force keeps us off balance; we never feel secure. There is an excitement with each wave but no stability.

However, when we risk going deeper, past the breakers, lifting our feet off the sandy bottom, we find an amazing phenomenon. The ocean waves rise and fall, rocking us as we float and tread water. We're in deep, cold water, but we find a sense of calm in floating on the surface with the ups and downs of the waves.

Such is the art of recovery. If we wade in only to our knees, the waves of food obsessions, special occasions, emotional turmoil, and fear will keep us off balance. We will hardly progress with weight loss.

It is our trust in God that helps us to go deeper, to the place where we must lift our feet from the bottom. There we are held by Him and find ourselves floating—rising and falling on the waves of recovery. We are not exhausted from fighting these waves or struggling for balance, but simply at one with the sea of life. It is the ride of a lifetime!

Today, Lord, grant me courage to wade past the breakers and swim in Your ocean.

JUNE 24

"Beware of practicing your righteousness before men to be noticed by them." —MATTHEW 6:1 NASB

Outside show is a poor substitute for inner worth. —AESOP

An Inside Job

In the past we may have wanted the outside of us to look good because we felt worthless inside. Rather than working on internal issues and dealing with our feelings of loneliness, shame, and worthlessness, we tried to lose weight in order to feel better. But it is virtually impossible to maintain a lighter body weight when we carry the heaviness of emotional pain in our soul.

Now we are learning that life is an inside job. As we learn to apply the key of forgiveness to our lives, we find a spiritual freedom from the bitterness of the past. As we learn to accept of the total problem, we are freed to take action. As we surrender to life on God's terms, we stop fighting the work that has to be done both inside and out.

Ironically, our physical appearance begins to improve, though our focus is centered on our spiritual condition and the next right action to take each day. Our outer appearance begins to reflect how positively we feel about ourselves, yet without being preoccupied with our looks.

Today, Lord, I ask for the grace to focus on forgiveness, surrender, and acceptance for this day.

JUNE 25

Facing the Fiery Furnace

These young men showed incredible faith and courage by refusing to bow to another god. Even if it meant dying for their beliefs, they would not compromise.

For those struggling with overeating, every day becomes an opportunity to bow to the god of appetite, comfort, and gluttony—or not. Bowing to food puts us under the threat of spiritual and physical death. And thankfully, this threat brings out our own defiance—we will no longer bow to this god. Standing against the threat means we will stand in a "fiery furnace" of feeling alone when we can't eat like other people do, or in the discomfort of saying no when we would rather eat the whole thing.

If we catch the vision of God's power shown in the faith of these Hebrew men, however, we can stand firm in the face of that furnace, not allowing any food item to sway our commitment to Him.

Today, Lord, may I surrender so completely to You that I stand firm in the furnace of temptation.

And these three men, firmly tied, fell into the blazing furnace. Then King Nebuchadnezzar leaped to his feet in amazement and asked his advisers, "Weren't there three men that we tied up and threw into the fire?" They replied, "Certainly, O king." He said, "Look! I see four men walking around in the fire, unbound and unharmed, and the fourth looks like a son of the gods." —DANIEL 3:23-25

Refined in the Crucible of Life

We can be sure that whether we are eating healthfully or bingeing wildly, we will be thrown into life's fires. God always puts His children through trials and difficulties to refine and purify our character.

As we progress in our journey, we can take hope from the story of Shadrach, Meshach, and Abednego, letting it remind us that when we are in the midst of the fire, the Lord will be right in there with us. His presence, tender care, and protection in the crucible of life are a testimony to all of His power and love. This is yet another reason we can confidently take action toward bettering our health no matter what the circumstances: God will be with us, even in the fiery furnace.

Today, Lord, may I accept the refining fires of difficulty. By Your grace, may I take action toward my goals.

But if we walk in the light, as he is in the light, we have fellowship with one another, and the blood of Jesus, his Son, purifies us from all sin. —1 JOHN 1:7

Do you know what the smallest package in the world is? A person completely wrapped up in themselves.

—WILLIAM SLOAN COFFIN

Wrapped Up

When wrapped up in ourselves, we are wholly consumed with our own needs, wants, and desires. We have no interest in the concerns of others or in their personal situations. Yet since none of us can ever have all of life served on a platter, we have chosen to fill the gap with indulgent eating. Interestingly, though, instead of the food filling us, we find that our problems have intensified and become more complicated. We may also recognize our deep loneliness. Our overeating is an act of self-absorption.

We now have the option to stop playing small. In order to progress in recovery—for peace and serenity and physical success—we must start looking beyond our own little world. We can let others into our hearts and enjoy the sharing of ourselves in intimacy with dear friends.

The paradox is that by getting outside of ourselves, connecting with those around us, we are free to love and experience others at a whole new level. Previously, our overeating served as a barrier to true relationship—but now we are practicing letting go of extra food so we have more time and energy for fellowship and love to flow.

Today, Lord, may I let go of extra food and my self-focus. As I focus on You, may I also reach out to others.

JUNE 28

"For whoever wishes to save his life will lose it; but whoever loses his life for My sake will find it."

—*MATTHEW 16:25* NASB

Paradox

Deep spiritual truths are often delivered in paradoxes. Here Jesus points to the mystery of how one who tries to save his life loses it, while one who loses his life (for Jesus' sake) ends up finding it.

Lasting success with weight loss lies in the same paradox: When we lose our life—that is, when we let go of food and follow the will of God—we find true life. The weight/food issue dissolves. We must let go of all the things we have tried in the past and begin seeing the spiritual nature of our struggles. The key of acceptance is essential here. We must grasp these truths:

- By losing weight, we find life.
- To deny what we think we want (food), we gain what we truly want (life, relationships, and true joy at being alive).
- To treat ourselves with food is to punish our spiritual self by keeping us from the life God has for us.
- To let go of how we made life work (anesthetizing with food) is to gain a new skill of feeling all our emotions, even when they're painful.
- To surrender to God means to win, not lose, and . . .
- When we lose, we win!

Today, Lord, may I let go of excess food to find the life You meant for me to live.

JUNE 29

And the peace of God, which transcends all understanding,
will guard your hearts and your minds in Christ Jesus.

Guard Your Hearts and Minds

Keeping a positive outlook is vital for recovery. We need the peace of God to guard our hearts and minds!

It's easy to get off track emotionally by comparing our progress to others'. We may also be putting excessive pressure on ourselves by thinking that we should be farther along than we are. It is discouraging when our weight loss is happening slower than we'd like.

In recovery, our hearts and minds play an important role. When our outlook for the day is dependent upon how we feel at the moment or what our eyes tell us, discouragement is imminent. Looking to God for strength is an essential part of our spiritual routine. He provides us with the truth, guarding our hearts and minds, reminding us of our hope in Him. He is guiding even the smallest of our positive actions toward health in wholeness. When we realize that consistent small actions produce good fruit in time, peace sets in. Our spiritual "gains" are more important than our physical "losses."

Today, Lord, guard my heart and mind from discouragement, and keep me in Your peace.

JUNE 30

Turning his head, Peter noticed the disciple Jesus loved following right behind. When Peter noticed him, he asked Jesus, "Master, what's going to happen to him?" Jesus said, "If I want him to live until I come again, what's that to you? You— follow me." —JOHN 21:20-22 AMP

An Assignment from Jesus

Throughout the New Testament, Peter never failed to show his humanness. Here the risen Jesus has just commissioned him to "feed My sheep." So what is Peter's first response? He immediately turns and wants to know what will be required of another disciple. Jesus sternly replies to Peter, "No matter what he does or doesn't do, you follow Me!"

It seems natural to want to know whether God will do for us what He's doing for others. We look at people who seem to have little or no problem with eating sweets, chips, or fast food, and we wish we were like them. The truth is, Jesus is saying to us—just as sternly as He did to Peter—that what others have to face is none of our business. (Ouch!)

Rather than comparing ourselves to others, Jesus asks us to focus on following Him, heeding His call, and obeying Him. If that means giving up certain foods, or limiting them significantly, He wants us to be willing to do so, even when others around us are eating them. Whether someone else has to walk through the same struggles we do is truly not our business.

Today, Lord, may I focus on the assignment You've given me without comparing my journey to others'.

JULY 1

"But I say to you, love your enemies and pray for those who persecute you, so that you may be sons of your Father who is in heaven; for He causes His sun to rise on the evil and the good, and sends rain on the righteous and the unrighteous."

—MATTHEW 5:44-45 NASB

Drop the Bag

We have carried a bag of resentments with us while trudging through life. The longer we've carried these resentments, the heavier they've become—and the heavier we have become.

Jesus calls us to pray for those people who have harmed us, because they have their own troubles. Sunshine and rain falls on everyone, and they need mercy just like we do. When we resist this teaching from Jesus because we don't want to let some people off the hook, we can remember that forgiving someone is not the same as excusing their behavior. What they did to us may have been horrible, and there is no justification for their actions, but by dropping our bag of resentments, we release our hurts and pain to God. We open the door to healing, as God now has the freedom to miraculously heal our hearts.

When we hold onto our bag of resentments, we weigh ourselves down and our physical body shows that weight. But when we let go of that heavy burden, our spirits become lighter and our bodies reflect the change, too.

Today, Lord, I pray to find mercy and understanding toward those who have hurt and persecuted me.

JULY 2

When Jesus came into Peter's house, he saw Peter's mother-in-law lying in bed with a fever. He touched her hand and the fever left her, and she got up and began to wait on him.

This is what we're to do. We are healed to help others. We are blessed to be a blessing. We are saved to serve, not to sit around and wait for heaven.

—RICK WARREN, THE PURPOSE DRIVEN LIFE®

Purpose

This is the perfect picture of recovery and purpose: When we are touched by Jesus, the infirmity leaves and we are free to serve. With continuous food and weight difficulties, we have lived our life sluggishly, as with a fever—low on energy, unable to fulfill our purpose for God. But as we are touched by the Lord, we can feel the cloud lift, and we're left to discover our new lives, undefined by our weight.

Amazingly, we may even seem at first to have too much time on our hands, unaware as we were of how much time was taken up by thinking about food, preparing it, and eating it. Now, thankfully, we can simply plan our food and forget about it. We can live our lives with purpose, in service to others. The more we serve, the more we'll realize how self-centered our lives have been. It's also true that the more we now enjoy our "weightless" life—with food in its rightful place—the more we'll be centered on serving God and His people.

Today, Lord, I pray that as You touch and heal me, I receive strength to love and serve others.

JULY 3

Do you not know that those who run in a race all run, but only one receives the prize? Run in such a way that you may win.

—*1 CORINTHIANS 9:24* NASB

Run to win. All good athletes train hard.

—*1 CORINTHIANS 9:24-25* MSG

The Prize

In your mind, what is the ultimate prize? Goal weight? A diamond chip? A one-year token? What motivates you to work hard on recovering from the grip of compulsive eating, control of food, and extra pounds? Many weight-loss programs have their own types of motivational rewards and recognition. But this time, for us, it is different.

Losing weight for life is a race that all may run and all who train hard can win! The prize is a new life—free from food obsession, free from being controlled by weight, free from extra pounds. The prize is freedom!

There is training that must be consistent. There is action that must be diligent. There is emotional work that must be persistent. But we are learning that training for this race is also an ongoing discovery of who God wants us to be. We are recognizing God's purpose for our lives at a new level. We are learning to find our true value in Him while dethroning our own lordship around food.

This path of discovery and recovery is so exciting that it has become *the* reward!

Today, Lord, I put myself in training for the race, the journey that You have called me to. I commit to training hard and running to win.

JULY 4

Live Free

We have been enslaved to our appetites and cravings, and we have been in bondage to diets. We
have felt trapped by fear, shame, and hopelessness.
We have been in a prison of isolation.

But Christ has set us free so we may live free! We
can take a stand for our lives by saying no to certain
foods and behaviors. Yes, we have the opportunity
to choose to gorge on sweets, but that's not freedom;
that's slavery.

Today, we are rejecting the harness of food
addiction. These shackles brought guilt, remorse,
and hopelessness. Today, we have the choice to live
in freedom.

*Today, Lord, I am grateful for the opportunity to live
a free life and rejoice in the day You've given me.*

JULY 5

Work out your salvation with fear and trembling.

—PHILIPPIANS 2:12B NASB

He restores my soul.   —PSALM 23:3A

Work Out and Restore

The path of recovery from food and weight obsession is a path of salvation and restoration. The route we're on is arduous and winding, with only a few steps ahead visible at a time. Having a healthy respect for God's laws of grace, we must take action on this path every day, one step at a time, trusting that God will be there.

This is the "working out" that Philippians 2:12 encourages: When we move forward on our way to our spiritual, emotional, and physical recovery, our salvation and wholeness in Christ is made manifest. Our souls are restored.

Today, Lord, with reverence and trembling, I take action toward my spiritual, emotional, and physical recovery.

JULY 6

"For I tell you that unless your righteousness surpasses that of the Pharisees . . . you will certainly not enter the kingdom of heaven." —MATTHEW 5:20

The Righteous Dieter

Have you met the righteous dieter? The one who is doing everything right? This is the person who is counting every calorie, exercising daily, drinking eight glasses of water, logging every action. This person seems to have all the answers—just ask!

It's hard to ignore people like this, because they're having success and making it seem so easy, so doable. Yet it's also hard to be around them for very long. Pride and arrogance seep from their demeanor, and the people around them feel envious, or even judged.

The Pharisees of Jesus' day spoke piously about their righteousness. But then our hero, Jesus, said that all the righteous works in the world are still not enough to merit entering the kingdom of God.

It can be tempting for us to become rigid and perfectionistic in our dieting. But as soon as our ego or pride is tripped, our spiritual condition is stunted. Further, the success we have on our own, through perfectionism, will not last.

It is in looking deeper than surface actions that we recover from compulsive and emotional eating. We must place our attention on a deepening relationship with God rather than on rigidly following a diet. We must put on the righteousness that comes in our humble and grateful love relationship with Christ, and then we will find lasting recovery.

Today, Lord, I will not just follow my food and exercise plan; I'll go deeper into my spiritual recovery.

JULY 7

"For if you remain silent at this time, relief and deliverance for the Jews will arise from another place, but you and your father's family will perish. And who knows but that you have come to royal position for such a time as this?"

—ESTHER 4:14

For Such a Time as Recovery

As we lose weight—with our appearance improving and energy rising—we find ourselves able to do things we weren't able to before. People may ask, "How did you do it?" We find that we've been elevated to a position of respect, and we now seem to have a responsibility that makes us uncomfortable. To continue in our recovery, we must give it away. We must tell others what it takes to be free from the food obsessions that once cut into our effectiveness. We must tell of our deliverance from being controlled by our weight and our subsequent quality of life. By sharing our journey, we are sharing hope. And we know firsthand that hope keeps us all moving forward.

When asked about our personal successes, those with whom we share may still not be able to grasp how all-encompassing this process is. Most people will cling to the notion that this might be strictly a diet-and-exercise, quick-and-easy type of program. But this is where we let go and let them do their own exploring. Our call is to simply be an example, a living model of what happens when we allow God to be the center of our path to freedom from food and weight problems.

Today, Lord, may I not keep quiet at a time like this and instead be an example of Your deliverance.

JULY 8

"You are the salt of the earth. But if the salt loses its saltiness, how can it be made salty again? It is no longer good for anything, except to be thrown out and trampled by men."

—MATTHEW 5:13

Salty for Life

Salt is a seasoning that brings the flavors of foods to life. It can also make us thirsty. Jesus is calling us to be salty: bringing flavor to others and helping them thirst for life.

As we progress and begin to find some relief from our compulsive eating, others will see our new life taking shape. Losing excess weight, our recovery begins to give the flavor of hope to people who are suffering. As a result, they may become thirsty for Jesus in the same way that we are. With so many who are imprisoned and hopeless because of food and weight problems—even in the church—we have much opportunity to be effective salt.

Ultimately, our recovery is not just about us. Our victories are a testimony to God's power. As we continue on the path, putting one day of surrendered, serene food choices next to another one, our resulting saltiness will be a blessing to those around us. Continuing in recovery for our own purposes in Christ, we impact those around us for the kingdom. Though this is not our primary focus for recovering, it remains true that in our own successes and overcoming, other sufferers will find hope for themselves as well.

Today, Lord, I pray to be a salty person, surrendered to You instead of food, and excited about life.

JULY 9

*"You shall do no wrong in judgment, in measurement of weight,
or capacity. You shall have just balances, just weights, a just
ephah, and a just hin; I am the LORD your God, who brought you
out from the land of Egypt."*   —*LEVITICUS 19:35-36* NASB

The Scale: Ally or God?

For some of us, the scale becomes a type of god as
we are losing excess weight. The number on the
scale measures whether we are good or bad, and dic-
tates our mood accordingly. Many weight-loss programs have weekly weigh-ins that are intended to be
helpful and affirming but can become a time of
shame and disappointment. These humiliating
experiences ultimately result in another problem:
We avoid the scale because we associate it with
degradation and failure.

In our journey of overcoming, we need the scale
to be a method of honesty and integrity with our
weight, not a symbol of defeat. By transforming our
approach to the scale as something that helps us stay
out of denial, it can be an ally to measure progress.
The scale helps us stay honest about the amounts of
food we've consumed, but it must be unassociated
with our worth as a person.

The Lord is the One who is bringing us out of
the "land of Egypt"—the land of slavery to weight
and the scale, out of the bondage of measuring ourselves by a number on that scale. The scale is simply
a tool by which to view our progress, not something
that signifies worth and meaning for our person-
hood.

*Today, Lord, may I use the scale to measure my progress,
not my worth.*

Search me, O God, and know my heart; test me and know my anxious thoughts. See if there is any offensive way in me, and lead me in the way everlasting. —PSALM 139:23-24

Search Me

Self-searching is an ancient practice that allows us to bring new perspective, action, and grace into our hearts. We may have avoided self-examination due to a fear of finding painful issues or problems. Or pride may have convinced us that we are above it. After all, if we are a "new creature," then the past does not have any bearing on the present, right?

While we certainly are new beings in Christ, we must develop a level of humility that only comes from rigorous self-searching. That is what allows us to open our hearts to God's help with our food obsessions and struggles with heaviness.

Opening our hearts in self-examination is only done with God's assistance, and is an important time for us to be surrounded by supportive people. We will be assessing our faults and the resentments from our past. Our friends can help us be realistic and keep us from being overly shameful or, on the other extreme, overly prideful.

When we take this part of the process seriously and with determination, we invite God's grace on a deeper level than was ever possible before this step. He is able to make changes in us that will lead us in the everlasting way.

Today, Lord, I pray for a willingness to be searched by You, with the comfort of supportive people.

Now may our Lord Jesus Christ Himself and God our Father,
who has loved us and given us eternal comfort and good hope
by grace, comfort and strengthen your hearts in every good
work and word. —2 THESSALONIANS 2:16-17 NASB

The Ultimate Comforter:
Chocolate or the Savior?

A postcard from overseas had this message: "Things
are getting worse . . . send chocolate!" Most of us
laugh at this because we can relate. When life is
hectic and stressful, it's easy to reach for something
like chocolate to "get us through." But what are we
reaching for? What do we really need?

Will chocolate really get us through our dark
moments? Or will it derail our ultimate goals of a
healthy weight, clear mind, and stable emotions?
Those of us who struggle with overeating know
how easy it is for one bite of chocolate to quickly
become more—a box, a pound . . . instead of a bite.

When our lives become hectic and harried, we
have more to sustain us than chocolate. We can
reach for God's grace, which is often found in an
accountability partner or group. In those times
when chocolate is looking like the answer to our
problems, we need other people to help us through
the moment. To remind us that, ultimately, we
don't need a temporal creation, we need the Creator.

Chocolate may be a type of comfort, but we
want the ultimate Comforter, the Holy Spirit.

Today, Lord, may I seek Your grace to reach for Your
comfort when I'm stressed and distressed.

JULY 12

God, make a fresh start in me; shape a Genesis week from the
chaos of my life.   —PSALM 51:10 *MSG*

Dealing with Slips

There will be times when our lives are so chaotic,
and the emotional triggers to overeat so powerful,
that we will slip. It's unfortunate but true. Yet giving
in to the food and seeking from it what it cannot
provide, teaches us once again that this is not the
answer. The comfort, support, and understanding
we need do not come from food—they never have.
Our help is found in the grace of God and His love,
seen through compassionate people who understand and have "been there."

When slips happen, we must call on God for a
fresh start. We must reach for Him out of the chaos
of shame, guilt, and remorse, humbly asking for our
heart to be re-created. He responds because He is
faithful. And by realizing once again that this condition is chronic and a plan of action is essential, we
surrender our food and weight problems to God.

Today, Lord, I reach for Your love and understanding
in the midst of my slip. Create a fresh start in me as I
surrender once again to You.

JULY 13

My heart is not proud, O LORD, my eyes are not haughty; I do not concern myself with great matters or things too wonderful for me. But I have stilled and quieted my soul; like a weaned child with its mother, like a weaned child is my soul within me.

—PSALM 131:1-2

Surrendering into Healing

A slip or relapse can be an invitation to give up on ourselves. It can be an open door to self-recrimination, shame, and self-loathing. Accepting this invitation, however, is a sign that we have not totally surrendered to the reality of our situation. Struggling with food is a chronic condition, much like our sinful nature. We cannot combat this on our own.

Fortunately, God is powerful enough to deal with our struggles. Though we may feel like giving up on ourselves and scrapping the entire recovery process when we slip, this would be giving up our faith in God's mercy, power, and grace. Instead, we can surrender our pride, and still and quiet ourselves before God. When we do, our soul becomes like a small child's. Our attitude of humility and surrender allows us to choose healthier foods.

By not allowing the difficult battles and slips to deter us, our humility will usher in God's strength for victory once more.

Today, Lord, I quiet myself before You and accept how chronic my situation is. I surrender my progress to You and Your grace over time.

JULY 14

A thousand may fall at your side, ten thousand at your right hand, but it will not come near you. —PSALM 91:7

From Devastation to Gratitude

Compulsive and emotional eating can make life bleak and lonely, and many of us are unable to envision any other way of life. We may realize the devastation but have no faith for taking action. All around us there are people living in this land of despair.

But take heart! The Lord, as our ever-present guide, has allowed us to see into another realm—one with the opportunity for life apart from devastation. No longer controlled by food obsessions or defined by our weight, gratitude compels us to carry out His will and bring hope to the many others who still suffer. We have compassion for them, not judgment, because we once lived where they live now, and we recognize how easily we could live there again if we kept a cavalier attitude.

Today, Lord, may I remember the devastation of compulsive and emotional eating. May I remember the grace You've shown me in my effort to overcome my problem. Build my compassion for those who still suffer.

JULY 15

New Ways of Thinking

We need a new way of thinking! That's why we're in the Lose It For Life program. The diet mentality restricts and deprives. Compulsive and addictive eating brings painful, life-threatening consequences. It seems like we can't live with food and we can't live without it. There has to be an answer!

Once again, accepting God's help and His power is the only way out of the cycle of restricting and bingeing. We must realize that our best efforts were failures; our best thinking, though perhaps profound in knowledge of calories and exercise, only made the problem worse. This is a chronic condition that, over time and without intervention, will rob us of life options.

When our thinking is infused with this reality, we become willing to take whatever actions are necessary to live free. When we come out of denial about the seriousness of our self-defeating behaviors, we can then see the futility of our efforts to survive without God's power and strength.

Today, Lord, I pray to see the truth of my condition. I ask for the willingness to do whatever is necessary to live free of my food obsession.

JULY 16

Yesterday is gone. Tomorrow is but a dream. But today is here with all its infinite possibilities.

—*THE RT. REV. JOHN H. MACNAUGHTON*

Stay in Today

Stay in the present day. That is the only place we can build the future. It is the only place we can make amends, where possible, for the past. It is the only place where we can deal with feelings as they arise so they don't become triggers for emotional eating.

When we stay on track with our food plan for this day only—not allowing guilt and shame over what we ate yesterday, not allowing dismay at not getting to eat with abandon in the future—we create a safe place to enjoy today. We create the possibility for a great future, free of excess pounds and the emotional ups and downs of the binge-and-diet cycle.

Taking care of ourselves around food today brings a sense of accomplishment and self-respect. The Lord is with us in the present, so there is no need to bemoan the past or worry about the future.

Today, Lord, may I take action toward my recovery, letting go of the past and giving the future to You.

Therefore we do not lose heart. Though outwardly we are wasting away, yet inwardly we are being renewed day by day. For our light and momentary troubles are achieving for us an eternal glory that far outweighs them all.

—2 CORINTHIANS 4:16-17

Wasting Away

We must not lose heart about practicing our program to "lose it for life." When we have a plan for our food, exercise, and spiritual growth, and a structure of supportive people around us, we are on the pathway to success.

But that is just the beginning. Yes, starting is often easier than continuing. Beginning a new life toward healthy eating and exercising can be an exciting and hopeful time. But staying on that plan day by day over the long haul can seem boring and tiresome after a while.

This is where we all need renewal day by day. We need fresh inspiration and encouragement for pressing onward. As we "waste away," we must repeat our plan of action daily to be successful over time. We must review our ideas regarding food obsession to keep our mind focused, our heart teachable, and our life steadily on course.

Over time, we'll find that light and momentary trouble has become the tool that God used to bring us closer to Him. While we will have lost weight and gained victory over our struggles with food, the eternal glory gained will far outweigh the physical battles we've faced.

Today, Lord, help me repeat the plan of action to which I have committed, taking heart that You are working Your will in me for Your glory.

JULY 18

Jesus stretched out His hand and touched him, saying, "I am willing; be cleansed." And immediately his leprosy was cleansed. —MATTHEW 8:3 NASB

Faith and Willingness

In this exchange between Jesus and a leper, we find ingredients for our own healing: faith, willingness, and action. The leper approached Jesus with faith in His willingness and ability to heal. Jesus fearlessly responded to the request by reaching out to the man and touching him. And in that moment, the cleansing occurred.

Our healing occurs at the intersection of our faith with God's willingness and power. In the past we tried to steel ourselves to conquer our food and weight problems with willpower. But what we didn't have was staying power. Failed diet after failed diet taught us we couldn't sustain our efforts long-term. And believe it or not, we weren't meant to!

God's power must enter our life. As we approach Jesus daily with the same faith as this leper—as we align our will with God's will—we forfeit our limited strength and discover the infinite power of God.

Today, Lord, I come to You with my insufficient will-power and join it to Your infinite power, in faith and willingness to do Your will.

His master replied, "Well done, good and faithful servant! You have been faithful with a few things; I will put you in charge of many things. Come and share your master's happiness!"

—MATTHEW 25:21

Faithful in Small Things

For some, being faithful with our actions around food seems like a small, insignificant area of life. But we are now taking responsibility for what we put into our mouth, both in quantity and quality. As we establish a structure around our eating behaviors and attitudes, we are learning to be good stewards of the God-given resources around us.

God has given us a body to nurture. We are the only ones who can either fuel it for life through healthy choices or ruin it through junk foods and inactivity. By choosing to eat and move healthfully, we begin to feel better, think better, and live better. We are better prepared to face life on all levels: physically, mentally, emotionally, and spiritually.

This all begins, however, in the small choices— bite by bite, meal by meal, choice by choice, day by day. Like the servant to whom the compliment was given, when we are faithful in small areas of life, God then entrusts us with more. We find that life opens up as a daring, exciting adventure with God's hand upon us each day. And the Lord Himself will celebrate with us!

Today, Lord, may I be a good steward, feeding and nurturing the gift of my body.

Blessed be the God and Father of our Lord Jesus Christ, the Father of mercies and God of all comfort, who comforts us in all our affliction so that we will be able to comfort those who are in any affliction with the comfort with which we ourselves are comforted by God. —2 CORINTHIANS 1:3-4 NASB

The Circle of Comfort

Isn't it amazing that the Father of mercies and the God of all comfort is with us in our affliction? When we meditate on that, our hearts can be soothed, secure, and hopeful, knowing that even our food and weight problems are understood by our heavenly Father.

But that's not the only good news. Through our overcoming, we are able to come alongside others who suffer the same affliction, to comfort them and offer them hope. We are not alone, and we can share that hope with others!

Our experience and suffering can benefit others by bringing the encouragement of what God's power can accomplish. When we allow our affliction to become a source of strength and witness to God's power, we find that life truly is meant to be shared. One person's surrender may help others find courage to do the same. That's what happens in the sheer blessing of connection with one another: Lives change.

Today, Lord, as I receive Your mercy and comfort, may I pass this along to others who experience my same affliction.

JULY 21

O taste and see that the LORD is good; how blessed is the man who takes refuge in Him! O fear the LORD, you His saints; for to those who fear Him there is no want. —PSALM 34:8-9 NASB

Taste and See

When we begin our recovery, the food plan we choose may seem that it is missing something: food! We may be concerned about not having enough to eat and feeling hungry between meals.

In the past, we dealt with this by snacking throughout the day to keep hunger at bay. We never experienced an empty stomach because we kept ourselves full all the time! In essence, we were protecting ourselves from the emptiness that might have triggered feelings of loneliness, sadness, or grief. That emptiness was a cue to eat in order to keep those feelings from surfacing.

This response has always been the struggle of emotional eating. So what do we do with those feelings when we are hungry?

There is no deprivation with the Lord. When we take refuge in Him, when we fear or respect Him and His will regarding our food intake, there will be no want or lack. This is how we may "taste" the Lord's provision: to live between meals without snacking. We can ask God to "feed" and nurture us when we are hungry, and by His grace, we can stay the course with our food plan.

Today, Lord, as I turn to You for refuge from food cravings and hunger, I ask that You feed me with Your loving care.

Then Jesus was led by the Spirit into the desert to be tempted by the devil. After fasting forty days and forty nights, he was hungry. The tempter came to him and said, "If you are the Son of God, tell these stones to become bread." Jesus answered, "It is written: 'Man does not live on bread alone, but on every word that comes from the mouth of God.'" —MATTHEW 4:1-4

Resisting Temptation

Fasting for just a few days is exhausting, so we can imagine that Jesus was probably ravished with hunger after forty days and nights without food. But He didn't let Satan get the best of Him, even in that physical deprivation. Jesus also didn't die from hunger. He suffered, but He didn't die.

Sometimes it seems hard for us to make it from breakfast to lunch without feeling like we'll expire. But that small sense of suffering can teach us a great lesson in perseverance. Our High Priest knows what it's like to be hungry, and yet He said no to food.

When we feel overwhelmed with hunger, we can learn by Jesus' example to wait. We can trust that we will make it through whatever emotion we face, whatever situation we deal with, or whatever tempting delicacy sits in front of us—without giving in to temptation.

We can do it because Jesus has done it before us, and He will be our guide. We now turn from the temporal to the spiritual—from the food to Jesus— because life is more than food.

Today, Lord, as I refrain from tempting foods, I will remember that You understand what it's like to be hungry, to be tempted. I seek the strength of Your Spirit in these moments.

JULY 23

We have one who has been tempted in every way, just as we are—yet was without sin. Let us then approach the throne of grace with confidence, so that we may receive mercy and find grace to help us in our time of need. —HEBREWS 4:15B-16

He, Too, Was Tempted

It's easy to rationalize that our food problem is not significant to God. It's also painful to admit that giving in to overeating has often kept us from the kingdom work God has for us. Yet acknowledging this is crucial in order to move into a place of surrender and service to God.

We have this hope: When it feels like a particular food is calling us to indulge, we can boldly approach the throne of grace and ask for the strength to not act on that craving. Jesus understands this type of suffering because He experienced it in the wilderness. The first test He faced from the devil had to do with food. Before His public ministry, He experienced the temptation to use His power for self-fulfillment on a physical level.

He dealt with it by remembering God's Word and waiting on Him. As we do the same, deepening our reliance on and intimacy with God, we are more ready to participate in meaningful ministry and to live in the freedom that comes in the power of Christ.

Today, Lord, I take comfort in knowing that You understand my suffering with food temptations, and I ask for Your mercy and grace to help me.

Jesus, full of the Holy Spirit, returned from the Jordan and was led by the Spirit in the desert, where for forty days he was tempted by the devil. He ate nothing during those days, and at the end of them he was hungry. The devil said to him, "If you are the Son of God, tell this stone to become bread." Jesus answered, "It is written: 'Man does not live on bread alone.'"

—LUKE 4:1-4

Remember His Victory

After fasting for forty days, Jesus was weary and His hunger intense. He was vulnerable to the attacks of the enemy, and in that desperate state, He experienced what it was like to have an outside force tempting Him with food. But this temptation wasn't just physical; it was deeply spiritual as well. Would He use His power to fill a basic human need for Himself?

Jesus, of course, did not give in to the temptation. He knew what was at stake, and He answered with authority. He understood that though bread is a symbol of life, it is not all there is to life. Satisfaction does not come from filling our physical hunger but from filling our spiritual life.

Knowing that Jesus experienced these temptations, we can go to Him in moments of struggle with food. He doesn't just know a little about being hungry; He suffered hunger more than we ever have! So when it seems like indulging can be justified, consider what is at stake. This isn't just about healthy eating; this is about our spiritual health. In the midst of our hunger, we can remember Jesus' triumph over temptation.

Today, Lord, I turn to You in my moments of struggle, and I surrender my own justifications for overeating.

He cried out with a loud voice, "Lazarus, come forth." The man who had died came forth, bound hand and foot with wrappings, and his face was wrapped around with a cloth.

—*JOHN 11:43B-44A* NASB

Hearing the Loud Voice

When we suffer from food and weight problems, it can seem like we are lying in a tomb, hiding from the pain of life. Somehow we buy into the belief that carrying extra weight will protect us from getting hurt by people as we have been in the past. But the result is that we are bound up with the graveclothes of fear, resentment, and failure. All confidence that we can make any lasting difference in our weight seems lost. The final layer wrapped around us is a hopelessness and an inability to envision the chance at life as a normal-sized person.

Yet Jesus comes to us in our self-constructed tomb and cries out to us with a loud voice, "There is more to life! You are not done! Come forth!" Upon hearing His call, we "who had died" limp forward into the light of day to present ourselves as new, resurrected people.

Today, Lord, may I be willing and courageous enough to do my part when I hear Your loving voice call me out of my tomb of fear and pain.

JULY 26

Jesus said to them, "Unbind him, and let him go."

—*JOHN 11:44B* NASB

Letting Others Unwrap You

As we emerge from our tomb as Lazarus did, we are filled with new life. Unfortunately, we are still bound, still wrapped, and unable to move because of our pain, disappointments, resentments, and fears. In the midst of this, however, Jesus speaks again, this time to the ones around us: "Unbind him, and let him go."

We really do need other people to unbind and unwrap us so we can truly be free and live. As we accept the call to life and courageously come out of our tomb, we are also making ourselves ready to have others unbind our pain. Dealing with feelings, issues, and events of the past, we need counselors, group members, and understanding friends to support us.

Living outside the tomb means making ourselves available to the help of others, despite our fear of being known. Thankfully, when we do our part to step out, Jesus and others are there with us on the journey.

Today, Lord, may I be willing to step out and allow others to unwrap the graveclothes that keep me from fullness of life.

And do not be conformed to this world, but be transformed by the renewing of your mind, so that you may prove what the will of God is, that which is good and acceptable and perfect.

—*ROMANS 12: 2* NASB

Transformed, Not Conformed

One of the ultimate reasons we are in the Lose It For Life program is because we are seeking transformation—of our mind, our attitudes, emotions, behaviors, and of course, our body. This is a tremendous task. We cannot do it alone! Transformation happens from the inside out. As we turn away from "this world" of food and our claim in it, the process begins.

God's power flows in as we surrender our will and allow our mind to be renewed with acceptance and ownership of our condition. The miracle emerges as we take action toward fulfilling the will of God, shifting our attitudes from victim to victor. We deal with our emotions—past and present—head-on and with vigor. Then we may find that we also behave differently around food, letting go of what is unhealthy and choosing healthier items and portions.

From these steps, transformation in our body occurs. We are enabled to act differently around food, and those excess pounds are gradually shed. So with our entire being, we declare that God's will is "good and acceptable and perfect."

Today, Lord, I turn away from the world of food and allow Your transforming power to be proven through me.

"Do not store up for yourselves treasures on earth, where moth and rust destroy, and where thieves break in and steal."

—*MATTHEW 6:19*

What Do You Treasure?

These famous words of Jesus may make us think of money rather than food, since we may be unaware of how food has become our treasure. We must ask ourselves in all honesty: How much does food light up my day? How much time do I spend treasuring the thought of a good meal or a particular dessert or snack? Am I willing to drive across town and pay whatever price it costs to experience a certain type of ice cream, pizza, or buffet?

Often without knowing it, our hope for the day can revolve around food. It can become the center-piece of our lives. Even if we deny it, our body shows the world that we treasure food more than our spiritual connection. We store up pounds rather than heavenly crowns.

Food is an earthly prize. It is temporary and it deteriorates. The moths and rust of despair over unhealthy eating are also destroying our energy. The thieves of excess weight, high blood pressure, dia-betes, and heart attack break in to steal our lives.

Jesus calls us to let go of our earthly treasures and to begin storing up heavenly treasure—perma-nent treasure that lasts forever. Surrendering to Him is key.

Today, Lord, I surrender my food to You, and I confess my treasuring of it.

JULY 29

"For where your treasure is, there your heart will be also."

—*MATTHEW 6:21*

Spiritual Treasures

Our mind may be set on shedding pounds, but our heart must lead our stomach in losing weight for life. We cannot give up our treasure for a period of time (such as with a diet), only to prize and nurture it again later. The path of recovery is such that we reevaluate what we are treasuring on a daily basis.

In place of those earthly prizes, we can begin to store up treasures of spiritual character—such as compassion, mercy, forgiveness, and love—through relationships with those who will walk the path with us. We must keep our hearts focused on God, turning to Him in humility, admitting that we have treasured food in the past.

Above all, our relationship with the Lord will become our most priceless prize as we know Him more intimately.

Today, Lord, may I seek to treasure my relationship with You rather than food.

For I am the LORD, who heals you.   —EXODUS 15:26

The Gift of Healing

We want to be healed from our sicknesses! Many of us have finally come to realize and accept that we have physical, emotional, and mental problems. We've made poor choices, wounding others and ourselves. We may now be so determined to recover from our defects and losses that healing has become our primary focus in life.

While it is good to seek healing and recovery, our drive to fix our lives can become a controlling obsession. We are missing the point if we expect to work hard enough to bring about our own healing, trying again to force something that is not ours to control. Yes, we must participate and be actively involved in the process, but we must seek first to know God.

Let us not lose focus. We do not choose our own healing. Rather, we choose God and find that He heals us.

Today, Lord, may I live to know You more deeply. May I know healing from food and weight issues as a beautiful gift from You.

It is God who works in you to will and to act according to his good purpose. —PHILIPPIANS 2:13

Higher Power

We cannot choose God's will without God's help! We always gravitate toward our own wishes and desires regarding who we want to be, how we want to live, and what we want to have. Without God's work in us, we serve our own destructive ways.

Even when we try to "will" ourselves into wanting what God wants, it just never works. We can't muster up enough willpower to act according to His good purpose. It just isn't in us for the long haul. As this law applies in a general sense, it certainly applies to our habits with eating and exercise!

But God is at work in us! He grants us His power for change. As He moves in us today, we have what it takes to choose wisely for spiritual, emotional, and physical health. By God's grace, we can make choices toward His purpose.

Though we ourselves might never choose to get up early for aerobic activity, we know from whom to draw our strength. We have *the* Higher Power working in us.

Today, Lord, work in me to act according to Your good purpose.

AUGUST 1

Have nothing to do with godless myths and old wives' tales;
rather train yourself to be godly. — 1 TIMOTHY 4:7

Basic Training

Superstition has no place in the life of one who truly seeks for health and wholeness. We have tried enough diets, "miracle" weight-loss products, and other false hopes to be convinced of this! Left with no more energy for yet another "fabulous" solution, we are now willing to learn what it really does take to live a life of recovery from food and weight issues. We're now recognizing we have work to do.

Bingo! In this verse Paul tells us to get into training. We can teach our whole self—spirit, mind, and body—to be godly. It involves action, like the daily surrender of our will to God's, meditation on His truths, talking about spiritual principles with others, and getting educated about how to nourish our bodies. The fruit of all this will be seen in healthier eating and exercise choices that will strengthen us physically. Each part of us has growing to do, and all parts will benefit as the others mature.

Today, Lord, I will work to teach at least one part of me to be godly. I will let go of superstition and instead focus on training.

Live in harmony with one another. Do not be proud, but be willing to associate with people of low position. Do not be conceited. —ROMANS 12:16

So, I Need Help—Big Deal!

When faced with any sort of problem, many of us first try to fix it ourselves, not wishing for others to know our personal affairs. And most of the time, with enough thought, prayer, and hard work, we've been able to resolve our share of challenges in life. But not all challenges. Some problems have plagued us for years and we are still plugging away, determined that somehow, by our own efforts and wisdom, we will figure out a solution.

How long will we resist our legitimate need for help? What will it take for us to lay down our pride and ask another human being for guidance? We have prayed to God and read His Word, but we've been unwilling to heed what it says about our need for connection with the body of Christ. His Word explains that we each have unique gifts that bring blessing to others, and that there are those among us who are gifted with wisdom for solving problems, discerning truth, and offering guidance and support.

Instead of isolating in pride, we can admit that we're unable to find all the answers. We can freely associate with others at ground level and discover the great insight and support we've been missing for so long.

Today, Lord, may I lay down my pride and connect with another person who has known my need.

AUGUST 3

As the sun went down that evening, people throughout the village brought sick family members to Jesus. No matter what their diseases were, the touch of his hand healed every one.

—LUKE 4:40

Jesus, the Perfect Healer

"Why haven't You healed me, Lord, just by the touch of Your hand? You were so willing before; don't You care anymore?"

We can get tunnel vision when considering the ministry of Jesus. It's not abnormal that we would yearn to be healed of our food and weight issues by a touch from Him. After all, we believe in His ability to cure us instantly. So we are easily discouraged and often angry when He leaves us to the process of recovery instead.

But when Jesus was on the earth, there were many regions where He did not travel to bring His healing touch. For every person that He gave special attention to, there were multitudes that He ignored. Some He healed immediately, and others He did not. Yet Jesus lived the perfect life—He made no mistakes in His ministry on earth; He made no mistakes with His love. He still is perfect in His love and care. So we can remind ourselves that each person Jesus has healed will eventually die, but He will accomplish His purposes in us by our willingness to take the path toward healing that is ours.

Today, Lord, may I trust in Your plans for my healing. You know just what kind I need, and I know that You care for me perfectly.

AUGUST 4

I will give you a new heart and put a new spirit in you; I will remove from you your heart of stone and give you a heart of flesh. And I will put my Spirit in you and move you to follow my decrees and be careful to keep my laws. —EZEKIEL 36:26-27

Heart Transplant

Has your heart been damaged? Have you been so wounded, so hurt, that you've hardened it in defense? Has it turned cold so that others won't get too close? So that it can't get bruised by improper handling? Have you boxed your heart up? Is it still beating . . . ?

When our heart has quit functioning, we may eat from pure apathy. Dead to all hope and passion in life, we may no longer care about our health. Life has become meaningless, and we fill the emptiness with the slow suicide of gorging. But God wants to give us a new life and a new heart.

God has not only seen our wounds, but He has lived through them with us. Caring very deeply and personally, He offers us a new heart and spirit. He promises to remove the lifeless stone inside us and replace it with a heart of flesh—soft, strong, warm, teachable—beating. His Spirit inside will move us to follow His ways and truly live. It is time for our spiritual surgery!

Today, Lord, begin to remove this heart of stone. I want a heart that beats again!

AUGUST 5

"Be careful, or your hearts will be weighed down with dissipation, drunkenness and the anxieties of life, and that day will close on you unexpectedly like a trap." —LUKE 21:34

Light-Hearted

We sometimes get stuck dragging around the burdens of life, the fears of the future, and the pains of the past. Unexpectedly, our hearts become heavy. We carry this weight in various forms, and it creates even more despair and depression.

Jesus warns us against such a trap. Our goal is not just to lose excess weight from our bodies but to lose extra pounds from our hearts! We must guard our hearts with all diligence, protecting our serenity, trusting in God's sovereignty. We must live within His will for our abundance of life.

When our heart is weighed down, so will our body be. We will eat from anxiety, lounge in dissipation, and overindulge to make ourselves numb. But true peace is found in the heart that carefully remains in God's daily provision and love. Let us be careful each day to keep our heart light.

Today, Lord, help me be careful and protect my heart from excess weight. May I pray with a friend, seek wise counsel, listen to worship music, or take a walk in an effort to remain in Your provision and love.

Then the man and his wife heard the sound of the LORD God as he was walking in the garden in the cool of the day, and they hid from the LORD God among the trees of the garden. But the LORD God called to the man, "Where are you?"

—GENESIS 3:8-9

Come Out, Come Out, Wherever You Are!

Remember playing hide-and-seek as a child? It was exhilarating to hide while the person who was "it" passed so closely, looking for us. "Where are you?" they may have called. Then came the thrill of being found, chased, wanted, pursued—running for dear life toward home base. We may also recall a time, however, when no one found us. Was that quite as exhilarating?

We in recovery from food and weight problems are often very good hiders. We know just where to go to isolate and hide in shame, never to be found. Yet God seeks us out. He knows where we're hiding and calls us out of shame, in spite of our sin and brokenness. The thrill awaits us—to be chased by God, who wants us, who loves us, and who pursues us toward health and wholeness, homeward.

Today, Lord, may I be found by You. May I come out of hiding and know the thrill of running homeward, pursued by Your love.

AUGUST 7

I can do everything through him who gives me strength.

—*PHILIPPIANS 4:13*

I've Got the Power!

Sometimes we get stuck waiting on God to fix everything. We believe in His power and yearn for His healing touch in our lives. When healing is delayed, however, we may convince ourselves He is holding out because we haven't prayed hard enough, trusted enough, or had faith enough for Him to move in our lives. But very often, while we're waiting on God to move, He, too, is waiting on us to move.

Our relationship with God is not one-sided, where we simply depend on Him to do everything for us. We are not puppets. He has invited us into partnership with Himself. God will do what only God can do, and we must do what only we can do.

In our desire to achieve weight loss and healthy living, we must not just pray, trust, and believe that God will move—we, too, must get moving. As we acknowledge our dependence upon God, He will grant us the strength we need to exercise and to eat healthy foods in appropriate portions.

Today, Lord, I know that You will strengthen me to participate in my healing. May I be faithful to You and get busy with my responsibilities.

AUGUST 8

"I have swept away your offenses like a cloud, your sins like the morning mist. Return to me, for I have redeemed you."

—ISAIAH 44:22

Listen to What He Says

It is already done! God has already redeemed us from the dark pit that our sins have created.

This may feel like too great a gift for those of us who feel such guilt for being overweight. So we resist the mercy and grace, preferring instead to continue punishing ourselves, claiming we are unworthy of any help from God. When He calls to us, bidding, "Return to me," we want to hide under a rock in shame.

But listen to His call: "Return to me." What a beautiful thing for Him to say! He could say anything He chooses, for we completely deserve to be separated from Him. Yet instead of leaving us to die in our sin, He speaks to us with passion and great encouragement: "I have swept away your offenses like a cloud, your sins like the morning mist." We can hear Him reaching for us in excitement because of what He has done!

Today, Lord, I praise You and thank You for calling to me with passion and encouragement.

AUGUST 9

And we rejoice in the hope of the glory of God. Not only so, but we also rejoice in our sufferings, because we know that suffering produces perseverance; perseverance, character; and character, hope. And hope does not disappoint us, because God has poured out his love into our hearts by the Holy Spirit, whom he has given to us. —ROMANS 5:2B-5

Lord, We Rejoice

Lord, today I simply rejoice in the hope of Your goodness, Your glory, Your holiness, Your power, Your splendor, Your love. There are many great reasons to celebrate because of who You are.

I expect that today will bring a certain amount of suffering as I face my emotional eating temptations and surrender my will to Yours. I want to heal and grow today, Lord, but it may not be easy. Yet I will choose to rejoice in my suffering, because it develops my perseverance.

I rejoice because, through perseverance, my character will mature, and then I will find hope once again—hope that it is all worth the effort; hope that You bring about change through obedience; hope that my cravings will lighten; hope that I will lose excess weight by combining faith with stamina—and none of this hope will disappoint me. Once again I find Your love poured into my heart, filled to overflowing by the Holy Spirit You have given to me.

Thank You for loving me every minute and for causing my heart to rejoice in all things.

Today, Lord, I rejoice in the hope of Your goodness, Your glory, Your holiness, Your power, Your splendor, Your love.

"Call upon me in the day of trouble; I will deliver you, and you will honor me."   —PSALM 50:15

Dare to Call Upon Him

Revel in this great promise from God! We may feel like our whole life is a day of trouble, so this is just the promise we need!

Coming to recognize our need for God's help with weight loss is an entire process in and of itself. We may have spent years convinced that surely we have the power within us to control our eating, or we've been convinced that God would not care to help us in these matters. We could not have been more wrong! We are powerless over our urges to binge, and He is absolutely ready and willing to help us in every aspect of our lives.

Whatever it is that causes us trouble, we must get to the place of surrender. The next time we are faced with the opportunity to misuse our food, we can immediately call out for His hand instead of struggling to control the situation. He promises to come through, to deliver us from trouble.

Our daily experience of God brings honor to Him as we trust in His power and express our deep, deep gratitude for His help.

Today, Lord, I will dare to call upon You before I choose trouble.

AUGUST 11

If you, O Lord, kept a record of sins, O Lord, who could stand? But with you there is forgiveness; therefore you are feared.

—PSALM 130:3-4

With You There Is Forgiveness

We can barely stand to think of all the ways we've misused food and mistreated our bodies over the years. Guilt and shame may overwhelm us as we consider all that has led to our overweight and unnecessary physical ailments. We are suffering the consequences of neglecting our health, and we are disheartened enough that we haven't even tried to change at all.

What would we do if God kept a record of our sins? Who could stand? Oh, but praise be to God— He doesn't keep a list. This may be a hard concept to grasp, but God does not just forgive our sins; He wipes them away, and there is no record held against us. Not only is God holy enough that He could keep a record of our wrongs, but He is also powerful and mighty enough to blow it away for all eternity, erasing it even from His own memory. He is loving enough to have actually done this. That's why we fear Him and revere Him! In His holiness He does not shun us but comes close—and saves us.

Thank You, Lord, for Your forgiveness. You are all-powerful, yet so loving.

AUGUST 12

He is not far from each one of us. For in him we live and move and have our being. —ACTS 17:27B-28

He Is Ever Present

Some days it seems as though God is far away, watching us struggle from a distance. We know He created the whole universe, and at times we may feel insignificant. So we ask, "How could God be directly involved in my life?" We wonder if He really cares about us personally or if He is even paying attention. Yet we mustn't lose hope. God is not absent or unaware!

In Acts 17 Paul reminds us that God is not far from us. In fact, He is ever present, every minute of our life. Yes, He is the Creator of the universe, but as such He has chosen to be not only God Almighty, but "God With Us." It is truly in Him that we live and move and have our being. Among His many blessings, He gives us our very life and breath. He gives us whatever movement we have and a soul that can live with Him forever. Our very existence reveals that God is with us, for it is by His design that we are alive.

Today, Lord, may I remain in the truth that You are not far from me. With each breath, may I be reminded that You sustain my very being.

"Ah, Sovereign LORD, you have made the heavens and the earth by your great power and outstretched arm. Nothing is too hard for you. . . ." Then the word of the LORD came to Jeremiah: "I am the LORD, the God of all mankind. Is anything too hard for me?"   —JEREMIAH 32:17, 26-27

Nothing Is Too Difficult for Thee

Let us harness this praise from Jeremiah that it might lead us through our most desperate moments. When our goals seem unreachable and we devise reasons for quitting our program, when progress seems slow, may we shout to the Lord, "Nothing is too hard for You!" In our weaknesses and resignation, may we hear God return His word to us, "I am the Lord, the God of all mankind," and find encouragement once more.

We will have our days of doubt and despair, but God is our sovereign Lord. We are on His team, and He has all power to do more than we could ever dream in a lifetime. Let us trust in His might, rest in His arms, and hope—just for today.

Today, Lord, I personalize Ephesians 3:20: "Glory be to You! By Your mighty power at work within me, You are able to accomplish infinitely more than I could ever dare to ask or imagine."

"Now my soul is deeply troubled. Should I pray, 'Father, save me from what lies ahead?' But that is the very reason why I came! Father, bring glory to your name."

—JOHN 12:27-28A *(JESUS SPEAKING)*

The Dreadful Task Before Us

We who seek spiritual healing and truth are in for excruciating pain at times. Encountering the reality of our lives, our mistakes, and the mistakes of others can be gut-wrenching. Pulling back the blinders of denial can cause distress and turmoil that may seem unbearable. Often, even the mere thought of facing our issues can be debilitating, but we know it is the only path to wholeness.

Jesus has been there. As the time approached for His torture and crucifixion, His soul became deeply troubled to the point of dread. He had the most dreadful task imaginable before Him and was sickened by it. Yet look at how He reasoned through His plight. He considered asking the Father to save Him from the horror that lay ahead. But He then rejected His own desire, for He knew the suffering must occur to bring about God's purposes. He surrendered Himself, praying, "Father, bring glory to your name."

May we be as centered as Jesus while facing our own difficult path toward resurrection. May we identify with Jesus in His sufferings and also in the hope that lies ahead.

Today, Lord, I am dreading some of the tasks before me. Yet through this journey, Father, bring glory to Your name.

Then the LORD answered Job from the whirlwind: "Who is this that questions my wisdom with such ignorant words? Brace yourself, because I have some questions for you, and you must answer them. Where were you when I laid the foundations of the earth? Tell me, if you know so much. Do you know how its dimensions were determined and who did the surveying? What supports its foundations, and who laid its cornerstone as the morning stars sang together and all the angels shouted for joy? Who defined the boundaries of the sea as it burst from the womb, and as I clothed it with clouds and thick darkness? For I locked it behind barred gates, limiting its shores. I said, 'Thus far and no farther will you come. Here your proud waves must stop!' Have you ever commanded the morning to appear and caused the dawn to rise in the east?"

—JOB 38:1-12 NLT

Brace Yourself

Then Job replied to the Lord, "I am nothing—how could I ever find the answers? I will put my hand over my mouth in silence. I have said too much already. I have nothing more to say" (Job 40:3-5 NLT).

Job's response here is so fitting: "Oops . . . uh . . . pardon me. . . . Here, let me just put my hand right over my mouth for safekeeping. I think I'll just go ahead and zip it from here on out." Job, who suffered many tragic losses and much physical anguish in life, had given to questioning God's performance and wisdom. And God made His point with dear Job. In the midst of our trouble, God knows all . . . and God knows best.

Today, Lord, when I am tempted to complain of my torment with food and weight issues, may I remember Your sovereignty and choose to trust You instead.

At this, Job got up and tore his robe and shaved his head. Then he fell to the ground in worship and said: "Naked I came from my mother's womb, and naked I will depart. The LORD gave and the LORD has taken away; may the name of the LORD be praised." In all this, Job did not sin by charging God with wrongdoing. —JOB 1:20-22

You Give and Take Away— Lord, Blessed Be Your Name

Job knew suffering. Within one day, God allowed Job to lose everything valuable in his life. He lost his farm animals, his farmhands, all his sheep and shepherds, his camels, and his servants. Even his sons and daughters were killed. His livelihood and all he held dear were destroyed, obliterated with one fell swoop.

Yet Job also knew God. He knew God and loved Him. He believed in God's sovereignty. Did Job grieve for his horrifying losses? Terribly! But even in his most tragic reality, he gave praise to God. And later, when Job's body was brutally afflicted and he had many despairing questions, he refrained from cursing God in any way.

Meditate on this praise once more: "The LORD gave and the LORD has taken away; may the name of the LORD be praised." How pure was Job's love for God! As we grieve about our challenges with food and weight and the trials of life, may we declare such praise to God at all times, in every circumstance. He is sovereign, and He is good.

Today, Lord, and every day, blessed be Your name. You give and take away, yet will I praise You.

But when the kindness and love of God our Savior appeared, he saved us, not because of righteous things we had done, but because of his mercy. He saved us through the washing of rebirth and renewal by the Holy Spirit, whom he poured out on us generously through Jesus Christ our Savior, so that, having been justified by his grace, we might become heirs having the hope of eternal life. —TITUS 3:4-7

Unbelievable Mercy

In our past efforts to lose excess weight, we have failed many times. Although our intentions have always been strong, we have never been able to do this perfectly. We have felt ashamed of our over-eating and disappointed in our track record with exercise. Critical voices inside our head tell us we're pathetic or worthless as a human being—that we don't deserve to lose weight because we haven't wanted it badly enough. We have believed these voices as if they came from God, but they do not.

Here is the heart of God our Savior—it is kindness and compassion for the helpless. Seeing us desperate, unable to live perfectly, He poured out His Spirit so generously that we might have the hope of life with Him eternally. This is the tenderness of our God: As we have failed and will surely fail again, He does not condemn, but pours out His love on us to fill us with hope once more. May we be so brave as to exchange our shame for the mercy and grace of this God who makes us clean.

Today, Lord, I will dare to trust in Your love for me despite all my failures.

For the kingdom of God is not a matter of what we eat or drink, but of living a life of goodness and peace and joy in the Holy Spirit. —ROMANS 14:17 NLT

The Big Picture of Wellness

In trying to lose weight, we can become obsessed with all the details involving food and drink. We can get so focused on our goals that we micromanage our eating to a fault, neglecting to nurture the rest of our personal needs. We can miss the bigger picture of wellness in life. Our imbalance results in fluctuating weight or damage to our relationships, faith, moral strength, or even a lack of joy.

Let us be diligent to care for our whole person— spirit, mind, and body. We don't need to fix everything at once. But we can simply and gently tend to our different parts, treating ourselves with love. For this is the kingdom of God—to live lives of goodness, peace, and joy in the Holy Spirit.

Today, Lord, help me to see the bigger picture. May I live today in goodness, peace, and joy in You.

I can really know Christ and experience the mighty power that raised him from the dead. I can learn what it means to suffer with him, sharing in his death, so that, somehow, I can experience the resurrection from the dead!

—PHILIPPIANS 3:10-11 NLT

To Really Know Christ

At times the intensity of our pain is overwhelming. We feel hopeless, like it's all for nothing—that our struggle with food and weight is just useless agony. We search for meaning and purpose in the hurting times.

In his letter to the church at Philippi, Paul wrote passionately on the value of our pain. He taught that we can embrace suffering as a treasured opportunity to identify with Jesus, prizing the chance to "really know Christ." Our hope can abound, for as we endure pain with Christ, dying to our own flesh, the awesome resurrection power enables us to live new lives in Him. It is never for nothing when we allow ourselves to more closely identify with Jesus, in suffering and in resurrection.

Today, Lord, may I know You more deeply in the suffering and find hope in Your resurrection power.

For the LORD does not abandon anyone forever. Though he brings grief, he also shows compassion according to the greatness of his unfailing love. For he does not enjoy hurting people or causing them sorrow.

—LAMENTATIONS 3:31-33 NLT

He Takes No Delight in Our Suffering

Have you ever felt as though God must delight in your suffering? That He is purposefully declining your requests just for the fun of it? We can feel cursed by God at times, abandoned in our agonies and trials. We think, *If He really cared, He would not allow me to suffer this type of pain.* Yet this is not the heart of God.

As Jeremiah writes in Lamentations, the Lord is not abandoning us. It is true that sometimes He brings grief, but it is never for His pleasure. If indeed God brings on the grief, it is only what's necessary for our benefit. As we endure sorrow, He holds us in His unfailing love and compassion. He may be bringing a time of grief to help move us toward the joy that awaits us. We can trust in God's motives for our well-being.

Today, Lord, may I find solace in Your unfailing love and compassion. May I trust in Your will for me.

AUGUST 21

Listen, for I have worthy things to say; I open my lips to speak what is right. My mouth speaks what is true, for my lips detest wickedness. All the words of my mouth are just; none of them is crooked or perverse. —PROVERBS 8:6-8 (WISDOM SPEAKING)

A Season for Stillness

We could spend our days in idle chatter and gossip, but to what end? Wisdom calls to us instead. She urges us to listen. When we are truly seeking answers to our food and weight challenges, one of the most important things we can do is to quiet ourselves entirely. This is not a time for random interaction and noise or for constant output. It's a time for input. While there are certainly occasions when we must process our thoughts aloud, now may be a time for us to listen.

Getting quiet may prove to be somewhat of a challenge, but we are fighting for our health here. We can decide to dedicate ourselves to stillness for a season. Wisdom is speaking, and our job is to seek her through prayer, Scripture, and the voices of those who will share their journey with us.

This proverb can bring such hope to us who fret about having no answers. There are answers; there is justice and truth. Wisdom is accessible to all who will listen.

Today, Lord, I will quiet myself and listen for wisdom.

AUGUST 22

I love you, LORD; you are my strength. The LORD is my rock, my fortress, and my savior; my God is my rock, in whom I find protection. He is my shield, the strength of my salvation, and my stronghold. I will call on the LORD, who is worthy of praise, for he saves me from my enemies. The ropes of death surrounded me; the floods of destruction swept over me. The grave wrapped its ropes around me; death itself stared me in the face. But in my distress I cried out to the LORD; yes, I prayed to my God for help. He heard me from his sanctuary; my cry reaches his ears. —PSALM 18:1-6 NLT

Safety in the Battle

We have found ourselves in grave condition, too . . . overweight, under-exercised, disabled from the fullness of life intended for us—the death of our vibrance staring us in the face. We are too exhausted to participate in fun activities, too embarrassed to go to the beach, too intimidated by others who are more physically coordinated than we are. So we resign ourselves to what's easy, what's comfortable, what's "safe."

But what does "safe" mean? The psalmist reminds us that it's God—our rock, our fortress, our savior from that which drives us toward death. In our distress, we do not just ball up and die. We cry out to the Lord, praying for help. He hears our voice. Paradoxically, by staying in the battle, we find true safety.

Today, Lord, rather than aiming for safety in my own comforts, I will instead take a risk. I will engage in life, in the battle. I cry out to you, my Rock, my Fortress, my Savior. You are my Strength; in You I take refuge.

AUGUST 23

Show me your ways, O Lord, teach me your paths; guide me in your truth and teach me, for you are God my Savior, and my hope is in you all day long. —PSALM 25:4-5

The Path of Recovery—Today

This heartfelt prayer shows all the elements of recovery: humility, asking for direction and guidance, a search for truth, and complete trust in God as the Savior—all day long.

One day at a time, we can ask to be shown God's direction for following our food plan and staying out of the deprivation-and-diet mentality. With God's guidance we can learn new ways of dealing with feelings and relationships. We can ask to see truth, no longer living in denial about the seriousness of our condition.

By having a teachable spirit, we are humble enough to see that in turning away from unhealthy food choices, we're drawing closer to living out God's will for our life. We are able to have a deeper trust in His ability to save us from the despair of compulsive eating and an overweight body. Our hope is grounded in who He is, not our own unpredictable and failing willpower. We develop an even greater humility when we realize that we must do this all day long, every day.

God's salvation is in the present—not tomorrow, or Monday, or the beginning of next year. We are taught in the present and guided now.

Today, show me Your ways, O Lord. I humbly ask You to bring me out of denial and to show me the truth of my condition. I trust in Your grace to save me from the despair of compulsive eating.

AUGUST 24

*Dear friends, I urge you, as aliens and strangers in the world,
to abstain from sinful desires, which war against your soul.*

—1 PETER 2:11

Aliens and Strangers

No one ever said it was a sin to eat a chocolate donut! The sin is when we replace God with worldly solutions and pleasures.

It is not a problem to enjoy a donut occasionally when we are faithfully caring for our body with sleep, exercise, and nourishment. It is not a problem if we are connected and thriving in relationship with God and His people. It is not a problem as long as we are not using the donut to escape from some pain we'd prefer to avoid—or that one donut does not turn into a dozen.

As followers of Christ, we are strangers to the ways of this world. When sinful desires urge us to flee from discomfort, it is a war against our soul. Instead of surrendering to the easy way out that the donut represents, we can look to God for His answers. As we abstain from overindulgence, our soul becomes stronger, free from bondage to sinful desires. We may one day even choose to enjoy the donut—with no sin at all.

Today, Lord, I will live as a stranger to the ways of this world.

A gentle answer turns away wrath, but a harsh word stirs up anger. —*PROVERBS 15:1*

Choose Gentleness

While attempting to change our lives, we may find that suddenly we're easily irritated by those around us. Our friends' and family's habits and character traits that never bothered us before may start to get on our nerves. We may begin to see the ways we were influenced into overweight and how others choose to remain in the lifestyle we are trying to leave. This can cause us to be bitter and resentful, especially when our new food choices are criticized by those who modeled overeating for us.

We may be tempted to reciprocate the harshness. Yet we can choose to be gentle in our relationships, first with care and compassion in our hearts, and then in our actions and words. We can consider our own need for love and acceptance, right where we are. We can offer that love to others in gentleness—turning away anger that is in ourselves, and then turning away the anger in others.

Today, Lord, when I want to be harsh with others, or even with myself, may I instead choose gentleness.

AUGUST 26

A man's own folly ruins his life, yet his heart rages against the Lord. —*PROVERBS 19:3*

The Greatness of Victimhood

Isn't it great to be the victim? There is so much benefit in this position. We get to be innocent. We get to be right. We are free from guilt, shame, remorse, responsibility, and accountability for where we are in life. We receive attention and sympathy from those around us who enjoy rescuing, and we feel very valuable as the wounded sufferer, forever afflicted by the indecency of God and others. Yes, it's great to be the victim.

However, if we plan to mature in our journey toward weightlessness, then the victim-plan-for-life is of no avail. We must own our choices that have brought us misery. Though significant people in our lives have hurt us in the past, sometimes severely, we are responsible for seeking help for those injuries and healing in our lives. We are responsible for our own recovery.

By taking ownership of the choices we've made, unjust anger toward God can also be relieved. We can partner with Him today for our well-being and remember that He never works for our destruction.

Today, Lord, I resign from the role of victim. I will responsibly seek help for my problems with food and excess weight.

Above all, love each other deeply, because love covers over a
multitude of sins. —1 PETER 4:8

Love Deeply

If we spend our time on earth resenting those who
have harmed us; if we hold on to anger and pursue
revenge; if we shut down our hearts in defense
against pain, what is our gain? If others hold us in
contempt and offer no forgiveness when we make
mistakes, what is our gain? Why should we care for
ourselves when there seems to be no hope of recon-
ciling relationships?

With this mindset, things can look bleak
enough that there is temptation for us to give up
caring for our health. That's why we are called in
God's Word to choose love instead. It's not a simple
task, but it's one that brings hope. We are not only
called to love, but to love one another deeply—
above any other decision. It is an act of our will, not
merely a warm feeling we find on the inside. A
choice we make in spite of the wrongs we've suffered. To acknowledge our own weaknesses and
walk humbly, ready to forgive and be forgiven in
Christ Jesus—to love and be loved—is our highest
standard.

Today, Lord, when I want to resign in futility and
overeat, may I instead walk humbly with You. May I
love myself and those around me, by choice. I know
this alone will solve many of my problems.

Praise the LORD, O my soul; all my inmost being, praise his holy name. Praise the LORD, O my soul, and forget not all his benefits—who forgives all your sins and heals all your diseases, who redeems your life from the pit and crowns you with love and compassion, who satisfies your desires with good things so that your youth is renewed like the eagle's.

—PSALM 103:1-5

Addicted to Heaviness

Though it may be difficult for us to imagine, we can actually be addicted to carrying excess weight. It does provide us with several benefits. We may be terrified of what life would be like in a healthier body, and so we avoid getting well. We use our weight to avoid sexuality, to excuse us from others' high expectations, to "protect" us from closeness, and to distract us from dealing with our deeper issues. We focus on working around overweight rather than working on what causes it. We need our weight; we're addicted to these benefits.

But let us not forget all of God's benefits. He redeems our life from the pit of dependence upon overweight. He forgives the sin of neglecting our body and heals our diseases, our addictions. He crowns us with love and compassion; He satisfies our hunger with good things so that we will truly live with energy like we had in our youth. We can start letting go of excess weight and trust that He will bring us great blessing, providing for all of our needs.

Today, Lord, help me to see all Your benefits. May I continually let go of my hidden fears of being thinner and healthier. Help me to trust in You to provide for me. Praise Your name!

If I could speak in any language in heaven or on earth but didn't love others, I would only be making meaningless noise like a loud gong or a clanging cymbal. If I had the gift of prophecy, and if I knew all the mysteries of the future and knew everything about everything, but didn't love others, what good would I be? And if I had the gift of faith so that I could speak to a mountain and make it move, without love I would be no good to anybody. If I gave everything I have to the poor and even sacrificed my body, I could boast about it; but if I didn't love others, I would be of no value whatsoever.

—1 CORINTHIANS 13:1-3 NLT

Love in Practice

In today's journey of recovery from food and weight challenges, we examine our hearts for love. How are we doing in the love department?

In reading the succeeding verses of 1 Corinthians 13 (4-7), insert your name in the blank provided, where the word "love" would normally appear. Lord, speak to our hearts through this passage . . .

(___) is patient and kind. (___) is not jealous or boastful or proud or rude. (___) does not demand (___ 's) own way. (___) is not irritable, and (___) keeps no record of when (___) has been wronged. (___) is never glad about injustice but rejoices whenever the truth wins out. (___) never gives up, never loses faith, is always hopeful, and endures through every circumstance.

Today, Lord, teach me ways that I can share Your love. Help me practice what I'm receiving from You. Help me to LOVE!

Let us therefore make every effort to do what leads to peace and to mutual edification. Do not destroy the work of God for the sake of food. —ROMANS 14:19-20A

Reach Out in Peace

Changing our behavior around food can cause tension in our relationships. Those who are close to us may boldly share their opinions about our new lifestyle. They may be resistant to what we are doing because it reveals to them their own weaknesses or need for change. They may get defensive or be disappointed when we choose not to consume the foods they want to share with us. They may feel rejected or inhibited from eating what they want in our presence. A flurry of weird relationship dynamics can be set into motion the moment we start to live differently! But in compassion, we can reach out with peace and edification.

When we sense tension, sadness, fear, anger, or anything different in those around us, we can immediately respond with grace and warmth. Regardless of how we are treated, we can always choose to speak with humility, love, and confidence. We can be ministers of reconciliation, even when someone is angry, because we know that God may be doing a work deep inside the heart of that person. Let us not destroy His work in us or in others over our behaviors with food.

Today, Lord, may I be a minister of peace. I pray to build up those around me, especially when I sense there is tension.

AUGUST 31

Then he said to them, "Watch out! Be on your guard against all kinds of greed; a man's life does not consist in the abundance of his possessions." —LUKE 12:15

Guard Against Greed

We may have never considered our overeating to be a form of greed, but it has proven to be such. For many of us, food has been the unhealthy focus of our attention for years. We've obsessed over meals, hoarded our portions, and perhaps even set our sights on the plate of the person next to us. We have been sent into panic when our pantry was not filled to the brim with options for desserts, midnight snacks, and on-the-go munchies. Yet the goodness of our lives is not measured by the abundance and variety of our diet and pantry supply.

So while it is quite fine to enjoy the pleasures that food can bring, it is not so fine for us to rely on our storehouse and large servings to provide us with fullness of life. Food always fails us when we use it to replace what only God can truly be for us. So let us be on our guard against greediness in our use of food. God uses food to sustain us, to bring pleasure, but above all, to teach us to look to Him as the source of all life . . . and our greatest abundance by far.

Today, Lord, I know that You are the Giver of Life. You provide all my needs in appropriate measure.

SEPTEMBER 1

Even while we were with you, we gave you this rule: "Whoever does not work should not eat." Yet we hear that some of you are living idle lives, refusing to work and wasting time meddling in other people's business. In the name of the Lord Jesus Christ, we appeal to such people—no, we command them: Settle down and get to work. Earn your own living.

—2 THESSALONIANS 3:10-12 NLT

Settle Down and Get to Work

There is a difference between hard work and busyness. We can easily fill our days with crises, relational triangles, and chitchat. We can exhaust ourselves with meaningless activity and scurrying about, never accomplishing one solid, worthwhile task.

This may be a hard pill to swallow, but we might be living the idle life. Busy all day to no avail, and perplexed by our lack of healing and growth, have we given up? Do we declare, "All of life is a busy day —when could I possibly think about my health?"

In 2 Thessalonians Paul commands us to "settle down and get to work." What a statement! It's time for us to get moving on the work that earns a true reward for our life. We must disengage from busyness, settle down, and focus our efforts on what's really important.

Today, Lord, may I walk away from busyness, settle down my scurrying, and, with Your help, get to work on me.

Since we have these promises, dear friends, let us purify ourselves from everything that contaminates body and spirit, perfecting holiness out of reverence for God.

—2 CORINTHIANS 7:1

Let Us Purify

Why does "purify[ing] ourselves from everything that contaminates the body and spirit" sound like something we would not want to do? Why wouldn't we want to get rid of the things that contaminate? Probably because purification often involves losing something we've depended on or something we've enjoyed in place of God and His ways. However, we also know this enjoyable thing has produced negative results and has held us back from the fullness that God intends for us.

Our hesitation might stem from a fear that giving up our impurities will leave us void. This is not what will happen! God has given us many promises for the life lived purely before Him. He promises He will be with us, walking with us, filling us and living in us—the Almighty Lord. We can bravely pursue the perfecting of our holiness and trust in Him to fill us to overflowing with His love and good promises for our life.

Today, Lord, as I turn from impure food and impure thoughts, I trust You to fill me with good things. If I feel scared to let go of my excess, then I will call on a friend to help me.

SEPTEMBER 3

An anxious heart weighs a man down, but a kind word cheers him up. —PROVERBS 12:25

The Cost of the Chaos

When we eat out of anxiety, we are relying on food to satisfy more than just physical hunger. We are seeking some relief from our distress, hoping food will compensate for our lack of serenity. But our anxious eating usually backfires. We feel the weight of poor eating choices, and our anxiety is increased all the more.

It may not be easy, but we must consider the cost of the chaos and oppose the frenzy. Today, for one meal, we can call a truce with the whirlwind of life. If our homes are filled with distractions and stressful relationships, we can find another quiet place to dine. We may want to appeal to others for help in creating a safer eating environment. We can call a beloved friend for kind words and gentle prayer just prior to eating. As we slow our breathing and quiet the noise, our eating will be healthier and we'll find some peace at the table.

Today, Lord, may I plan for serenity while eating. May I share peaceful moments and kind words with loved ones.

SEPTEMBER 4

In your anger do not sin: Do not let the sun go down while you are still angry. —EPHESIANS 4:26

But certainly God has heard; he has given heed to the voice of my prayer. —PSALM 66:19

I'm Angry Today!

Do you ever just want to stand up and protest, "I hate this! I hate being heavy . . . and I hate getting healthy! I don't *want* to face my issues! I just want to eat what I want and not have to think about it!"?

You are not alone! We who rage today are bothered that we need help from God and others. We are frustrated by the pace of progress and have decided we hate the concept of surrendering our will. We resent letting go of what we want to control, working on deep issues, exercising our body, and limiting our foods. We are generally peeved that this process hurts. It's difficult, and we want it to be easier.

Now inhale . . . and exhale. Then say it: "Lord, I am angry today."

Give God the reality of your heart, and find out what happens. You will not shock Him in your rage but more likely please Him in your authenticity. It is more humble to share your heart than to suggest that He can't handle it. Your Creator is not appalled by your grief but cares for you deeply. He already knows what's inside you, and as you confess your feelings, you can know you've been heard. When our protest is heard, then our fury subsides.

Father, I'm so glad You are big enough to handle my fiercest moments. Today, I'm in a rage.

SEPTEMBER 5

Do your best to present yourself to God as one approved, a workman who does not need to be ashamed and who correctly handles the word of truth. —2 TIMOTHY 2:15

Half the Work, Half the Benefit

Adjusting our old eating style to a healthier format will bring results in our desire to lose excess pounds. We may lose weight consistently for a time and rejoice in our progress, then suddenly hit a wall. We get stuck, still heavier than we want—though we've come a long way toward reaching our ideal body weight. We've been diligent with our food plan but seem able to only go so far in our goals.

It is at this point we must remember that "about half the work" brings about half the benefit. We can do more to affect our weight than merely change our eating. If we understand our needs for exercise, connection with others, and spiritual and emotional healing, then we also know our diligence in these areas is vital to our continued health improvement. When we stop halfway in our efforts, then we'll stop halfway toward our goal.

Today, Lord, may I increase my diligence in an area I've neglected.

SEPTEMBER 6

"Oh, there is so much more I want to tell you, but you can't bear it now. When the Spirit of truth comes, he will guide you into all truth." —JOHN 16:12-13 NLT (JESUS SPEAKING)

You Can't Handle the Truth

It is easy to become discouraged by our lack of knowledge when we yearn so much to get well. We have accepted that we have problems and now beg for answers on how to make the changes that will improve our life. However, the ability to improve will never come from an information download into the brain, for it's not just information that we need.

As someone once said, "You can't go through college in a week." How true that even if our every question was answered immediately, we would not be able to apply all our new knowledge at once. The quest for truth is more involved and much slower. It is a lifelong process whereby we absorb information over time.

Jesus Himself knew that answering the disciples' many questions all at once would be too over-whelming and counterproductive in that moment. He wanted to tell them so much, but in wisdom He refrained.

In our progress toward healthy living, it's okay that we don't know everything right this moment. As we seek for answers, we will learn what we need for today. With practice, and in God's time, our lives will improve.

Today, Lord, may I accept the reality that healing takes time. Help me to stay in the process and trust that You will reveal new information to me when You know I am ready to receive it.

*"If my people, who are called by my name, will humble them-
selves and pray and seek my face and turn from their wicked
ways, then will I hear from heaven and will forgive their sin
and will heal their land."* —2 CHRONICLES 7:14

Partner with God

We have prayed for years that God would intervene
in our struggles. We've pleaded with Him for help
in every aspect of our lives, including our diet and
weight-loss programs. This is good, because He has
called us to prayer. But more than that, God has
invited us to partner with Him in transforming our
own lives.

This partnership with God begins with humility.
We must not only pray but humble our lives before
Him. When it's hard for us to recognize our lack of
humility, it is helpful for us to examine our behaviors. Our resistance to God is found in our unwill-
ingness to put action to our prayers. We are called
to seek His face, pursue Him, know Him. We are
called to turn from our wicked ways—from unhealthy foods, an inactive lifestyle, isolation, and
the destructive patterns we've identified thus far.

As we walk in humility, God will make good on
His promises. And by partnering with Him, our
lives will be transformed in every way.

*Today, Lord, I will put action to my prayers. May I
walk in all humility.*

If it is possible, as far as it depends on you, live at peace with everyone. —*ROMANS 12:18*

Let It Begin with Me

Live at peace with everyone? Impossible! "You don't know my mother," you might say.

Everyone interacts with difficult people in life. We have each been wounded, sometimes deeply, by someone significant to us. Perhaps we are confronted daily by a person with whom we'd rather have no contact at all. Convinced we cannot make peace because of their issues and behaviors, we then feel trapped and powerless. In misery, we turn to food for the escape we need. Yet we have other options.

While we are never able to change or control another person, we can always make choices for our own behavior. Instead of being victimized and indignant that another person refuses to move toward peace, we can let peace begin with us. No matter how unfairly we are treated by another human being, we are not sentenced to a life of only one response. We have the freedom to respond peaceably, surrendering our need for them to be someone other than who they are. We can let their hurtful words fall to the ground as we preserve our serenity today.

Lord, when I am challenged by a difficult person today, help me to do my part to live at peace. Bring serenity to my soul, Lord, so I will not turn to food for escape.

Can anything ever separate us from Christ's love? Does it mean he no longer loves us if we have trouble or calamity, or are persecuted, or are hungry or cold or in danger or threatened with death? . . . No, despite all these things, overwhelming victory is ours through Christ, who loved us. And I am convinced that nothing can ever separate us from his love.

—ROMANS 8:35, 37 NLT

Nothing in All Creation

Nothing can ever separate us??? What about our doubt in God's love? . . . Surely, that's unlovable. What about the way we sometimes let down our family, the way we fail our friends? What about our delight in bingeing on junk food and the ways we mistreat our body? What about the ways we hide from people . . . from God? What about our perfectionism and desire to control others? What about the way we lose our temper toward those we love, or the chaotic mess of junk in our home, or how we oversleep instead of reading our Bible? What about the way we loathe helping our children with their homework, or withdraw from our spouse? What about the sexual sins we've committed? What about the lie we already told today? What about how ugly we feel at times? . . . Yet despite all these things, overwhelming victory is ours through Christ, who loved us.

NOTHING in all creation—including everything wrong with us—can ever separate us from His love!

Today, Lord, I see that You will always love me, no matter what!

As obedient children, do not conform to the evil desires you had when you lived in ignorance. But just as he who called you is holy, so be holy in all you do; for it is written: "Be holy, because I am holy." —1 PETER 1:14-16

With Knowledge Comes Responsibility

For many years we had the pleasure of pleading ignorance. We were uneducated about healthy eating—and rather preferred to be so, in order to avoid the responsibility that comes with knowledge. As far as we understood, the desires we had for excessive junk foods were merely random cravings that could only be filled, of course, with whatever we wanted at that moment.

This was a comfortable way of life! Until we wanted to put on a bathing suit, or shoot hoops with our kids, or have our picture taken, or attract a desirable date, or be uninhibited in private moments with our spouse. Then, after enough of these not-so-pleasant experiences, we were miserable enough to look for some answers. But . . . oh, no! We forgot that with knowledge comes responsibility! No more pleading ignorant! (It didn't really work for us anyway.)

As we start to have a clue about our behaviors around food, we can walk in obedience, moving toward holiness. We can step away from that which defiles and instead become holy because He is holy.

Today, Lord, may I walk obediently in what I already know to do for my health.

SEPTEMBER 11

Be gracious to me, O God, be gracious to me, for my soul takes refuge in You; and in the shadow of Your wings I will take refuge until destruction passes by. —PSALM 57:1-3A NASB

A Terrorist On Board

There is a destroyer among us. Like a terrorist and his sinister plot to lay waste to a country, our compulsive eating has invited destruction into our life. In a sense, we are all on a hijacked plane, and we all have a terrorist on board. It is Satan himself saying, "Don't worry; everything will be okay. You can trust me. That little donut won't hurt you this time! Eat, drink, and be merry!"

We may think we have lots of time to change the way we eat, the way we approach life, the way we use food to avoid life. Truly grasping the seriousness of our situation and wayward eating behaviors is often difficult. But destruction is imminent if we do not take heed.

Will we choose captivity on a hijacked plane headed for destruction? Or will we gather our courage, take charge of our plane, and make a stand for health and wholeness—a stand for life!

Today, Lord, I have been in captivity too long. By turning over control of compulsive and emotional eating to You, I am courageously making a choice for freedom from food and weight. I am making a stand for my life.

SEPTEMBER 12

"Be glad, O people of Zion, rejoice in the LORD your God, for he has given you the autumn rains in righteousness. He sends you abundant showers, both autumn and spring rains, as before." —JOEL 2:23

Autumn Rains

The prophet Joel rejoiced in bringing hope to Israel. In his book of the Bible, we read that Israel experienced famine and the judgment of God following a terrible drought and an infestation of locusts. In the midst of this calamity, the nation came to realize that they had to completely depend upon God. The people and the land were dry and empty because of prideful attempts to live according to their own will. But Joel's words foretold the Lord's mercy and grace that would come.

When we have associated enough pain with our obsessive food thoughts and compulsive behaviors, we, too, come to a place of drought and famine. Our spirit is no longer in touch with God, and we are spiritually dried up and starving—even as we seek comfort by eating!

When we realize that food will not fill our emotional and compulsive needs, Joel's words remind us that we must completely depend upon God. At the point of acceptance and surrender are we ready for the autumn rains of righteousness and open to receive God's abundant showers of love and grace. We need only ask in honesty. As we receive the rain in autumn, the spring of renewal and growth will come.

Today, Lord, I realize I am dry and hungry. I am ready for Your abundant showers of love and grace.

"Have I not commanded you? Be strong and courageous. Do not be terrified; do not be discouraged, for the LORD your God will be with you wherever you go."

—JOSHUA 1:9 (THE LORD SPEAKING)

We Have a Choice?

How can we be commanded regarding our feelings? Do we have a choice about how we feel? This scripture tells us that we do.

Working this Lose It For Life program will elicit every emotion we have ever experienced—and more—as we face not only our physical problems but the spiritual and emotional hurts that drive our destructive behaviors. This can be terrifying if we have avoided these past pains for years.

However, we do not have to let our fears and insecurities run amuck. We can feel what we feel and then harness emotion with the reins of truth. Jesus calls us back to the knowledge of who He is and of His promise to soothe our anxieties. He calls us to be strong and courageous in light of these truths.

Today, Lord, may I remember that You are with me and that You are the Lord. I will walk boldly in strength because of who You are.

Get rid of all bitterness, rage and anger, brawling and slander, along with every form of malice. Be kind and compassionate to one another, forgiving each other, just as in Christ God forgave you. —EPHESIANS 4:31-32

It's All About Humility

Today, it's all about humility. The only way for us to be rid of all bitterness, rage, and anger is to first acknowledge our own guilt. This may be hard if we tend to be naive about ourselves. While the sins of those around us seem glaring, we may not notice our own sins, which appear just as blatant to others.

By examining our hearts with utter humility and honesty, we can admit that at times we are guilty of many forms of malice. We may be able to confess a spirit of judgment, insensitivity, stubbornness, manipulation, blame, thoughtlessness, avoidance, and so on. We sure don't enjoy viewing the junk inside of us, though! It's not a pretty picture! We would prefer to be innocent and right—the victim. However, when we acknowledge that we, like everyone else, have fallen short of the mark, we can gain enough humility to initiate reconciliation.

Whether or not we are provoked by another person, we can let kindness, compassion, and forgiveness begin with us—just as in Christ, God forgave us.

Today, Lord, to improve my physical health, may I walk in humility and be ready to forgive. Let kindness and compassion begin with me.

Therefore, I urge you, brothers, in view of God's mercy, to offer your bodies as living sacrifices, holy and pleasing to God—this is your spiritual act of worship. Do not conform any longer to the pattern of this world, but be transformed by the renewing of your mind. Then you will be able to test and approve what God's will is—his good, pleasing and perfect will.
—ROMANS 12:1-2

In View of God's Mercy

Lord, I worship You today. You have been merciful to me; You have saved my life from sin and death. Jesus, You gave Your life on my behalf. I am so grateful to You for Your love.

I offer You my body today. You live within me, and I am Yours. Have Your own way, Lord; have Your own way in me. May I eat to please You and to honor the temple of my body, Your dwelling place. Let me be a living sacrifice, surrendered to You in every way. May I be holy and pleasing to You.

I pray against mindless eating and inactivity. Transform my behaviors as I meditate on Your Word and study Your principles. Teach me to know Your will for my life and to live it against the grain of this world.

Today, Lord, and every day, You are worthy of all worship, adoration, and praise. I surrender all to You.

SEPTEMBER 16

"I have heard all about you, LORD, and I am filled with awe by the amazing things you have done. In this time of our deep need, begin again to help us, as you did in years gone by. Show us your power to save us."

—*HABAKKUK 3:2* NLT (HABAKKUK'S PRAYER)

Show Us Your Power to Save

As we look for God to work in our own lives, we find hope in the testimony of others. Scripture records the history of God continually saving His people. By hearing the stories of deliverance told by those who have traveled the path before us, we gain faith that He will help us, too. When we see God's hand at work in their lives, we can be filled with awe. God has done great things in the past, and He has the power to save us today.

Now is the time of our deep need. We are fighting for our lives regarding food and weight, and it is a good time to be praying like Habakkuk. At any moment that we are low on faith, we can ask God to grant us that, too.

Today, Lord, show me Your power to save, and increase my faith!

. . . because by one sacrifice he has made perfect forever those who are being made holy. —HEBREWS 10:14

Make Me Holy

When Jesus became our atoning sacrifice, we were made perfect in the eyes of God. Oh, if we can grasp this, how life-changing it would be! By accepting the gift of Jesus, we are adorned in His righteousness. Through Him we are no longer unsightly but wholly acceptable and flawless before God. No amount of overeating or inactivity could ever stain our perfection, and no amount of our good behavior could ever create it. It is solely what Christ has already done that cleanses us from all unrighteousness.

But God is not finished with us yet! Since we are now made perfect in Christ, the rest of our life is about being made holy. This is a process that occurs day by day for a lifetime. Holiness comes as we turn our life over to God's care and grow in our desire to serve Him. It comes as we increasingly stand apart from sin and evil, engaging in God's good and pleasing and perfect will. It is not the total absence of mistakes and failures that makes us holy, but the presence of Jesus in our lives. It is the process of growth and increasing faith, of healing and deepening love, of taking on the nature of Christ and resembling Him more each day. This is how we are being made holy.

Today, Lord, use my food and weight issues to make me more like You.

SEPTEMBER 18

Beloved, I pray that in all respects you may prosper and be in good health, just as your soul prospers. —3 JOHN 2 NASB

When We Are Beloved

Being in good health is important, not only for ourselves but for those who care about us. We have friends and family in our lives who are invested in us, who care for our well-being, and who love us. While it is important for us to desire healing for our own sake, we can find extra motivation as we consider the relief and joy we will bring to our loved ones. This is not about earning points with anyone or, conversely, about the guilt of letting others down. It is about our health first and then the byproduct of witness and reassurance to others.

Losing it for life testifies of God's power and faithfulness to heal and restore us as we offer our lives to Him, even in our eating behaviors. We will be a role model to our children of a surrendered heart to Christ. We may bless our spouse with renewed libido and find that our own has improved! In one way or another, others will see the work of God in our lives. We can lose excess weight and increase our energy for ourselves and for those who call us "Beloved."

Today, Lord, I find extra motivation when I think of blessing those around me with evidence of Your work in me.

To keep me from becoming conceited . . . there was given me a thorn in my flesh. . . . Three times I pleaded with the Lord to take it away from me. But he said to me, "My grace is sufficient for you, for my power is made perfect in weakness." Therefore I will boast all the more gladly about my weaknesses, so that Christ's power may rest on me.

—2 CORINTHIANS 12:7-9

This Thorn Is a Gift?

After years of diligence in our quest for "weightlessness," we may be tempted to feel shame for the cravings we still have and for still dreading exercise each morning. Yet this may not be a failure on our part or an indication of stunted growth. It may not mean that we lack faith, or diligence in prayer, or maturity. It may instead be the very thing that Paul describes in his second letter to the Corinthians: an intriguing gift from God. A gift that, while very annoying, may be the one reason we will stay connected with Him.

As we acknowledge that we do not make healthy choices on our own, we are more securely bound to Him each day. We might wander away and stray from our love relationship with God were it not for the knowledge of our utter weakness and dependence on Him. We might cease to praise God if we were confused into thinking we've progressed on our own. So our thorn is actually a blessing that keeps us humble and relying on Him.

Today, Lord, and every day, I praise Your name for perfecting Your power in my weaknesses. I gladly boast of my inabilities and fall prostrate in worship before You.

Trust God from the bottom of your heart; don't try to figure out everything on your own. —PROVERBS 3:5 MSG

The Solution Is Spiritual:
Trust God; Don't Overeat

We have tried "figuring out" weight loss on our own. We have the books, magazines, videos, and other media that tell us the how to's of fitness. If it were a matter of merely having the right information, then we would have merely a one-step program: Get educated. But we are educated, and we may even realize that our overeating is often rooted in emotional needs. Yet our knowledge of that fact is not enough to affect consistent change in our behavior.

This proverb teaches us that the solution is trusting God, not "figuring it all out." The problem may be physical. The cause may be emotional. The solution is spiritual.

Trust God from the bottom of your heart to take care of you, even when you are hungry—especially when you are hungry! When you are scared, anxious, angry—no matter what happens, no matter what you feel—just don't overeat. Pray. Call a supportive friend. Get out of the house. Chew a stick of sugarless gum. Do what it takes to live in the place of surrender, and trust that the help will come if you are serious in taking action.

Today, Lord, I give up trying to figure this out. I trust You to hold me when I refrain from overeating.

Do you not know that your body is a temple of the Holy Spirit, who is in you, whom you have received from God? You are not your own; you were bought at a price. Therefore honor God with your body. —1 CORINTHIANS 6:19-20

His Choice of Residence

We have a wonderful opportunity to worship God throughout the day today. We belong to Him, and He dwells within us. This is good reason to treat ourselves well: We honor God by caring for His temple.

Often, today's verse has been a source of shame for those of us who have struggled with eating and exercise. Now we can let it be a beautiful blessing! It can serve to remind us: God could live anywhere He wants, and He desires to live within me!

As we begin to receive the deep meaning in His choice of residence, we can be filled with the warmth that comes from being so loved. We can honor His presence in us and return His love by nourishing ourselves with good food and enjoying the thrill of activity today.

Today, Lord, I will honor You with my body. Thank You for loving me so much.

SEPTEMBER 22

*And he will be called Wonderful Counselor, Mighty God,
Everlasting Father, Prince of Peace.*   —ISAIAH 9:6

We Need Him in Every Way

In what ways do you need God today? He has provided for us by His Son, Jesus Christ. When we despair in our suffering, He is the Prince of Peace. When we are feeble and weak, He is Mighty God. When we need guidance, He is our Wonderful Counselor. When we are abandoned, He is our Everlasting Father.

With each new step as we journey toward weightlessness, we will find new emotion. We're facing our weaknesses, grieving our losses, becoming vulnerable with others, moving our bodies, submitting to partners in accountability, laughing . . . We are bound to need God in every way possible. Let us praise Him not only for being our Savior but for generously filling our needs in every other way.

Today, Lord, may I know You more deeply for all that You are. I praise You for generously meeting my need in this day.

SEPTEMBER 23

David and all Israel were celebrating before God with all their might, singing and playing all kinds of musical instruments—lyres, harps, tambourines, cymbals, and trumpets.

—1 CHRONICLES 13:8 NLT

Passionate Joy

We need to celebrate more! Have you ever truly celebrated "with all your might"? Doesn't it just sound amazing, liberating, honest, simple, untainted, unrestrained, pure, and joyful? I want to be a part of that!

The intricacies of life have a way of zapping the passion right out of us. We are learning and growing on our road to "weightlessness," but often this is a serious course that can bring out pains from the past. Surely David and the Israelites were not all living the easy life either. No, they each had trials and challenges of their own. Yet they were somehow able to rejoice, worship, and celebrate . . . with all of their might. They made room for joy amid all of their heartache. I want to be like that.

Today, Lord, I will celebrate what's good in my life and what's great about You.

"It will be like a woman experiencing the pains of labor. When her child is born, her anguish gives place to joy because she has brought a new person into the world." —JOHN 16:21 NLT

Embrace the Pain

In this passage, Jesus speaks to His disciples regarding the sadness they will feel as He suffers and dies . . . and the joy they will feel when they see Him again. He likens it to a woman's experience of childbirth.

We who are recovering from food and weight problems are also in the process of delivering a new person into the world. It is not easy to give birth! It often involves anguish, perseverance, and tremendous effort on our part. There are times of agony and despair as we ache and push through our most painful realities.

With new challenges before us, we may feel as though we can't continue any longer—that the task is insurmountable—and we want to give up. Yet we are reminded that through all of the distress, our anguish is turned to great joy as the new person emerges. Transition is painful, but we can allow and embrace these labor pains as a wonderful sign that new life is coming forth.

Today, Lord, may I embrace the pain that comes with making positive changes in my life. May I receive it as evidence that my new life is emerging.

And I pray that Christ will be more and more at home in your hearts as you trust in him. —EPHESIANS 3:17A NLT

Come In, Lord

Though we may have invited Christ into our hearts and received His gift of salvation, it may take a while before He is truly at home within us. This is not because Jesus withholds Himself at all, but because we have not yet opened every door in our hearts to Him. He is in the house, but it is not yet a home. We have hidden the areas we don't want Him to see—the basement and closets where our clutter abides . . . our appetite and obsessions, anger and fears, sadness and sinful desires. These are the places where He has not yet been welcomed, where we withhold our private treasures and shame.

Unlocking the bolts and turning on the lights in a closed-off room can be terrifying. "What will He think of my mess? I don't want to get rid of these things!" It requires a step of faith.

As we dare to trust God and crack one of the doors we've held shut, He does not blast through to destroy us. Instead, His love restores the damaged areas. He fills us with light and warms the coldness within. He makes our heart His home.

Today, Lord, I pray to trust You more. I pray that soon I will trust You enough to let You into a room I've kept locked.

"And you must commit yourselves wholeheartedly to these commands I am giving you today. Repeat them again and again to your children. Talk about them when you are at home and when you are away on a journey, when you are lying down and when you are getting up again. Tie them to your hands as a reminder, and wear them on your forehead. Write them on the doorposts of your house and on your gates."

—DEUTERONOMY 6:6-9 NLT

Bring It to Life

Have you ever heard the most life-changing sermon, been moved to tears with revelation and insight, only to discover you've lost what you learned before you even left the parking lot? Have you gone to a seminar on weight loss and healthier living, been given an entire program of great information, but then laid down your notes and materials, never to be looked at again? It is not so uncommon—times of great intention, great inspiration . . . and a lifetime of not-so-great dedication.

It does take dedication. If we want to see change, we can no longer expect it to happen through osmosis. God has outlined for us what to do, and it involves drastic measures. It is not enough simply to hear His truths and commands or helpful information in a seminar. We must get it all into our heart. He tells us to talk about it frequently and in every setting. We must interact with others who have insight to share, and we must process all that we're learning. We are to write it down, to have notes all around us—even with us—in an effort to bring the truth to life.

Today, Lord, I will structure my day to integrate what You're teaching me about healthy living.

Therefore confess your sins to each other and pray for each other so that you may be healed. The prayer of a righteous man is powerful and effective.　　—JAMES 5:16

Houston, We Have a Problem

We can easily inhibit our own healing and growth with a lack of honesty and realism. By trying to cover up our weaknesses and pretend that all is well, we hope to avoid exposing our secret shames and brokenness. But when our best efforts have produced such a mess, and we're not willing to reach out for help, how do we plan to find any answers?

Managing our image and hiding our shame has not benefited us as we had hoped. In fact, it has entirely backfired. People can look at us and perceive by our overweight that we have some problems. We might find relief in finally acknowledging to others what they can already see. It is time for confession.

In our humility and true desire for healing, we are likely to discover that safe people embrace us and identify with us at many levels. We can then join in powerful and effective prayer, one for another, in the righteousness of Christ.

Today, Lord, I will confess my misuse of food to a friend. I will ask for prayer and offer it in return.

SEPTEMBER 28

Give us this day our daily bread. —*MATTHEW 6:11* NASB

Plenty Today and More Tomorrow

For compulsive overeaters, it can be difficult to release our grip on food. When it's time to eat, a temptation may be triggered by the thought that this might be the last chance to eat for a long time. We may quickly consume all the food in front of us and even stash food in our pockets for later.

What makes us think we must survive on this one meal for days? Is there a legitimate reason to believe we won't eat again in just a few hours? When we want to stash and hoard food, we need to remember what Jesus taught us to pray: "Give us this day our daily bread." We need not accumulate food, for we can trust that God will fill our needs for today—and that tomorrow He'll do just the same.

Today, Lord, may I calmly partake of Your daily bread.

Daniel made up his mind not to defile himself by eating the food and wine given to them by the king. He asked the chief official for permission to eat other things instead. Now God had given the chief official great respect for Daniel. But he was alarmed by Daniel's suggestion. "My lord the king has ordered that you eat this food and wine," he said. "If you become pale and thin compared to the other youths your age, I am afraid the king will have me beheaded for neglecting my duties." —DANIEL 1:8-10 NLT

Facing Opposition

When some of us were young, we were constantly told to "Clean your plate!" We may even yet have others urging us, "Have some cake!" "You can have some of that, can't you?" "You're looking pale today. Have you had enough to eat?" "Don't you want more?"

While these may be well-meaning people, their words can easily sabotage our goals of eating nutritious foods and appropriate portions. It may be difficult for others to understand what we're trying to accomplish in avoiding the foods that defile us— and that's okay. Not everyone has to understand. What's important is that *we* understand, and that we remain connected to those who can support our mission. Then, when we feel overwhelmed by the pressure from others, we can remember that we're not alone. As we dedicate time to pray and interact with fellow strugglers, our hearts and minds are better prepared to enter a challenging setting.

Today, Lord, I will remain dedicated to what's good and healthy for me, even in the face of opposition.

The thought of my suffering and homelessness is bitter beyond words. I will never forget this awful time, as I grieve over my loss. Yet I still dare to hope when I remember this: The unfailing love of the LORD never ends! By his mercies we have been kept from complete destruction. Great is his faithfulness; his mercies begin afresh each day. I say to myself, "The LORD is my inheritance; therefore, I will hope in him!"

—LAMENTATIONS 3:19-24 NLT

It's Not All Weight Loss

As we seek to develop a healthy body, weight, and lifestyle, we experience loss of more than just excess weight. In the recovery process, we also suffer the loss of what food has provided for us in place of God. We lose the medicating effect that emotional eating had on our pain, and we are forced to acknowledge our wounds again.

Though we are on a path of growth and healing, it can be a real time of suffering. We have coped with life using emotional eating for so long that to abandon this lifestyle can be like leaving our homes for the wilderness. We will never forget this awful time.

"Yet I still dare to hope when I remember this," says Jeremiah. "The unfailing love of the Lord never ends! . . . The Lord is my inheritance; therefore, I will hope in him!"

Today, Lord, Your mercies truly are new. When I feel homeless and despairing, I will remember Your unfailing love for me. You are my portion today and my inheritance for eternity. Renew my hope in You!

OCTOBER 1

"Thy will be done, as in heaven, so on earth." —LUKE 11:2B KJV

"But how can we hasten the coming of that Kingdom for the world that needs it so desperately—for our own lives that need it no less? Jesus tells the method. . . . Through the doing of God's will. . . . Not merely reverencing it or intellectually assenting to it, but doing it, just exactly as far as we can see and understand it for our own lives. . . . Jesus says very clearly that growth in spiritual understanding comes primarily, not through the intellect, but through the will. . . . Christianity is laboratory work, not a lecture-course; it is life, not theory."

—MABEL N. THURSTON, THE OPEN GATE TO PRAYER, PP. 41-42

Doing the Will of God

It is common to think that when we intellectually assent to the will of God, we are doing the will of God. But Jesus and the Scriptures are clear: We must not confuse knowing with growing.

In struggling with food and weight problems, we have asked God to help us figure out, understand, and thereby control our food in hopes of losing excess weight. All our understanding, though, has been fruitless in the long-term. "Knowing" has not been our problem; "consistent action" has.

Taking on faith that it's God's will for us to daily care for our body with nutrition, exercise, and rest, now is the time for action. As we walk in His will, one meal, one moment, one day at a time, we grow spiritually in ways where we have not previously matured. We actually hasten the kingdom of God into our lives and become examples of the kingdom for others.

Today, Lord, may I not just know Your will but do it.

OCTOBER 2

But what could I say? For he himself had sent this sickness. Now I will walk humbly throughout my years because of this anguish I have felt. Lord, your discipline is good, for it leads to life and health. —ISAIAH 38:15-16 NLT

His Discipline Leads to Life and Health

Sometimes children will only learn valuable lessons through a time of discipline. Likewise, we adults sometimes need pain in order to learn. This can be very humbling, and rightfully so. In a form of arrogance, we stray from God's plan for our health, but with humility we can come back in the confidence of our Father's loving hand upon us.

After years of neglecting our body and personal care, we may now be in the good discipline of God. It may be a great struggle for us to return to health again. However, the moment we choose to embrace our need for His discipline is the moment our life will begin to improve. We know God's guidance will lead us to life and well-being once more.

If we will allow it to, all of our anguish will serve a positive purpose.

Today, Lord, may I walk humbly with Your guidance.

OCTOBER 3

Do not be surprised, my brothers, if the world hates you. We know that we have passed from death to life, because we love our brothers. Anyone who does not love remains in death.

—1 JOHN 3:13-14

Where's the Love?

From a very young age many of us received either deep hatred from our parents and family or, just as harmful, indifference. This was devastating to us, as we instinctively knew that these were the people who were supposed to love us the most. Now as adults, we're realizing that this affected every part of our life—we see our resulting battles with feelings of unworthiness, inferiority, shame, abandonment. All of it has influenced our decision to overeat; and in that, we continue the mistreatment that began long ago.

Coming to terms with our family history can be shocking to us—even baffling. Today, however, we can begin to see things for what they are. For starters, we can accept that our parents were not and are not healthy people. If they do not know the love of Christ, they will not have that love to share. Even if they do know the love of Christ, they still will not be able to share it perfectly.

For our own benefit and progress in recovery, we can release our indignity, our confusion, and try not to take their actions so personally. By courageously taking this view, we are more grounded, more realistic, more ready for living and moving forward.

Today, Lord, help me begin to accept that my parents were not able to give love in every way that I needed it. May I receive whatever love they do give and release my surprise at their inabilities.

For instance, one person believes it is all right to eat anything. But another believer who has a sensitive conscience will eat only vegetables. Those who think it is all right to eat anything must not look down on those who won't. And those who won't eat certain foods must not condemn those who do, for God has accepted them. —ROMANS 14:2-3 NLT

Level Ground

As we are learning about healthier living each day, our eyes are being opened. We are discovering a new world of options for eating and activity. We are noticing that not everyone is on the same path of learning and growth. Family members and friends may continue to eat foods that are destructive to their health, unaware that there is another way to live. We are observing, too, that not everyone struggles with weight issues. Some people are just thin by nature, and they can eat whatever they want without even a thought to their weight.

It would be easy to criticize those who either don't struggle with food issues or don't care about their health, especially if we've been criticized about our own food and health choices. However, no condemnation is helpful in any way. We can instead choose to embrace one another, right where we are, just as God is embracing us.

We certainly don't have life all figured out. Neither does anyone else. As we grow in humility, we are better able and more eager to accept others in Christlike love, no matter our differences.

Today, Lord, when I want to judge others for how they are eating, may I instead just accept them. I pray that the people in my life can start to accept me, and I will not argue them into it.

And this world is fading away, along with everything it craves. But if you do the will of God, you will live forever.

—*1 JOHN 2:17* NLT

The Downward Escalator

Without getting gloomy, we must come to understand that we are on a downward escalator—all of nature is in a continual state of decay. If we are not purposeful about upward movement, if we are merely content to stand still in one place, then we, too, will fade into oblivion. All of our feeding on the things of this world, all of the ways we avoid healing and growth, will bring about exactly what we've settled for—distance from God and despair.

But this does not have to happen to us. Instead of allowing our cravings to pull us away from the Lord, we can allow our cravings to move us *toward* Him. It will take a concerted effort on our part, but as we live within the will of God for our physical well-being, then our spiritual lives will improve, and vice versa. This is not about earning salvation, which is impossible. It is about living in the abundance of life promised to us by our Creator. It is about living on purpose and choosing to strive for closeness with God.

Today, Lord, I will be diligent to move closer to You.

But the LORD is in his holy temple; let all the earth be silent before him. —HABAKKUK 2:20 *(THE LORD SPEAKING)*

Silent Before Him

We are very good at avoiding silence. The quietness is just too loud for us at times, too scary, or just plain unfamiliar. Instead of silence before God, where we simply rest in His presence, we often talk and fidget about. We mention losing weight and having food plans and exercising; we talk about goals and dreams, disappointments and struggles—all things worth sharing when the time is right. But it's almost as if we prefer our own busyness and drama over what we may find in the stillness.

Yet the Lord is in His holy temple. He is sovereign over all. He is holy. Oblivious to His sheer majesty, we often miss the privilege of just being with the Lord of heaven and earth. Today, however, we can make a decision to quiet our heart and life before Him. We can return to reverent awe and bask in His presence. In our stillness we can simply be with Almighty God in serenity and surrender.

Today, Lord, I will be silent before You.

OCTOBER 7

Elijah was a man just like us. He prayed earnestly that it would not rain, and it did not rain on the land for three and a half years. Again he prayed, and the heavens gave rain, and the earth produced its crops. —JAMES 5:17-18

Bold Elijah

Do you trust in the power of God for great miracles? Do you walk in the confidence that God will bless your prayers, even in the face of great opposition? Consider the prophet Elijah, who modeled such boldness. In the presence of a king who worshiped Baal, Elijah declared that his God—the God of Israel—was really the one in charge! He prayed in the face of great opposition, knowing that God's will would prevail.

May we walk in the same boldness as Elijah, trusting in God's power and will. When negative voices and people try to derail us, may we all the more confidently walk in God's ways and trust in Him for the results.

Today, Lord, I believe in Your power to do great things in my life.

So I decided there is nothing better than to enjoy food and drink and to find satisfaction in work. Then I realized that this pleasure is from the hand of God. For who can eat or enjoy anything apart from him? God gives wisdom, knowledge, and joy to those who please him. —ECCLESIASTES 2:24-26 NLT

Who Can Enjoy Anything Apart from Him?

King Solomon searched down many paths for pleasure and purpose in his life—even pursued fulfillment through food and drink—yet he came to the same conclusion many of us have reached in our own experiences with bingeing: Nothing ever provides enough pleasure to bring the joy that we seek long-term. Not even food. Indeed, any true and lasting fulfillment must come from the hand of God. "For who can eat or enjoy anything apart from him?"

For every path taken, Solomon discovered one recurring truth, and this is what it boils down to: Life is meaningless apart from God. As we please God—the giver of wisdom, knowledge, and joy— we will be satisfied, and food won't have such a big job to do!

Today, Lord, may I be pleasing to You.

OCTOBER 9

Give me neither poverty nor riches; feed me with the food that is my portion, that I not be full and deny You and say, "Who is the LORD?" Or that I not be in want and steal, and profane the name of my God.   —PROVERBS 30:8-9 NASB

Enough Is Enough

Enough is enough. It really is. How simple and how refreshing . . .

Eating enough is like being paid fairly for a job well done. Our body earns a certain amount of food each day for living. We can serve ourselves an honest and reasonable portion of food for the work it's performing and feel very good about it. Treating our body with respect and caring for its proper functioning brings a sense of rightness and evenness to our life. A confidence that things are as they should be.

When we are tempted toward the poverty of rapid weight loss or the "riches" of bingeing, we can pause and ask God for our portion today, knowing He will provide it—as much as we need, when we need it. Just enough.

Today, Lord, may I remember: Enough is enough.

I know whom I have believed, and am convinced that He is
able to guard what I have entrusted to Him until that day.

—2 TIMOTHY 1:12 NASB

On Guard

Do you trust God? Do you know whom you have
believed? Paul did! As he writes to Timothy about
the amazing trustworthiness of the Lord, Paul
speaks with absolute confidence in God's reliability.
Whatever it was that Paul had entrusted to God for
that day, he was convinced of God's capacity to
guard it.

Whatever we surrender to the Lord today—our
eating and exercise, our desire to lose weight, our
feelings of helplessness—we can rest assured that
He will come through for us. God is able to guard
what we entrust to Him, each and every time. He
never fails to provide us with just what we need as
we give up control of our lives to Him.

Today, Lord, may I walk in the confidence of Your
power. I trust You with my food and weight challenges.

"You know with all your heart and soul that not one of all the good promises the Lord your God gave you has failed. Every promise has been fulfilled; not one has failed."

—JOSHUA 23:14

The Promise I Have in You

God is a promise keeper, and here are a few promises He has offered to us:

· If we are in Christ, we are a new creation. The old has passed, and the new has come (2 Corinthians 5:17).
· We can give all our cares to God, because He cares about us (1 Peter 5:7).
· We will receive a great harvest at the right time if we do not give up (Galatians 6:9).
· When we confess our sins to each other and pray for each other, God will heal us (James 5:16).
· Whoever accepts correction is on the way to life (Proverbs 10:17).
· God will do what is right (2 Thessalonians 1:6-7).
· We have freedom now, because Christ made us free (Galatians 5:1).
· God will direct our paths as we trust in Him (Proverbs 3:5-6).

Today, Lord, bring to mind Your promises to me. When I begin to despair, I will trust in Your Word. Nothing compares to the promise I have in You.

You may say, "I am allowed to do anything." But I reply, "Not everything is good for you." And even though "I am allowed to do anything," I must not become a slave to anything. You say, "Food is for the stomach, and the stomach is for food." This is true, though someday God will do away with both of them.

—*1 CORINTHIANS 6:12-13A* NLT

I Can Do Whatever I Want

We are free to enjoy all sorts of choices in life, including all types of foods. God allows it and He created it this way. We are free to make whatever choices we want, but some options have proven to be of no benefit to us.

It may be very reassuring to know that we need not ban a favorite food for all eternity. Yet if we are wise, we'll live so as not to be mastered unexpectedly. Enjoying a soda and popcorn at the movies can be so much fun, but does it create an insatiable craving for more? If we become slave to the foods we enjoy, then what has become of our freedom? While everything is permissible, not everything is beneficial. May God help us to discern which is which.

Today, Lord, I will live wisely within my freedom.

I have directed you in the path of wisdom; I have led you in upright paths. When you walk, your steps will not be impeded; and if you run, you will not stumble.

—*PROVERBS 4:11-12 NASB*

What Are We Exercising?

Sometimes exercising our bodies is really an exercise of our will. So many times we have had great intentions to walk, run, or work out at the gym for an hour every day. Yet we did not last for more than a month, or two weeks . . . or less. Just as we must learn to surrender to healthier eating, so also we must learn to surrender to the wisdom of activity. Increasing our heart rate and building muscle is a physical routine, yes, but it is born in the spiritual exercise of willingness and surrender.

No matter our current physical condition, we must gradually increase our daily activity. By picking a realistic beginning point, such as walking for twenty minutes a day before breakfast, we are not so overwhelmed and are better able to maintain the structure for lasting change. Once our routine is set, we are able to eventually add simple body resistance or weight-lifting elements to our program. In time, as we have more energy and a clearer mind, we come to appreciate and look forward to exercise. Affirming God's gift of movement becomes a great part of our day.

Today, Lord, may I surrender my will around exercise and move my body for Your glory.

When Moses came down from Mount Sinai with the two tablets of the Testimony in his hands, he was not aware that his face was radiant because he had spoken with the LORD. When Aaron and all the Israelites saw Moses, his face was radiant, and they were afraid to come near him.

— *EXODUS 34:29-30*

Shine Through Me

Do you know someone who absolutely radiates the goodness of God in his or her countenance? Consistent prayer and time spent with God has produced a wellspring of joy and a river of peace within this person, and it is noticeable, perhaps shocking. The influence of God upon that individual is visible and desirable to those around him. Even a person in the depths of personal struggle and despair will radiate the presence of God if God is living within.

As we seek to know God more deeply through our struggles with food and weight, *our* countenance will change. God's transforming power in our life will be evident to those around us as we surrender our will toward eating and exercise. By practicing His principles, which we discover more richly through time spent with Him, our lives will begin to reflect His very presence and beauty. We are suddenly more attractive than we've ever been, not just from a trimmer body but because we are radiant with the goodness of God.

Today, Lord, begin to shine through me.

OCTOBER 15

This is what the LORD Almighty says: Do not listen to what the prophets are prophesying to you; they fill you with false hopes. They speak visions from their own minds, not from the mouth of the LORD. They keep saying to those who despise me, "The LORD says: You will have peace." And to all who follow the stubbornness of their hearts they say, "No harm will come to you."

—JEREMIAH 23:16-17

Grant Me Discernment

God has warned against false prophets. They attempt to lead us away from His path and good will for our lives. Many of us have been fooled by more than one magical weight-loss program offered by those who were hoping to profit from us. And though it's difficult to admit, we fell for it because we so wanted to believe that achieving and maintaining a healthy body weight could really be easy; that there might be a shortcut or a way to bypass hard work. Oh, to be so fortunate!

Honestly, moving toward true health and wholeness involves a good deal of effort but also a good deal of joy. It brings great blessing and encounters with God at the deepest levels. We can be thankful that God is challenging us and that we've embraced the hard work for our benefit. Instead of believing false prophets who offer what appears to be a quick fix, this time we can choose to dig deeper, to live for the long-term, and to make progress at the spiritual level, too.

Today, Lord, I pray for discernment about how to live for my long-term well-being. Thank You for challenging me to dig deeper and for inspiring me to work hard.

"Choose for yourselves this day whom you will serve. As for me and my house, we will serve the LORD."

—JOSHUA 24:15

Fear God

"Fear God" seems like a command. It sounds like something we should do. Today, however, we will read these words as a title, a type of god—a fear-god. Consider for yourself: Do you have a fear-god?

When we take an honest look at our behaviors, we can see that many times we have chosen to bow to our fear-god instead of revering the one true God. We've laid in bed instead of getting up to exercise, afraid to start a program we would not maintain. We've snacked at parties rather than interacting with people, for fear of being too vulnerable. We've hidden beneath layers of fat, afraid of being truly seen by anyone, or lived within guilt and shame, fearing that God would never really offer His grace to us. We have given power to these fears, allowing them to dictate our choices, our behaviors, our being.

How can we live within God's will and receive direction from Him when we are consistently serving our fear-god? In the book of Joshua, God's people were issued a challenge. We are now faced with the same challenge, often several times per day. In serving God's plan for our life, we begin to find answers for each moment and gain access to His ultimate power for living. Gradually, we watch our fears lose authority. The true God becomes greater, and the fear-god becomes less.

Today, Lord, I am scared but willing to face one fear. Help me to remember that this fear is not my God.

OCTOBER 17

O Lord, you preserve both man and beast. How priceless is your unfailing love! Both high and low among men find refuge in the shadow of your wings. They feast on the abundance of your house; you give them drink from your river of delights. For with you is the fountain of life; in your light we see light.

—PSALM 36:6B-9

The Abundance of God's House

We love to feast. Concerned that we wouldn't have the chance to eat later, we have consumed vast portions of food at a sitting and even encouraged our children to do the same. Past the point of full, into sickness at times! We think we're stocking up energy for later, but when "later" arrives, we just feast again with the same distorted thinking.

Most of us interested in losing excess weight need not be concerned with feasting for preservation. Eating an appropriate portion may feel scary, like we're depriving and neglecting our body's needs, but this is not the case. Notice the word *appropriate*. When we eat responsibly, then we are freed to feast on the abundance that comes from God. He provides for us from His unlimited resources and fills the deeper cravings that we have stuffed with food for so long. He will fill us with life and light in His unfailing love and preserve our hearts for eternity.

Today, Lord, may I eat my next meal appropriately. May I spend time in Your Word and talking with You. May I feast from the abundance of Your house and experience Your love more deeply than ever.

Though the fig tree does not bud and there are no grapes on the vines, though the olive crop fails and the fields produce no food, though there are no sheep in the pen and no cattle in the stalls, yet I will rejoice in the LORD, I will be joyful in God my Savior. The Sovereign LORD is my strength; he makes my feet like the feet of a deer, he enables me to go on the heights.

—HABAKKUK 3:17-19

Lighten Up

"Though the Fig Newton is not my 'bud,' and grape jam is my vice, though too much olive oil fails me and the fields produce no chocolate, though there is no lamb on my plate and no steak at the table, yet I will rejoice in the Lord and be joyful in God my Savior."

Let us laugh! Today we may need to lighten up emotionally more than we do physically, and take a few things less seriously. Of course, we are not to make a mockery of God's Word or to disrespect Him or His people in any way. But we can appropriately use the sense of humor and gift of laughter He's given to us for times of rejoicing amid the trials. When we appreciate the ironies, absurdities, and sheer comedy of life, we often find great relief from even our heaviest burdens. Laughter amid pain is an amazing emotion!

Today, Lord, may I find the humor in my need for a food plan. May I laugh with a friend about how much I'm craving a deep-fried Twinkie.

OCTOBER 19

Can a man scoop fire into his lap without his clothes being burned? Can a man walk on hot coals without his feet being scorched? —PROVERBS 6:27-28

Fire Safety

Stocking a vast supply of junk foods within our home and workplace is like playing with fire. We have the desire to eat healthy foods and appropriate servings but yet continue to purchase the types of foods that we hope to avoid. We set up our very failure, creating hazardous conditions and danger all around us! How can we continually go to our pantry and say no to Twinkies and chips, or to our refrigerator and say no to cheesecake and soda? Insanity!

If we are to have any hope of progress in our quest for healthy living, then we can no longer play with fire and expect not to get burned. It's time for some preventive maintenance, for fireproofing our home, our office, even our car. While it's not possible for us to make every environment totally safe, we can at least improve the areas where we spend a majority of time. This will not be easy, and we may need a friend to help us toss the junk and select healthier foods, but as we do, a sense of freedom and hope will emerge because we took a stand for health and sanity today.

Today, Lord, I will fireproof my home. I will join You in protecting my life!

OCTOBER 20

"You search the Scriptures because you believe they give you eternal life. But the Scriptures point to me! Yet you refuse to come to me so that I can give you this eternal life."

—*J O H N 5 : 3 9 - 4 0 NLT (JESUS SPEAKING)*

The Scriptures Point to Him

In search for answers to our challenges with food and weight, we can become obsessed with trying to find what's right and what's wrong. Even in other areas of our life, we search the Scriptures for answers —yes and no, black and white, jot and tittle, direction. We trust in the Word of God to bring us eternal life, yet often we miss Jesus in the process.

More than answers, more than a prescription for the healthy life, more than a list of things to do and not to do, we need Jesus Himself. All of Scripture points to Him. Rejoice that God has provided us with answers for living . . . but more than that, He has provided Himself as revealed through His Word, His people, and our hearts in Christ Jesus. Let us follow the direction of Scripture and come unto Jesus, the giver of eternal life.

Today, Lord, I will not be consumed with my need for answers in Scripture. I will see that it all points to You and be consumed with who You are!

When he has brought out all his own, he goes on ahead of them, and his sheep follow him because they know his voice. But they will never follow a stranger; in fact, they will run away from him because they do not recognize a stranger's voice. —JOHN 10:4-5

Know His Voice

Walking with Jesus and following His voice makes us feel safe and sound. We are not left to wander alone aimlessly through life. We are part of His flock, and we can trust that He is always guiding us and speaking into our lives. Are you listening?

Knowing the voice of Jesus happens as we spend time with Him and His people. He walks ahead of us each day through every decision, every trial, and every joy. He is speaking. He is not silent; He's actively and daily calling us to follow Him. By actively listening, we become more familiar with His voice. We grow to sense His gentle guidance, even in the mundane things of life, and thus more clearly recognize when a stranger tries to lead us astray.

Today, Lord, I will actively listen for You through Your Word, Your people, and Your Spirit in me. I want to hear and know Your voice.

I keep working toward that day when I will finally be all that Christ Jesus saved me for and wants me to be.... I am focusing my energies on this one thing: Forgetting the past and looking forward to what lies ahead ... —PHILIPPIANS 3:12-13 NLT

To Win the Game, Step Out

In Philippians Paul passionately teaches believers the importance of living deliberately for the cause of Christ. The mission of Paul's life is to become all that Christ wants him to be, and he has a plan for how to accomplish that: by forgetting the past and looking to what lies ahead.

Consider the inseparability of these two endeavors. How can we look forward to what lies ahead when we continually serve our old lifestyle? How can we forget our past when we have no aspirations? The two work simultaneously, creating one solid plan for achieving God's call on our life. So we must move past the misery of our failures and disappointment.

Now is the time for us to step out of our familiar, destructive habits and into God's grace and healing power for an abundant life. It is a process. Fortunately, we can follow the example of Paul, who clearly identifies the mission of his life and gets on with it. We can live deliberately and aim toward becoming all that Christ saved us for and wants us to be, if only we'll forget the past and focus on what lies ahead.

Today, Lord, I will move out of one destructive habit and into Your healing power. Please help me to focus my energies on becoming all that You want me to be.

OCTOBER 23

You gave your good Spirit to instruct them. You did not with-hold your manna from their mouths, and you gave them water for their thirst. —NEHEMIAH 9:20

The Gift of Food

An obsession with health and fitness can be a destructive force, but learning to use food as God intended can produce great blessing and pleasure. Consider these examples where God used food to portray His glory and bring people together:

- God commands Israel to celebrate the Passover with a feast. This was a reminder of His protection and provision for the people during the Exodus (Exodus 12:42-51).
- As the Israelites wander in the desert, God provides quail and manna, meat and bread, for them (Exodus 16).
- Jesus shares communion—a time of intimate fellowship—with His disciples (Matthew 26:20-25).
- Jesus tells the story of the prodigal son, who left home and squandered his inheritance. Upon the son's repentance and return, his father celebrates with a feast (Luke 15:11-24).
- Jesus uses five barley loaves and two fish to feed thousands of people at once. He shows His glory and compassion for the people by filling their hunger (Matthew 14:13-21).

Each time we eat, let us meditate on God's love and provision in our life. Let us praise Him for the many ways He uses food to bless us.

Today, Lord, I will remember that food is a blessing from You.

"What have you gained by worshiping all your man-made idols? How foolish to trust in something made by your own hands!" —HABAKKUK 2:18 NLT (THE LORD SPEAKING)

Serving Food

We are overweight because we have trusted in idols. Instead of trusting the one true God with our bodies and living by His principles, we have chosen to worship other gods, the most obvious of which is our food. Instead of serving *food* to our body at mealtime, we are *serving* food—our body has been chained to whatever our cravings demanded of us.

But we can break free. It requires the admission that we are powerless to choose well for ourselves with our eating. We must believe that God can do all things, and then we can trust Him to grant us His power to change our behaviors. We can end our service to the gods of food, sloth, busyness, idleness, apathy, fear, and hopelessness. We have an almighty God who will fill us with life and energy as we seek to worship Him only.

Today, Lord, I worship You alone.

So whether you eat or drink or whatever you do, do it all for the glory of God. —*1 CORINTHIANS 10:31*

Simple Changes That Honor God

We can glorify God through every aspect of our life, and we can bring Him dishonor as well. This can be a sobering thought to those of us who know we've blown it so many times. We can think of a hundred ways we have dishonored God, and we know we have not eaten for God's glory! We have hoarded portions, treasured junk food, eaten over harbored resentments, and perhaps even starved ourselves at times.

Rather than living in the shame of our past failures with food, though, we can start where we are today. We can make simple changes and take baby steps toward glorifying God with our lives. With our food today, we can first give thanks for our portions, even the smaller ones. We can drink a glass of water instead of a can of soda. We can choose fresh produce over canned. We could even dare to make amends with someone we've resented—and find that our eating improves. Glory be to God!

Today, Lord, may I eat and drink and live to glorify Your name in whatever I do.

*He humbled you, causing you to hunger and then feeding you
with manna, which neither you nor your fathers had known, to
teach you that man does not live on bread alone but on every
word that comes from the mouth of the LORD.*

—DEUTERONOMY 8:3

We Live on Every Word from God

We've often heard the first part of this scripture:
"Man does not live on bread alone," but we less frequently hear the rest of it, "but on every word that
comes from the mouth of the Lord."

God may be using our insatiable appetites to
humble us and point to our need for His guidance.
When we realize that we can't eat enough to solve
our own hungers—when we reach a desire for
answers—we can allow those longings to drive us
straight into His Word and in fellowship with those
who speak truth and encouragement.

True life comes by God's Word! We will always
be hungry and lost in our attempts to substitute
what only God can provide for us. So let us seek
Him for sustenance.

*Today, Lord, I will see my deep need for Your Word
and truth. Instead of merely surviving, I will thrive in
the fullness of life that is nourished by You.*

OCTOBER 27

May you experience the love of Christ, though it is so great you will never fully understand it. Then you will be filled with the fullness of life and power that comes from God.

—EPHESIANS 3:19 NLT

Experience His Love

We've been living on empty. In spite of our history of overeating at meals and bingeing on snack foods, we have yet to become truly full. Oddly, though we may even recognize our issues with hunger at the spiritual level, we continue to suffer from feelings of perpetual emptiness. It's not enough for us to simply recognize our need for Christ's love; we must experience it if we desire the fullness of life.

If we are hungering for His love today, we are not limited to seeking Him in seclusion. We can diligently reach out to trustworthy people who will be His arms and His voice of unconditional acceptance. We need not miss even brief opportunities to be encouraged. In doing so, His love will become more and more tangible, less and less obscure. The experience of His love, in whatever form, will fill the emptiness and satisfy our spiritual hungers. We will then have power from God to choose wisely for our life today.

Today, Lord, I want to be filled by Your love. When I feel empty, I will reach out for even five minutes of connection and support.

OCTOBER 28

"What good will it be for a man if he gains the whole world, yet forfeits his soul? Or what can a man give in exchange for his soul?" —MATTHEW 16:26

Have I Gained the Whole World?

"Gaining the whole world" is easier than it sounds. Daily we are presented with a smorgasbord of reasons to overeat: We are broken people with problems, character defects, fears, illnesses, injuries, and wacky families! We are trying to cope, but we often use food to escape, thereby creating more problems.

We must ask, "Have I (weight-) gained the whole world, eating from emptiness, apathy, anger? Have I forfeited my own soul, living for my destruction instead of my well-being?" It may be painful to really slow down and answer these questions honestly, but it's an essential step in recovery. By unlocking the mysteries to our unhealthy eating, the monster of compulsion loses some power. Be brave. You are fighting for your soul, and God is with you.

Today, Lord, I will examine the patterns behind my eating. Please grant me insight in this fight for my soul.

So the Word became human and lived here on earth among us. He was full of unfailing love and faithfulness.

—*JOHN 1:14* NLT

Putting Flesh on His Love

Though many of us with food and weight issues tend to isolate ourselves, the very thing we need is God's embrace of love through the hearts and arms of His people. It's not enough to just know that God loves us when we feel abandoned by everyone else on earth; we desperately need the acceptance of warm faces, touch, interaction, caring, and guidance from real people.

God recognizes the importance of putting flesh on His love. He did not stay separated and isolated from this world full of sinners. He put skin on and came to embrace and enfold us in His arms. He spoke with us, wept with us, prayed for us, touched us, healed us, and suffered with us. He became flesh and dwelt among us.

Let us learn from this act of God, who believes in love with skin on it. Let us step out of isolation and into community, where we can give and receive in relationship. May we dwell among others and come out of hiding, a day at a time.

Today, Lord, may I receive Your love through relationships with Your people.

OCTOBER 30

"You shall love your neighbor as yourself."

—MATTHEW 22:39B NASB

Self-Care Is Not Selfishness

It's easy to read this passage and locate the simple lesson, "Be good to others." Yet we may be missing another important aspect of God's command here.

We can be so focused on "love your neighbor" that we dismiss "as yourself." Our days are spent helping others and saving the world, often to the detriment of ourselves. We find a sort of value in the martyr role and use this verse to justify the neglect of our own needs. Perhaps unknowingly, we keep the focus on everyone else's issues because we do not want to face our own. We use service to hide our truth.

Jesus knew the importance of those last two words "as yourself." A hard truth to grasp is that what's best for us is also what's best for others. Self-care is not selfishness. As we spend time caring for our own needs—caring for God's creation in us—we are then more stable and able to offer love and service to others.

Today, Lord, may I partner with You in meeting my food, exercise, and relational needs so that I may then give to the needs of others.

OCTOBER 31

Just as each of us has one body with many members, and those members do not all have the same function, so in Christ we who are many form one body, and each member belongs to all the others. —ROMANS 12:4-5

Each Part Belongs to the Others

Usually a person has a thing or two (or twenty) that he doesn't like about his body. Most of us would trade-out certain parts if we could just blink and have it done. Some of us may even despise our entire body. But consider the church, the body of Christ. It has members that are not entirely likable. Yet God has declared that each member belongs to the others; that we are all important to the function of the whole. One member or several may be drastically underdeveloped, needing the love and discipline from the others to bring transformation. So, too, the parts of our physical body that are underdeveloped, untoned, or overweight need the love and discipline that produce health and wholeness.

Hating our body is of no avail and negates God's good creation in us. We can give thanks for each part of our body and take care to develop each member so that the whole body may thrive and function at the highest level.

Today, Lord, thank You for every part of my body. It is all a gift from You. May I take time and care to develop myself today.

Then Jesus declared, "I am the bread of life. He who comes to me will never go hungry, and he who believes in me will never be thirsty." —JOHN 6:35

Bread of Life

How wonderful! Jesus is our ultimate low-carb bread!

These days, so many people are focused on the negative effects of eating bread. Yet in order to understand this passage, we must transcend the current buzz on the subject. In Jesus' time, bread was seen as a fundamental part of every meal. For people who were poor, it was often the main entrée. When Jesus described Himself as "the bread of life," He was associating Himself with what many people relied upon for their very survival.

Regardless of what we eat, no matter how elaborate or basic the food, our body will always become hungry and thirsty again. Just as we must feed our physical hunger daily, we must more importantly feed our spiritual hunger. As we devote ourselves to relationship with Jesus, our spiritual hunger will be satisfied by the Bread of Life. He so ultimately fills our spiritual emptiness that we are never left wanting; instead, we are nourished with His life-giving provision.

Today, Lord, may I know You as the Bread of Life.

"Test us for ten days on a diet of vegetables and water,"
Daniel said. "At the end of the ten days, see how we look com-
pared to the other young men who are eating the king's rich
food. Then you can decide whether or not to let us continue
eating our diet." So the attendant agreed to Daniel's sugges-
tion and tested them for ten days. At the end of the ten days,
Daniel and his three friends looked healthier and better nour-
ished than the young men who had been eating the food
assigned by the king. —DANIEL 1:12-15 NLT

Loyal to Our Food Plan

Our food plans may look too restrictive to those
around us, but then again, they are not for the benefit of those around us. This scripture is not about
dieting on only vegetables and water, but it can
apply very directly to our need for loyalty to our
food plan, whatever it is—even if it seems foolish to
others. We must know ourselves and what's beneficial or harmful for us to consume. This plan is for
our benefit.

In this scripture, the king's chief official was
alarmed by Daniel's request to eat in this manner,
but Daniel persisted. He suggested that the official
open his mind and examine the results of this
regimen. When others are confused by our food
choices, we can encourage them to be open-minded,
too. They may begin to see not only our physical
health improve but our emotional and spiritual
health as well. Regardless of whether or not they
open their minds, we have done our part by remaining loyal to what's good and healthy for us.

Today, Lord, may I walk in the confidence of Your
plan for me.

NOVEMBER 3

Do not be deceived: God cannot be mocked. A man reaps what he sows. The one who sows to please his sinful nature, from that nature will reap destruction; the one who sows to please the Spirit, from the Spirit will reap eternal life.

—GALATIANS 6:7-8

The Law of Sowing and Reaping

How more obvious can it be? If we sow to physical heaviness, then we will be heavy. If we sow damage to our health, we will be unhealthy.

We need not be shocked at our weight or at our struggle to lose it, but instead take responsibility for where we are in our struggle. We have made our own choices to get to this point.

Thankfully, the same law applies on the other end of the scale. When we sow to healthier living, then we will reap a healthier life. In seeking to please the Spirit, we care for our body—His temple, His dwelling place. Not only eternal but abundant life is here for us today.

Today, Lord, may I sow to please the Spirit in how I care for my body—Your temple.

But as I looked at everything I had worked so hard to accomplish, it was all so meaningless. It was like chasing the wind. There was nothing really worthwhile anywhere.

—ECCLESIASTES 2:11 NLT

The Clock Is Ticking

For what cause are you giving your life? Often we live our days wholly unaware that we are serving a cause we may never have defined. Our time on earth is fleeting, and we're living merely to mark off a to-do list . . . or to work and pay bills . . . or to loaf around. We're spending our precious days criticizing others or playing the role of victim or trying to be everyone else's "Holy Spirit." We're hiding from people . . . pursuing material pleasures . . . holding grudges. Is any of this worthwhile?

Wise Solomon, king of Israel, asked the same question. He was the wisest man in the world, with power and wealth and access to whatever he wanted. Yet looking back on his life and accounting for his days, Solomon concluded that time spent absorbed in his own drama was futile—that the only real meaning in life is to fear God and obey His commands. True meaning and joy are found only in God and His ways.

Today, Lord, I ask the question, "For what cause am I giving my life? Is any of this worthwhile?"

NOVEMBER 5

And let us consider how to stimulate one another to love and good deeds, not forsaking our own assembling together, as is the habit of some, but encouraging one another.

—HEBREWS 10:24-25A NASB

The Fellowship of "Losers"

One of the great things about following Christ is that we are part of a worldwide support group. From all walks of life, members of His body gather together for worship, for teaching, for laughter and tears, for tangible love and encouragement. Whatever challenges we face, we are not without resources or companions in our struggle.

As we "lose it for life," may we receive the same benefits of gathering together for encouragement. It is unnecessary and dreadfully miserable to go it alone. Instead, let us stimulate and motivate one another to love, and to exercise, and to choose our foods wisely. Let us build each other up and find hope in spending time with friends on a similar path.

Today, Lord, may I enjoy the fellowship of another "Loser."

NOVEMBER 6

For the grace of God has appeared, bringing salvation to all men,
instructing us to deny ungodliness and worldly desires and to
live sensibly, righteously, and godly in the present age . . .

—*TITUS 2:11-12* NASB

Grace for All Stages

A young girl, after spending the night at a friend's
house nearby, ran home to tell her mother some
great news: "Mom! Mom! Guess what? I know who
the Tooth Fairy is!" Surprised and shocked by her
daughter's announcement, the mother eagerly asked,
"Who is it?" The young girl replied, "It's Mrs. Putt!"

Coming to grips with reality often happens in
stages. Like the darling child in this story, we, too,
are unlocking life's mysteries in phases. After years
of feeding our worldly desires for food, we now seek
understanding for healthier living. It involves
unlearning falsehoods and finding truth for taking
godly, sensible action in the present age, and at our
present stage. As we gradually absorb new insight,
we can embrace God's grace for where we are today.
This is a process that we can rejoice in.

Today, Lord, may I take another step toward godliness
and wisdom with food. I receive Your grace today.

"My food," said Jesus, "is to do the will of him who sent me and to finish his work." —JOHN 4:34

Real Nourishment

For many of us, daily living is so cumbersome that it completely drains our energy. We feel tired and trapped by our many obligations. So much so that it is often all we can do to just "maintain the minimum." How can we even think about applying ourselves toward fitness goals when we are starved for hope in every other area? There are many things we "should" and "shouldn't" be doing, but we are simply too tired to face any of them. So we eat.

In our dissatisfaction, we turn to food to provide the flavor—the spice in life that we are missing. Our food is always available and pleasing when emptiness presents itself.

What Jesus says in this verse, though, is intriguing: "My food is to do the will of him who sent me and to finish his work." He gives us valuable insight for gaining the fulfilled life. It is not extra food and snacks that will replenish our energy or provide us with flavor. Real nourishment comes from living in the center of God's will for us.

By devoting even a few moments per week to using our spiritual gifts and talents, we will find new joy in our created purpose. Carrying out God's plan for us brings a surprising amount of energy, and our cup becomes full and then runs over . . .

Today, Lord, please show me a piece of Your created purpose in me. May I spend a few moments applying myself toward Your call on my life and finding new energy for the tasks at hand.

... and clouds are the dust of his feet. —NAHUM 1:3B

Above the Clouds

If you've ever ridden in an airplane, you can attest to this basic truth: The sun is always shining above the clouds. Down below, it may be the worst, blackest day you've seen, or the coldest, grayest sky imaginable, but get that plane above the clouds, and the sun is visible in all its splendor and majesty, with bright skies of beautiful blue all around.

We've each encountered darkness in our lives. We've been let down by others, neglected, ridiculed, even wrongly accused. We've been embarrassed, left behind, and attacked from all sides. We've suffered pain and disappointment, sorrow and despair, rejection and fear. We may be feeling those things today, but take heart! The sun is shining above these looming clouds of darkness. The Lord is on His throne as our light and our salvation from the despair of this broken world. While darkness prevails on earth, there is yet light, hope, and assurance in the heavenlies. It exists right now!

Today, Lord, when I reach for food in despair, may I set my thoughts on Your glory. Remind me of Your shining presence beyond my darkness.

"I make known the end from the beginning, from ancient times, what is still to come. I say: My purpose will stand, and I will do all that I please." —ISAIAH 46:10

A Work in Progress

God is working His purposes, and He always has been. Our battles with overweight are no exception to this truth. We may feel confused and wonder, *Lord, is this struggle in my life pleasing to You? How can this be part of Your purpose in me? It is so painful!*

God's purposes do not usually concern our comfort but our character. We must remember: He does not delight in pointless suffering. Read His Word and see how He mourns when we are hurting, how He hates injustice, and how He loves and feels compassion for those who are weak. Yet when our struggles produce integrity, humility, health, and wholeness in our lives, then this is pleasing to Him. The fulfillment of God's purposes is in progress much of the time, so we must be careful not to confuse the end with the means.

Today, Lord, I trust that You are bringing about Your purposes in me. I will open myself to believe that this pain is achieving something good in me.

Jesus said to him, "If you wish to be complete, go and sell your possessions and give to the poor, and you will have treasure in heaven; and come, follow Me." But when the young man heard this statement, he went away grieving; for he was one who owned much property.

—MATTHEW 19:21-22 NASB

Leaving Our Possessions

We can become so caught up in trying to do things the right way that we end up missing what God would really ask of us. The rich man in this passage thought he was doing everything required of him. He had even kept the law since the days of his youth. But like him, we can become so complacent in our routines that we miss the gentle call of God, asking us to let go of what we hold so dear.

Jesus knew that this young man was too attached to his riches, and so the man walked away from the path that God had for him. In our own lives we may not be attached to material things, but we could be too attached to food and thus missing our path from God.

As we come to realize this, we may find ourselves dismayed at the thought of God asking us to put down the desserts, the chips, and even the quantity of foods we have enjoyed. But it would be more tragic for us to hold onto food instead of holding onto Jesus and following His call to us.

Today, Lord, help me to release my grip on food and the grip of food on me. In letting go of my will, may I hear Your voice calling, "Come, follow Me."

The Lord God called to Adam, "Where are you?" He replied, "I heard you, so I hid. I was afraid because I was naked." "Who told you that you were naked?" the Lord God asked.

—GENESIS 3:9-11 NLT

Out of Hiding

Can you imagine being naked and unashamed? As children, most of us once knew such freedom. We ran in the sunshine through sprinklers and had no shame when others changed our diapers. We were uninhibited by our shortcomings and inabilities. We openly relied on others to do for us what we could not do for ourselves. We were unashamed, free to receive love and assistance from those whom God provided.

So who told us we were naked? When did we stop turning to God and His people for help in our messes? From enough time spent in this fallen world, we've learned shame and cover-ups, secrecy and hiding. Yet God is calling, "Where are you?" He does not call in order to find us but so that we may find Him.

As God bids us back to Him, may we reply as honestly and simply as Adam did. May we come out of hiding and remain in communion with God, bringing even our most secret shame to Him and His safe people for help.

Today, Lord, please help me answer, "Where am I today? Am I hiding in excess weight?" Lord, may I step toward You and connect with safe people.

Then David's anger burned greatly against the man, and he said to Nathan, "As the Lord lives, surely the man who has done this deserves to die. . . ." Nathan then said to David, "You are the man!" —2 SAMUEL 12:5, 7A NASB

Calling a Spade a Spade

Nathan was a prophet and adviser to King David. After David had committed several serious offenses against God, Nathan confronted the king. David was ignoring the severity of his actions until Nathan spoke clearly and effectively to him through a striking parable. In this, David easily perceived the wrong of the man in the story, and he burned with anger. Then Nathan revealed to David the rest of the story: "You are the man!"

Often, we are blinded to our own sin. Not only have we offended others at times without recognizing it, but we have also offended ourselves and God by mistreating our physical and spiritual health. So while it is good to have lighthearted friendships and acquaintances, we also desperately need those around us who will tell it like it is. We need the accountability of those who are more interested in telling the truth than they are in being polite—who will clearly and effectively call us out of denial and into reality. We need others to reveal our blindspots to us! Let us discard our need for flattery and take up with those who will call a spade a spade.

Today, Lord, I will seek out accountability in my life.

As Jesus and the disciples continued on their way to Jerusalem, they came to a village where a woman named Martha welcomed them into her home. Her sister, Mary, sat at the Lord's feet, listening to what he taught. But Martha was worrying over the big dinner she was preparing. She came to Jesus and said, "Lord, doesn't it seem unfair to you that my sister just sits here while I do all the work? Tell her to come and help me." But the Lord said to her, "My dear Martha, you are so upset over all these details! There is really only one thing worth being concerned about. Mary has discovered it—and I won't take it away from her." —LUKE 10:38-42

Lose the Melodrama

Many of us are crippled with Martha Syndrome. It is the melodramatic life of crisis. We are so upset over all our mistreatment . . . over all our chores! We regard our problems as unique, unfair, unsolvable, and we are sure to complain.

When we get swallowed up in daily drama, we must take time to rest and step out of the soap opera. Mary knew the importance of this. She let go of all the hype in exchange for some quiet time with Jesus. Not every challenge needs to be a massive struggle. As we mature, we become less absorbed with swirling details and more concerned with God's grander scheme.

In our challenges with food and weight, we can do as Mary did and exchange the flurry of circumstances for quiet moments at Jesus' feet. There will always be challenges, but there is really only one thing worth being concerned about. May we daily discover that one thing and lose the melodrama.

Today, Lord, I step out of my soap opera. May I see the grander scheme and calm myself at Your feet.

NOVEMBER 14

Afterward Jesus appeared again to his disciples, by the Sea of Tiberias. "I'm going out to fish," Simon Peter told them, and they said, "We'll go with you." So they went out and got into the boat, but that night they caught nothing. —JOHN 21:1-19

Going Fishing?

One would think that after the crucifixion and resurrection of Jesus, the disciples would have been on fire, ready to change the world. Yet Peter says he's going fishing, as if he's heading back to his old life! It's hard to imagine that after all Peter and the other disciples had experienced, they would simply return to their lives as if nothing had changed.

We can do that same thing, though, with our food and weight problems. We may experience success for a week, a month, or even a year and think that life is great. We might be losing weight and feeling so much better, more centered and serene. Yet we slip, we binge, we go back to life the way it was, as if nothing has affected us. We return to food as if the crucifixion had not occurred and the resurrection power of Jesus was not real.

However, like the disciples, we will find that the old ways produce no results. "Fishing" for life in food is not the answer anymore! We need Jesus to show us where to throw the nets to catch the life He has for us.

Today, Lord, may I turn from my old life of misusing food. Help me to open myself to Your wisdom about where to cast my nets for the life You have for me.

NOVEMBER 15

Therefore, there is now no condemnation for those who are in Christ Jesus. —ROMANS 8:1

Neither Shame nor Pride Can Reign

Condemnation may have been a significant part of our lives in the growing-up years. It may still be significant now. We may feel we are being judged or evaluated, condemned in our heaviness and struggles with food. We may feel excluded and rejected, even in our own homes. But perhaps we also engage in condemning others. Maybe we resent those who are thin or reject those who don't seem to have food issues. Perhaps we have diminished the worth of others based on their appearance or excluded them from true fellowship with us.

Yet in Christ Jesus, not only is there no condemnation upon us, but we are not to condemn others. It is to be no part of our lives! By accepting Christ, we have acknowledged our own weaknesses and the need of all mankind for a Savior. This puts us all on level ground, where neither shame nor pride can reign. We now live in the total acceptance of God, regardless of our messes or what others may think of us. Aware of His acceptance of us, we can humbly offer acceptance to others, free of all condemnation.

Today, Lord, I remember that there is no condemnation for those who are in Christ Jesus.

No discipline seems pleasant at the time, but painful. Later on, however, it produces a harvest of righteousness and peace for those who have been trained by it. —HEBREWS 12:11

Discipline:
A Harvest of Righteousness

Training our minds and taste buds not only to tolerate but to actually like healthier foods can be quite a process. We crave the sugar, salt, and fats that we've lived on for years because it's all we've known. There is one way for a burger to taste . . . we don't want a turkey burger. And we don't want to drink skim milk—it tastes like water! And we certainly don't want to exercise! The problem is that eating and drinking this way is actually what's stealing life away from us!

While no discipline is pleasant, the pain of continuing at status quo eventually becomes greater than the pain of changing. Both alternatives bring suffering, but which one will produce the harvest we seek in our lives? We can make one small change at a time to lessen the blow, and soon we find that the world is still turning, even though we ate a turkey burger.

As we test out healthier options, we may be surprised by what we find: a harvest of righteousness and peace in our hearts for honoring our bodies. Who knows? We may one day even prefer the taste of the healthier options!

Today, Lord, may I stick with this program and try one new, healthier food.

I know and am perfectly sure on the authority of the Lord Jesus that no food, in and of itself, is wrong to eat. But if someone believes it is wrong, then for that person it is wrong.

—ROMANS 14:14 NLT

To Each His Own

In learning how to care for our bodies, we can pay attention to what works for us and what doesn't. Certain foods may be totally acceptable for those around us, but affect us in direct opposition to our weight-loss goals. Very simply, for them, this food is okay to eat, and for us it is not.

We can pray that God will give us the grace to embrace our own body chemistry. As we seek to understand what our body needs, He will teach us how to nurture ourselves without depriving ourselves, and how to live and be filled with the good things He has for us.

We all have our battles, and we each have our joys. We must not compare ourselves to God's other children but live within what is right for us.

Today, Lord, I pray to live within what is right for me.

Not to us, O LORD, but to you goes all the glory.

—PSALM 115:1 NLT

All Glory to You

Working this program takes real effort on our part. Making healthy eating choices, exercising, and facing our deep-level issues are all things we have done in our quest for healing and wholeness in our life.

As the victories come, we want to celebrate. We want to congratulate ourselves on a job well done as we reap the benefits of our hard work and dedication. We light up in the admiration we receive from friends who acknowledge our progress. Yet if we've accomplished these things on our own, then why does our spirit yearn to give thanks?

By listening carefully to our heart, we encounter a basic truth—that all of it, any progress we have made, is an absolute gift from God as we have partnered with Him. May we never boast as though we, alone, have achieved this success. Rather, may we in all humility glorify God, who has blessed us with this program, helped us connect, and called us into abundant life.

Today, Lord, I thank You for being so good . . . and so good to me. Thank You for what You've done and for what You're doing in me. Be praised, and let me live to glorify Your name.

NOVEMBER 19

O Lord, you have searched me and you know me. You know when I sit and when I rise; you perceive my thoughts from afar. You discern my going out and my lying down; you are familiar with all my ways. —PSALM 139:1-3

You See All of Me

The Lord knows us better than we know ourselves. Some days we wake up to cravings that drive us insane. While eating a breakfast loaded with sugar, we begin to think about exercising. We have a real desire to start, but then continue to eat our waffles and syrup, only dreaming of how good it would probably feel to get moving. An article in the newspaper catches our eye, and we are suddenly captivated. Intending to read it quickly and then do some aerobics, we instead read it thoroughly and then check out the television, clearing the breakfast table with the morning news show as company. We notice our tennis shoes right by the door and then look at the clock and despair. Time has slipped away from us. We really did intend to exercise today, but now we must get in the shower. Maybe we can work it in tomorrow.

God has searched us and He knows us completely. He knows when we waste time; He perceives the battle within us. He hears and understands our thoughts and intentions, our feeble plans, from afar. He knows how disappointed we can be in ourselves. He is familiar with every part of us. He knows that we want to lose this extra weight; He knows we want to be healthy.

Today, Lord, teach me more about You and more about me. I find peace knowing that You understand, even when I don't.

For I have told you often before, and I say it again with tears in my eyes, that there are many whose conduct shows they are really enemies of the cross of Christ. Their future is eternal destruction. Their god is their appetite, they brag about shameful things, and all they think about is this life here on earth. —PHILIPPIANS 3:18-19

Living in Oblivion

This can be a rough passage to read for those of us who truly struggle with food and weight issues. We don't want our appetite to be our god, and we want others to look at our conduct and see Jesus, but we're still overweight.

The reassuring news is that this passage is not really for those who are on the path of recovery and healing. Paul is speaking with great sadness about those who live in oblivion, whose gluttony and insatiable appetite for "more" rule their lives. They brag and laugh shamelessly about what others would hide. They are consumed only with their own affairs and are completely unconcerned with the bigger picture. These people have no concept of care for self or others.

We must take caution not to fall into this way of living, where things that are important get tossed around as something of no value. Paul reminds us that this is a heartbreaking way to behave, and he labels this as an act of rebellion against the Cross of Christ.

Today, Lord, may I take seriously the implications of my behavior with food and exercise. May my life clearly show the evidence of my commitment to You.

We must pay more careful attention, therefore, to what we have heard, so that we do not drift away. —HEBREWS 2:1

Take Heed

It is good to gain knowledge for living. We can be very dedicated to taking in new information on a daily basis about health and fitness and about God. Then we must pay careful attention to apply what we can, since knowledge in and of itself is useless. Our problem isn't lack of learning, but lack of heeding what we've learned.

We will make better progress in recovery from food and weight issues if we let new knowledge penetrate our hearts. As information develops into true understanding, our lives begin to change. Paying attention and applying what we've learned at the spiritual level will keep us from drifting so easily from our plan for health.

Today, Lord, in relation to my physical health and learning, may I pay attention at the spiritual level. Reveal new truths to my heart so that my actions will follow.

But Daniel made up his mind not to defile himself by eating the food and wine given to them by the king. He asked the chief official for permission to eat other things instead.

—DANIEL 1:8 NLT

If Given the Choice

Daniel made an eating decision that was for his own benefit. Often we feel obligated to eat the foods offered to us by others. Someone brings brownies to the office, we're at a party with nachos and soda, or our mother baked a cake for our birthday. It is easy to let guilt dictate our eating choices, even though doing so may set us back in our fitness goals. On the other hand, we may love it when others supply unhealthy foods, because then we've found a good reason to cheat for the day.

Living in recovery from food and weight issues entails choosing our own well-being over reckless eating. We don't have to feel guilty about abstaining from foods that "defile" us; we are standing for our health. As we recognize our food boundaries as life-giving, not depriving, then we are more free to choose without guilt what we will and will not eat.

Regardless of what's available or who provided it, if a food is destructive to us, then we don't have to eat it. We can find something else instead and not feel deprived. We can feel great about standing for our health today, especially when it's not always "a piece of cake."

Today, Lord, may I stand firm when I have access to the foods that defile.

NOVEMBER 23

By faith Moses, when he had grown up, refused to be known as the son of Pharaoh's daughter. He chose to be mistreated along with the people of God rather than to enjoy the pleasures of sin for a short time. —HEBREWS 11:24-25

Hard Decisions

Moses was human just like us, with personal insecurities and uncertainties about God's plans for his life. He often felt unable to carry out what God wanted of him. Read through Exodus! We learn so much about his struggles with God's ways in these chapters. Yet Moses found the courage he needed to identify with fellow strugglers in the priority of living obediently rather than for comfort.

We can make the hard decisions with food. It will be uncomfortable, especially in the beginning as we get accustomed to a new routine. But as we make obedience our priority, we, too, will find the courage to walk away from the pleasures of misusing food and be able to identify with fellow strugglers instead.

We know that unhealthy eating is a temporary delight that causes us more harm than good. We can choose wisely for our health today, even though it may be a bit painful. Let us stand for what is good and right in our life instead of what destroys.

Today, Lord, I pray for courage to turn from the short-term pleasures of unhealthy eating.

For God did not give us a spirit of timidity, but a spirit of power, of love, and of self-discipline. —2 TIMOTHY 1:7

Surrender and Discipline

Sometimes we think we can do everything by our own power. If we want to lose excess weight, we don't need God's help. We are smart enough and strong enough to tackle the job on our own, and if we just have the willpower, we'll reach our goals.

Then there are times when we swing the other way into helplessness. Convinced we have no choices, we make no effort to change. We are intimidated and truly believe we will never make progress. So we quit altogether and resign in victimhood.

Finding a balance between strength and powerlessness can be tricky. It is in our timidity that we turn to God, and He provides us with strength for self-control. The two are interdependent. When we try life under our own power, we discover our need for God. When we discover our need for God, we find power, love, and self-discipline.

Today, Lord, may I see timidity as a reminder that I need You. May I dwell in Your provision of power, love, and self-discipline.

*For that which I am doing, I do not understand; for I am not
practicing what I would like to do, but I am doing the very thing
I hate.* —ROMANS 7:15 NASB

God Steps In

Our culture prizes independence and admires the
"self-made man." We want to control our own lives,
even when we are not doing it well. Even when God
begins to address our problems with weight, we
may know that we are beaten, yet we still attempt to
maintain control!

To discover our level of denial, we can look at
our track record. We've tried everything from
expensive fad diets and exercise programs to diet
clubs, pills, even shots. We've tried to pray it away,
"Take this from me, Lord!" but we've never been
willing to put down the excess food and do our
part. We've begged to be spared the consequences of
our food obsession, but we've not taken the hard
action of letting go of food.

We must admit that, left to ourselves, we cannot
permanently win over our food issues. We have to
have God's power—because we have none. What a
relief it is to admit powerlessness! It separates our
part of the equation from God's part.

Paradoxically, when we let go of power, God's
power flows in. It seems we can suddenly do what
we never could before, but it is actually God doing
for us what we cannot do for ourselves. God fights
the food and we let go—we are free.

*Today, Lord, may I admit powerlessness, accept my
part, and step out of Your way.*

NOVEMBER 26

About midnight Paul and Silas were praying and singing hymns to God, and the other prisoners were listening to them.

—ACTS 16:25

Unrestricted!

One of the most exciting and hope-giving passages in the entire Bible could be the experience of Paul and Silas in prison. They had been arrested, severely beaten, and thrown into jail unjustly. Many of us have experienced severe cruelty and "prisons" of our own. We are trapped in dysfunction and emotional pain, isolated in overweight, locked in by fear, closed off in anger, or even chained by apathy toward our health. But listen . . . do you hear the other prisoners singing?

This is how we often come to know God—through the sounds of worship offered by others who have been beaten and challenged yet who are unrestricted in passion and hope.

Regardless of our pain and confinements, God is so worthy of praise! When we see past our own afflictions to the compassion and great love of the Lord, then no prison on earth can restrain our worship or injure our confidence in Christ. It is this irrepressible hope that leads us out of imprisonment today.

Today, Lord, I worship You. You are worthy of all praise, and I give it—unrestricted!

We are hard pressed on every side, but not crushed; perplexed, but not in despair; persecuted, but not abandoned; struck down, but not destroyed. —2 CORINTHIANS 4:8-9

Our Source of Hope

What hope we have in Jesus (though sometimes we forget)!

It is easy to resign ourselves to believing that we will always be a certain body size rather than to anticipate results we can't yet see. Convinced we could never be thin or healthy or active, we've given up and quit trying.

This self-defeating mindset has got to go. It's a lie! We are not crushed. We are not abandoned. We may have been beaten down, perplexed, and persecuted, and we may have a long way to go in recovery, but we are not destroyed! If we're still breathing and in relationship with Jesus, then we have every reason to hope not only for our future but for this day.

By wholeheartedly jumping into the process of healing, we will see the pounds begin to drop. And after losing some weight, we'll realize that we didn't have to resign ourselves to hopelessness. We have the ability to partner with Christ and effect great change whenever we are ready to do it.

Today, Lord, may I walk in the victory that You have won for me. I will not defeat myself with lies!

The sluggard craves and gets nothing, but the desires of the diligent are fully satisfied. —PROVERBS 13:4

A Common Routine

Why is it that when we face an unpleasant task, our appetites suddenly begin to grow? We become unsettled and fidgety and can't think clearly. We crave a snack and migrate into our kitchen, looking for a tasty treat that might help us through the immediate discomfort.

Yet we aren't really hungry. We're procrastinating—looking for a nice distraction, a good reason to postpone our task. "I really must keep up my energy before I tackle this job!" The truth is, we're simply trying to put off whatever must be done for another fifteen minutes.

In the end, we are worse off than when we started. The quick sugar-fix was fleeting, and it didn't honor our body. In fact, we participated in damaging our body. We didn't boost our energy—and the task at hand is still incomplete.

Instead of spending energy avoiding the task, what if we took a step of faith and dove in fearlessly to work on whatever we're avoiding? What if we took a baby step toward completing the task? What on earth might happen then?

Today, Lord, I dedicate the next fifteen minutes to doing what is good and healthy for me.

How much more, then, will the blood of Christ, who through the eternal Spirit offered himself unblemished to God, cleanse our consciences from acts that lead to death, so that we may serve the living God! —HEBREWS 9:14

The Goal Is Progress

With each day we can choose behaviors that lead to either life or death. We long for transformation in our lives, yet there are still times when we sabotage our goals with food and weight. We slip into old patterns and find guilt and shame with the mistakes we make.

But there is good news. "Progress, not perfection" is a slogan in Twelve-Step recovery programs. It serves as a reminder that though we can't do all things perfectly, the goal is to make progress in the process of getting healthier. It means we dedicate ourselves to practicing the principles that lead to life.

When we fail to choose life and our conscience condemns us, we can remember the blood of Christ, which cleanses us. We can embrace the fact that we have a Savior. Let us live to make progress, not perfection.

Today, Lord, I know I need a Savior. You are perfect, and I am not. Thank You for saving me. I pray for progress and cleansing today.

So, as the Holy Spirit says: "Today, if you hear his voice, do not harden your hearts as you did in the rebellion."

—HEBREWS 3:7-8

Keeping a Soft Heart

We may cringe to acknowledge this, but unhealthy eating and living is rebellion against God. Without even knowing it, we have directly opposed His creative purpose for us with our emotional eating and inactivity. We have disabled our bodies from functioning at full capacity. And we have neglected to live in the freedom that Christ offers. But today His voice is calling us.

Often our problem with heaviness does not stem from lack of knowledge or clear direction but from our hardness of heart. We don't like that we struggle with food; it seems unfair, or it's just the way we were made. And we resist making any effort to change. But God calls us to keep our hearts soft for Him. He desires that we not turn away in anger, that we walk humbly and faithfully with Him in all things, even when we may not enjoy the process.

Today, Lord, may I soften my heart toward You and Your ways. Help me to live by Your principles in my eating and activities.

Reckless words pierce like a sword, but the tongue of the wise brings healing. —PROVERBS 12:18

The Salve of Truth

Many of us who are overweight have suffered for years from the piercing, reckless words of others. Our parents may have verbally abused us, calling us hurtful names, putting us down for our weaknesses, angry with us for existing—perhaps wishing we were never born. For some of us the injuries may have been subtler than that, where we simply lacked words of affirmation and care from others. Unkind words spoken by peers, even in childhood, may have affected us at various points of vulnerability. Even the media has wounded us, shaping our perception of self, striking our sensitivities.

So now let us listen to the words of the wise. We must find people who know the truths of God's Word and who will speak it into our lives. Spending time with a Christian counselor or mentor, involving ourselves in church and Bible study, and enjoying the fellowship of others on a common journey can usher in truth for healing. As we are saturated in this salve of truth, it seeps into our wounds, working into our very being and restoring us to health and wholeness.

Today, Lord, may I listen to words of wisdom for healing.

"Ever since the days of your ancestors, you have scorned my laws and failed to obey them. Now return to me, and I will return to you," says the LORD Almighty."

—MALACHI 3:7A NLT

Becoming the Right Kind of Rebel

For generations our families may have rejected God's laws and refused to live by His principles. Our heritage may be one of vehement rebellion or even apathy toward Him and His ways. In fact, learning how to mistreat our body may have begun decades before we were even born. Yet now we have the decision of whether to carry on the harmful behaviors or to break the family pattern.

With the same invitation extended in Malachi's day, God is calling out to us today: "Now return to me, and I will return to you." He bids each of us individually, regardless of our family heritage, to respond to Him. We can be the generation of change, where obedience and abundant life in the Lord begin. It is not our duty to simply live "the way we were raised." Emotional eating and inactivity may have been the way of our ancestors, but this is not a sentence upon us. Instead, we can rebel against ungodliness and end the pattern of destructive living. Let us choose for ourselves in this day what is beneficial for our own health and wholeness.

Today, Lord, I want to return to You. Help me to break the harmful patterns that have plagued my family for generations.

May your roots go down deep into the soil of God's marvelous love. And may you have the power to understand, as all God's people should, how wide, how long, how high, and how deep his love really is. —EPHESIANS 3:17B-18 NLT

Truly Grounded

Any attempts to effect positive change in our life must be rooted and grounded in God's marvelous love. This isn't merely a side issue; it is the basis for everything meaningful in our entire life. Our first mission in losing excess weight is to gain a deep, rich understanding of the vastness of God's heart for us—the breadth, depth, and full measure of His unending love.

As we nourish ourselves in this fertile soil, we will grow and mature through our challenges with emotional eating. We'll be less likely to believe the devaluing lies of the world that seek to destroy our hope and drive us to the "comfort" of bingeing. We will more firmly stand in the truth of our worth in the eyes of God, less needy of our food to save us from pain.

Today, Lord, I pray to be rooted in Your deep, rich love for me. I pray for the power to understand how wide, how long, how high, and how deep Your love really is.

DECEMBER 4

But whatever things were gain to me, those things I have counted as loss for the sake of Christ. More than that, I count all things to be loss in view of the surpassing value of knowing Christ Jesus my Lord, for whom I have suffered the loss of all things, and count them but rubbish so that I may gain Christ, and may be found in Him . . . —PHILIPPIANS 3:7-9A NASB

Rubbish

There is great freedom in knowing Christ. As we deepen our walk with Jesus, we become more centered, more grounded, and less attached to the things of this world. In the past we have treasured chocolate and sugar, prepackaged meals and fast foods, and anything fried or swimming in syrup. We clung to food and hoarded body weight.

But the more we practice the surrender of our eating to the care of God, what we once prized becomes nonsense. Our ultimate treasure becomes knowing Christ.

As we turn over this area of our lives, we know Jesus will meet us at our point of need. May we begin to see our love of food as but rubbish compared to our experience and life with Christ Jesus.

Today, Lord, may I deepen my walk with You and gain perspective for the other areas of my life.

DECEMBER 5

Then Joseph said to his brothers, "Come close to me." When they had done so, he said, "I am your brother Joseph, the one you sold into Egypt! And now, do not be distressed and do not be angry with yourselves for selling me here, because it was to save lives that God sent me ahead of you."

—GENESIS 45:4-5

God Brings About His Purposes

It has been said that one of the most life-threatening cancers of the human race is justified resentment. Many of us have suffered tragic losses and pain caused by significant people in our lives. We've been deeply wounded and have legitimate cause for the deep-seated anger and overwhelming sadness we feel.

The problem is that our resentments, while highly justified, are stealing years of joy and energy from our lives. Bitterness destroys our ability to truly live. We have turned to food for salvation in our despair. We have made our pain bearable with the comfort of food and yet created more pain by our overweight.

Consider the story of Joseph, who was sold by his brothers into slavery. He released them entirely from their action and acknowledged the sovereignty of God, who allowed it. Joseph reminds us that God is bringing about His purposes; we need not eat in despair. We can release ourselves from the burden of resentment by resting in God's sovereignty.

Today, Lord, when I want to eat junk food in bitterness, may I think about Your sovereignty and plans for my life. No one can sabotage Your purpose for me but me.

Indeed, in our hearts we felt the sentence of death. But this happened that we might not rely on ourselves but on God, who raises the dead. —2 CORINTHIANS 1:9

This Death Sentence Brings Life

We have felt the sentence of death in our attempts to lose excess weight. Many times we have come face-to-face with the fact that we cannot rely on our own strength to save us from overeating and inactivity. We will inevitably return to our old eating habits and lifestyle when we do not depend upon the grace of God to bring about the needed change.

Feeling the sentence of death, however, is actually a good thing. When we finally arrive at the end of ourselves and discover we cannot make a lasting difference, then we are ready to turn to the One who can do it for us. God has all the power we need to progress with weight loss and emotional healing. Now, instead of continuing to use our own limited strength, we can depend upon God's, and His is limitless. He can raise the dead, and He will raise us out of our death sentence into the newness of life that comes when we are sustained by His power. We first admit our own powerlessness, and then find all the strength we need for each task in moving toward health and wholeness.

Today, Lord, may I rely on You and Your strength for my life.

DECEMBER 7

Walking Through the Valley

While walking through a mall, we may be surrounded by aromas that set off a craving. Or we
might be driving down a road and suddenly find
we're surrounded by fast-food restaurants that
trigger a strong urge to visit the drive-thru window.

These moments can be like walking through the
valley of the shadow of death, calling us to give up
our resolve and our commitment to living on a spiritual plane. We are now choosing to live a life that
is free from excess food. We are refusing to eat
empty calories, refraining from deadly trans fats,
and avoiding killer sugar products.

There will always be urges that surge within us.
But when we turn to God from within for the
strength and courage to say no, we need not fear
these evils. God is truly with us.

Today, Lord, I am walking with You as You lead me
out of the shadow of death and into new life.

The LORD protects the simplehearted; when I was in great need, he saved me. —PSALM 116:6

Loose the Knots

Let us simplify our hearts. Instead of being so overwhelmed by all the changes we want to make, and feeling defeated before we even start, perhaps the first thing we could change is our approach to it all. It is our tendency to make things difficult and complex in nature, but we don't have to. Though our need for help with food and weight loss may be great, we can let go of the whirlwind inside of us in exchange for an innocent heart that simply asks for help at each step. God will save us!

The Lord "protects the simplehearted." What peace we can find in this truth! As simplicity extends into our behaviors, we can look at our bare necessities first and then go from there, having been loosed from the knots of anxiety, manipulation, and stress. As we merely take the next step in the right direction, we will be making progress. Each simple step makes a difference.

Today, Lord, I will be gentle in heart. Untwist my knots in exchange for simplicity. May I rest in knowing that You protect me and save me.

DECEMBER 9

Attitude of Gratitude

It is good to sing praise to our God. An "attitude of gratitude" will go a long way in our recovery from food and weight issues. With each morning our slate is clean and we can joyfully sing of His goodness. We can reflect upon His hand in our lives and praise Him for the journey toward weightlessness.

He is our stronghold and refuge in times of distress. We can praise Him for progress we've made mentally, emotionally, spiritually, and for His gifts of lovingkindness and compassion each day. With humble hearts we can praise God, for He is truly worthy to be praised in all things.

Today, Lord, I praise You for who You are and for what You're doing in my life.

DECEMBER 10

A little sleep, a little slumber, a little folding of the hands to rest—and poverty will come on you like a bandit and scarcity like an armed man. —PROVERBS 6:10-11

Diligence in Recovery

God has more for our lives than a passive existence. He made us with special gifts and talents, and He has given us the ability to influence others. It is tragic for us when we waste these gifts, sacrificing the life of meaning and purpose for our own self-centered will.

We've spent enough days making excuses and playing the victim to everyone else's cruelty. We have made our own poor choices, regardless of what anyone else has done to us. It's time for us to take responsibility for our lives and our problems with food and weight.

Our lazy days of eating and immobility have created poverty in our souls. The scarcity of real nourishment is attacking our very existence. If we remain sedentary, our very lives are at risk! Yet the good news is that we have the chance to change things today.

Today, Lord, I will not lounge around and overeat. I will feed my soul through diligence in recovery.

DECEMBER 11

Remember this: Whoever sows sparingly will also reap sparingly, and whoever sows generously will also reap generously.

—2 CORINTHIANS 9:6

Wholehearted, Even in Baby Steps

Degree matters. If we piddle around in our efforts with weight loss, then we can't expect to see a lot of results. Our goal is not just to lose excess weight quickly; we are concerned with losing it for life. This takes more than dabbling in a couple of areas that may need some attention. We are talking about progressively changing our lifestyle, one step at a time.

Taking baby steps toward progress is a matter of doing what we can do today, and refusing to become overwhelmed to the point of giving up. It is taking little steps that set an appropriate long-term pace. However, we take each step out wholeheartedly; this is how we sow generously to our recovery. When we step wholeheartedly, there will be a great harvest from our effort.

Today, Lord, may I sow generously and find that I reap the same.

DECEMBER 12

What a gift life is to those who stay the course! You've heard, of course, of Job's staying power, and you know how God brought it all together for him at the end. That's because God cares, cares right down to the last detail. —JAMES 5:11 MSG

Staying Power

Getting healthy and changing our lives is an obstacle course. Life comes from movement on that course, not from staying in one place or in one position. We can lie motionless, with no hope, no choices—a passive victim. Or we can function mechanically, doing what's always been done for the sake of routine. Or we can choose the course of healing and growth and receive God's gift of life.

"Staying the course" means that even when we don't want to, we get up and exercise. Even when we don't want to, we follow our food plan. It means we do the next right thing, take the next right action, despite how we feel. When we do, we find that God brings it all together for us, just as He did for Job.

God always comes through. He cares about each detail of our lives, even our food and exercise. Whenever we follow our plan of recovery, we embrace the gift of life given to those who stay the course.

Lord, today, may I stay the course of recovery with You as my guide. I want to embrace the gift of life.

DECEMBER 13

Do you not know? Have you not heard? The LORD is the ever-lasting God, the Creator of the ends of the earth. He will not grow tired or weary, and his understanding no one can fathom. He gives strength to the weary and increases the power of the weak. —ISAIAH 40:28-29

He Gives

Changing our life can be exhausting! The emotional energy it takes to live a single day facing our own issues rather than escaping to our choice comfort food is draining. It's not easy to face the craziness. But take heart.

God understands how tough it can be, and He never grows weary from helping us. He is always there, giving us strength in the moment we need it, increasing our power when we are weakest. In fact, being weary and weak is just about the best place we could be to receive God's richest blessing for living through today. He will give us the power to say no to harmful habits, and enough attitude to actually enjoy today's activity. He "gets" our whole situation, and He "gives" generously when we need Him the most.

Lord, today, I will live in the spark I get from You. Thank You for giving me all the strength and power I need today.

Now faith is being sure of what we hope for and certain of what we do not see. —*HEBREWS 11:1*

Life is either a daring adventure—or nothing. —*HELEN KELLER*

Adventure Unhindered

Helen Keller was an amazing human being, a teacher for all of us. She chose to live unhindered by her condition, even in the midst of her physical limitations. We can learn to do this as well: choosing to look at life as an exciting adventure, asking what it is that God is going to teach us next through our trial. We can view our situation—or any event in our life—with wonder and awe, daring to risk, get out of ourselves, and move forward into the unknown of life.

For Helen Keller, the alternative was nothing! She was cut off from the world, inhibited from connecting in the ways most of us do. Yet she chose to allow the limitations to motivate her to find new avenues of reaching beyond her little world and forward into life, learning, and relationship. The spirit within her, longing for more out of life, yearning for freedom from confinement, viewed this as an opportunity for adventure instead of a vacuum of nothingness. And Helen attained another level of living.

We have the same opportunity before us. To "lose it for life" is a daring adventure!

Today, Lord, help me to see my condition and my limitations as opportunity for life's adventure.

DECEMBER 15

The suffering you sent was good for me, for it taught me to pay attention to your principles. —PSALM 119:71 NLT

Pain: The Great Motivator

Suffering is good? As much as we may want to reject this notion, we know that suffering can bring positive results in our life.

It has been said that people listen to advice but obey pain. How true this is for so many of us. We often resist good, healthy choices until we hit the bottom of our discomfort. The suffering we experience by straying from God becomes our motivation, for life is better when we follow Him and His principles. Not always easier, but better.

Even a life lived right in line with God's will can be full of great pain. Consider Jesus, who perfectly executed God's plan yet was still beaten and crucified. No matter what kind of suffering we endure, may we allow it to point us toward God and His principles. Therein is a satisfying life.

Today, Lord, may I embrace my suffering as a gift from You. Teach me to know Your principles and find the peace therein.

In your unfailing love you will lead the people you have redeemed. In your strength you will guide them to your holy dwelling. —EXODUS 15:13

Headed to the Promised Land

In this passage Moses and the Israelites sing a song of praise to the Lord. They had just passed through the miraculously parted Red Sea, escaping from the pursuing Egyptians and the slavery of their rule. Although they faced a tough journey, they were headed toward the Promised Land. It was a time of rejoicing at God's protection, provision, power, and great love for His people.

Much like the Israelites, we, too, are in a fight for our life, escaping danger, headed for our own Promised Land of weightlessness. But as God's people, we know the Lord is with us. At times we may feel weak and hopeless, like we will never be free from slavery to excess weight; never escape the attacking persuasion of unhealthy foods; never survive today's regimen for exercise. But through all these difficulties, God is on our side. He is our redeemer. In His unfailing love, He will lead us; in strength, He will guide us.

Today, Lord, take me, lead me, and guide me. May I trust in Your unfailing love and almighty strength. Take me to places where You've promised my freedom from slavery.

DECEMBER 17

We all, like sheep, have gone astray, each of us has turned to his own way; and the LORD has laid on him the iniquity of us all.

—ISAIAH 53:6

I Don't Want to Be Textbook!

And we thought we were so unique! While God has definitely made each of us unique, we are often more like others than we want to believe. For years we thought that our problems were worse, that our joys were more meaningful, that our sorrows were much deeper than others'. We found value in being different. Common rules did not apply to us because we were one of a kind, so we resisted the advice and options presented to us by others. And it has left us isolated.

This verse reveals that we are not so unique. Like everyone else, we have problems and have turned to our own solutions. Our overweight condition has textbook characteristics that mimic those of millions of other overweight people. In most instances, we are just like every other heavy person who struggles with compulsive and emotional eating and inactivity. We have the same experiences with dysfunctional families and traumas. Though the particulars may vary, the effects are often the same.

We need not be let down in the ways we are similar to others, but be glad we're not the first to walk through these trials. We will glean from the experiences of others.

Today, Lord, I embrace the fact that I am often textbook instead of unique! May I humble myself to consider the advice I can find on getting well.

DECEMBER 18

Dear friends, do not believe every spirit, but test the spirits to see whether they are from God, because many false prophets have gone out into the world. —1 JOHN 4:1

Test the Spirits

We must not believe everything we hear—positive or negative. When the powerful voices in our life tell us that we are worthless, or that weight shouldn't matter, or that we are incapable of change, we must test these ideas to see if they line up with God's truth. As much as we may wish to believe that certain people know what they are saying and would never bring harm to us, we must be wise ourselves and develop discernment. People can say harmful things—sometimes completely unintentionally, but harmful nonetheless.

The same goes for when people speak words of flattery to us. They may inflate our ego by telling us we're wonderful or assure us that everything is fine when it's not. Some people will even say there's a product that will cure all of our weight problems, or that working through the tough emotions from our past will not help us "lose it for life." These spirits sound appealing; after all, who wants recovery to be difficult? But the truth is, no long-term benefits come out of false flattery. Again, we must test each spirit to see if it is from God, for not every false prophet is even aware that he or she is speaking untruth.

Today, Lord, I pray for discernment with the spirits around me. I pray to know what comes from You.

DECEMBER 19

Then the LORD said to Moses, "Behold, I will rain bread from heaven for you; and the people shall go out and gather a day's portion every day, that I may test them, whether or not they will walk in My instruction. —EXODUS 16:4 NASB

The Heart of the Matter

God uses food to test us? Oh, no!

If you are a parent, you may have done this very thing with your own children. Perhaps you've instructed your son to eat his vegetables at dinner if he hoped to play outside afterward. Maybe you've tested your daughter's fairness by entrusting her with a very serious job: dividing the cake for the family to share.

In each of these instances parents can learn a lot about the developing character of their child. God does not need tests to learn more about us; He already knows us completely and intimately. The testing is for us, not for Him. It allows us to encounter the truth about ourselves, our own character assets and defects, and our utter need for God. If we're paying close attention as God tests us involving food, we can often get right to the heart of our deepest issues!

Today, Lord, show me the heart of the matter.

DECEMBER 20

And my God will meet all your needs according to his glorious riches in Christ Jesus. —PHILIPPIANS 4:19

Chocolate Bliss

Oh, the joys of chocolate. Don't we love it? It is heavenly to smell and taste, it thrills the tongue, and it's a beloved companion in times of need. We have depended on chocolate for consolation in sadness, for celebration in victory, and for salvation from boredom. We've entered into fits when chocolate was unavailable. We love to eat it while we ponder life, when we're undecided on the dinner menu, or when we've earned a small reward. It can be our default craving for nearly every circumstance.

How in the world can something like chocolate have so much power? When did we decide that it should fulfill all our needs? We've obeyed its demands and sacrificed our health and sanity for a small high from sugar and caffeine.

Is it possible to satisfy a craving for chocolate with something other than chocolate? Yes. If we open our spirit, God will use our cravings to show us our deeper needs. He will reveal His truth to us and provide for us as we seek Him. His answers for our needs may even alter our cravings.

Today, Lord, may I look to You to supply all my needs.

But I am like an olive tree, thriving in the house of God. I trust in God's unfailing love forever and ever.   —PSALM 52:8 NLT

Growing to Trust

Can we trust God for today? We learned very early in life to be self-sufficient and keep to ourselves. We were let down, perhaps in our childhood, by those who should've come through for us in critical moments. So we struggle now with trusting God and other people. After all, isn't God in charge of the universe? If He let those people fail us, how can we rely on Him?

In order to grow our trust in God, we must first grow in the knowledge of His unfailing love for us. We can grow in this way by reading His Word, spending time with Him, and being open to tangible expressions of His love from His people. As our confidence in God's love increases, we aren't so dominated by the fear of being hurt by others.

Rather than isolating ourselves from people who will fail from time to time, we begin to believe and accept that whatever we experience today is part of God's work for our good. We begin to realize He's providing exactly what we need in order for us to grow into kingdom people, and He's using imperfect people as part of that program.

Today, Lord, as I walk in recovery, I will seek to know more about Your love for me. Grow my trust in You and in Your grand plan for me.

So, if you think you are standing firm, be careful that you don't fall! —1 CORINTHIANS 10:12

Continue in the Manner

Reaching our fitness goals and our appropriate body weight brings a feeling like none other! Knowing that we have persevered and that God has blessed us with weight loss is truly exhilarating and life-changing. We have such hope for our future and such gratitude to have found the system that works for us. Now we must continue to live in the manner that maintains our healthier physical and spiritual condition.

Now is not the time for us to lie back and rest on our laurels. We can celebrate and still be aware that we are losing it for life. In our rejoicing, may we dedicate ourselves to continuing the good work that Christ has done in us, bringing this message to others and remaining in the lifestyle that blesses us with health.

Today, Lord, may I be reminded that I'm losing it for life.

DECEMBER 23

Commit your works to the Lord, and your plans will be established. —*PROVERBS 16:3* NASB

Work to Live

Jack LaLayne said, "Most people work at dying. I work at living." This was the secret of a ninety-year-old man who had the body of a fifty-year-old.

We don't always think about the ways we choose to live our life—overstressed, overfed, under-exercised, overcaffeinated—and how these things are working us into an early grave. We blame early deaths on genetics and heredity. We use the excuse that we don't have time to exercise. Or we think that changing the way we eat is too overwhelming because it means changing the way we buy groceries, and to reorient our choices generally takes a huge amount of determination. It's just too much trouble!

But let's look at our choices: Are we working at dying or living? If we take the same energy we are using now to stay on the course we're on, and we channel that energy into new attitudes, new perspectives, and new behaviors around food, then new choices are more easily incorporated. Day by day we begin working ourselves into vibrant health and energetic activity. In other words, we are working at living!

In our new program, we have the tools and resources we need to take on this exciting endeavor with optimism, hope, and joy. Let's work!

Today, Lord, I take on the job of working to live under Your power and for Your glory!

Rend your heart and not your garments. Return to the LORD your God, for he is gracious and compassionate, slow to anger and abounding in love, and he relents from sending calamity.

—JOEL 2:13

Returning to the Lord

If you are struggling with food choices and find yourself in relapse, Joel's call to return to the Lord is for you! The shame and defeat we feel can be overwhelming and painful, and it's hard to admit to others that we are failing, but this is the perfect time to go deeper.

As we humbly surrender the things that are keeping us from living fully in the Spirit, God will remain true to His loving character. He promises us compassion rather than further destruction.

Knowing this, what holds us back from a life fully surrendered to God rather than food? Perhaps it is a resentment that has never been examined. Perhaps it is a fear of financial difficulty or need for acclaim—to be the "best," to be special or favored. Whatever it is, there is only one way to respond if we desire healing and compassion: We must fall before our Lord and admit the things that have brought us shame. Though He has every right to refuse us, the Lord is "abounding in love." He will welcome us with compassion. And when we face the deeper issues, we'll find that food will have less power in our lives, while God takes prominence.

Today, Lord, I am willing to look deeper into my heart and soul for those issues that have been hidden. By faith, I surrender them to You.

You prepare a table before me in the presence of my enemies.

—PSALM 23:5

The Table of the Lord

The Lord provides for us even when we are in the presence of enemies. The psalmist may have been talking about physical enemies, but our enemies are not always flesh and blood.

The media is filled with advertisements about food that can kill us! Then there are the enemies in the form of fast-food chains, whose neon signs attract our attention wherever we drive. These enemies cater to our compulsion to focus on a particular food item, making it difficult to refrain. They also incite the part of us that wants our fair share.

Even if we are in the presence of these enemies, we can be victorious if we sit at the Lord's table— the one He prepares for us. His table is spread with surrender, acceptance, and willingness. The table of surrender brings humility that says, "Not my will, but Yours," when it comes to our food choices. The table of acceptance brings serenity to be free from compulsion. The table of willingness brings the ability to refrain from food items that are not on our plan.

When we sit at the table of the Lord, we are filled by spiritual food that satisfies more than physical hunger. We experience spiritual connection with God and loving relationships with people. The enemies may always be there, but they have no power over us.

Today, Lord, may I sit at the table You prepare for me, even in the presence of "enemies."

We are destroying speculations and every lofty thing raised up against the knowledge of God, and we are taking every thought captive to the obedience of Christ.

—2 CORINTHIANS 10:5 NASB

Chattering Monkeys

A woman was talking about her problem with food and weight, which seemed to center in her mind. She said it was like a clan of critical, persistent monkeys chattering in her head, "Are you going to eat that? How do I look? You're too fat! What do they think of me? You need more exercise!"

This kind of mental obsession often burdens those of us with food and weight issues. Our thought patterns toward ourselves, our progress, and other people are usually negative. This negativity, if not stopped, can keep us chronically discontented and will likely lead to compulsive eating.

Sustained recovery must include dealing with the mental obsessions and silencing the "chattering monkeys." How else can we hear from God about our next step and where to direct our energy?

"Taking every thought captive" means submitting every thought to God as it occurs, and releasing our fear about our weight, appearance, and food to Him. We may need help to accomplish this, but we must not continue to dwell in the negativity.

Today, Lord, I submit the chatter in my head to You. Let my thoughts be obedient to Your will.

DECEMBER 27

"Blessed are those who mourn, for they will be comforted."

—MATTHEW 5:4

Mourn the Losses

In our journey out of bondage to food, many wounds may be uncovered. Some of us have lost childhoods to abuse. We may have lost parents and other loved ones who took our feelings of security with them. We may need to grieve about past mistakes and what we have missed by being overweight. Having used food to avoid our feelings, we have anesthetized our grief because it was so intense and overwhelming. But to become truly free, we need to learn to grieve. In fact, Jesus said we are blessed when we grieve because God will comfort us. The more grief and woundedness we bring out of hiding, the more God comforts and sets us free.

So when we are diving into the depths of loss, we must trust that He will be with us. Instead of running from the intensity of our feelings, we learn to deliberately feel them as deeply as they go. As we do this, we come to terms with the reality of loss. Acceptance brings peace. The blessing is that we are no longer haunted emotionally, and we are no longer triggered to eat in our grief.

Today, Lord, wrap Yourself around me as I allow myself to grieve and to move into acceptance.

DECEMBER 28

"Consider the farmers who eagerly look for the rains in the fall and in the spring. They patiently wait for the precious harvest to ripen. You, too, must be patient, and take courage."

—JAMES 5:7B-8A NLT

Small Commitments, Big Changes

Most of us want quick results, but if we want to make lasting changes, we must cultivate patience.

A woman described what helped her to achieve stable weight-loss results: "I found that committing to small changes over time was a key to making huge changes that last. My problem was that I ate continually throughout the day. So to provide structure, I started eating three distinct meals a day with no snacks. The meals I had were more like banquets, but I broke the binge/starve cycle that had been my pattern for many years. As I surrendered to this simple structure, I was able to let go of extra food a little at a time.

"As I made small changes over time, my body adjusted, and I began to lose the extra pounds. Emotionally, I was beginning to deal with feelings and issues from the past. Spiritually, I was surrendering my food choices to God's will each day. As the weight came off, I could face the fear of being thin and adjust to a new image slowly and gradually. I felt a spiritual connection with God that was deeper than I'd ever had before."

Today, Lord, help me cultivate the seeds of small commitments. Let them be watered by the rains of surrender and willingness, and bring to me the ripe harvest of recovery.

DECEMBER 29

*Now the Lord is the Spirit, and where the Spirit of the Lord is,
there is freedom.* —2 CORINTHIANS 3:17

Thirty-one Flavors

A woman spoke of her new life of recovery from compulsive eating: "I used to frequent certain ice cream shops that boasted thirty-one flavors. It was an exciting treat to survey the options and make a choice. There was a ritual about it and a sense of adventure having a different flavor each time. But the illusion of freedom was short-lived. I became imprisoned by an ice cream obsession that was never satisfied.

"To regain my freedom I had to begin a program of recovery. I saw that I needed to find a way to let go of this obsession, because ice cream was not part of my food plan.

"At first, this was a huge loss, and I actually grieved, missing the fun and entertainment of so many flavors. But I learned that by letting go of ice cream and making healthy choices within my food plan, I was freeing myself from a life of bondage to food. As I lost weight, I found that my *life* had more options. I was able to do things I had been ashamed to do before. I was not worn out all the time. My life was becoming full and exciting. Becoming free of food obsession and excess pounds, I received so many more choices about living. A new understanding of freedom and choice began to emerge: Freedom to live life has more flavors than thirty-one!"

Today, Lord, let me survey the flavors of life and live in spiritual freedom.

DECEMBER 30

I came so they can have real and eternal life, more and better life than they ever dreamed of. —JOHN 10:10 MSG

Enduring or Enjoying?

We may wonder whether all this "recovery work" is worth anything in the light of eternity. Will it add to our salvation? No, but it's not wasted either, because as Jesus said, He came so we may have not just eternal life but also "better life than [we] ever dreamed of."

Recovery from bondage to food, although painful and arduous, could mean the difference between merely enduring life to the end or enjoying the journey. Though recovery costs us the chance to eat whatever and whenever we want, it improves the quality of our life. We understand our desperate need for God more clearly. We reach out for Him more consistently. We open up to people more intimately and fearlessly. As our body sheds the extra pounds, we have more energy and fewer physical aches and pains. We are not just enduring life, we are experiencing the richness and abundance that Jesus promised.

Today, Lord, may I not just endure but enjoy life abundantly.

DECEMBER 31

Then Jesus said to his disciples, "If anyone would come after me, he must deny himself and take up his cross and follow me. For whoever wants to save his life will lose it, but whoever loses his life for me will find it." —MATTHEW 16:24-25

Keeping/Losing, Losing/Finding

We are on a journey with Jesus as our guide. Part of our journey is the desire for weight loss, and that has motivated us to seek guidance. How wonderful that we have the ultimate leader walking the road with us! This road, however, does not end with weight loss as our final destination. Rather, as we walk the path of surrender and saturate ourselves in God's grace, we may find we receive weight loss as a beautiful gift from God along the way.

Many of us will walk this path for some time while our bodies change at a pace we find discouraging. We may even demand results as compensation for our efforts. It is then that we realize we have not yet surrendered our life, putting aside our selfish ambitions for our cross.

This is not an easy road! Life with Christ is about losing our life, our will, our timetable, and our stubborn resistance to God's best for us.

We must not strive to lose weight more earnestly than we strive to align our will with God's. As we exchange our ambition for His will, we'll find true life and God's purpose for us this day! We can trust that He knows what we need, and perhaps today, it is the gift of peace that comes from letting go.

Today, Lord, I put aside my selfish ambition and receive the gift of You. I accept Your good gifts for me, in whatever form they come. I trust Your path for me.

THE TOTAL SOLUTION
—PHYSICAL, EMOTIONAL, SPIRITUAL—
FOR PERMANENT WEIGHT LOSS

LOSE IT *for* LIFE

STEPHEN ARTERBURN & DR. LINDA MINTLE

**No diet, pill or surgery can give you
God's tools to Lose It For Life.**

But this book can.

Most diet programs only tell you what to eat or how to exercise. And when you're done with them, the pounds return. *Lose It For Life* is a uniquely balanced, total solution that focuses on your mind, body and soul—and how the emotional, mental and spiritual factors affect your weight. Ultimately, this solution—developed by best-selling author and radio personality Stephen Arterburn, who lost 60 pounds 20 years ago and has kept it off—helps readers achieve what they desire most: permanent results.

Using the principles from the nationally recognized Lose It For Life Seminars, this groundbreaking book is the perfect companion to any weight-loss program—Atkins, South Beach, Weight Watchers, whatever! And it's co-authored by Dr. Linda Mintle, whose clinical work in eating disorders gives even more hope to those who have tried fad diets with disappointing results.

This book will give you the information and motivation you need to live a healthy life and to finally *Lose It For Life!*

ISBN: 1-59145-245-7
PRICE: $22.99 U.S.

Lose It For Life for Teens
Steve Arterburn & Ginger Garrett

Weight is such a critical issue with teenagers. They are overwhelmed with messages that present unrealistic and unhealthy body images. *Lose It For Life for Teens* will save them a lifetime of struggles and negative self-perceptions. It will help young people:

• set the right goals
• deal with emotional triggers for overeating
• understand how to lose weight in a healthy way and keep it off
• design a customized workout program
• realize the power, comfort and relational support God offers

ISBN: 1-59145-248-1   PRICE: $12.99

Lose It For Life Workbook

This companion workbook helps participants to better apply the program to their specific situation. It is also ideal for group study, helping facilitate meetings for those who want to encourage each other in their journey toward better physical and spiritual health.

ISBN: 1-59145-275-9   PRICE: $13.99 U.S.

Lose It For Life
Day by Day Devotional

God is interested in all of our problems, but surprisingly, many Christians neglect or are reluctant to bring their struggles with weight issues to Him. *The Lose It For Life Day by Day Devotional* will help Lose It For Lifers draw daily spiritual encouragement from the One who loves us most and is interested in every aspect of our lives—even our struggles with weight.

ISBN: 1-59145-249-X   PRICE: $13.99 U.S.

Lose It For Life
Journal Planner

The *Lose It For Life Journal Planner* is a vital tool that will help participants plan for success and record results on their journey toward optimum health. It also includes valuable specific support for those days when temptation is hitting hardest.

ISBN: 1-59145-274-0   PRICE: $9.99 U.S.

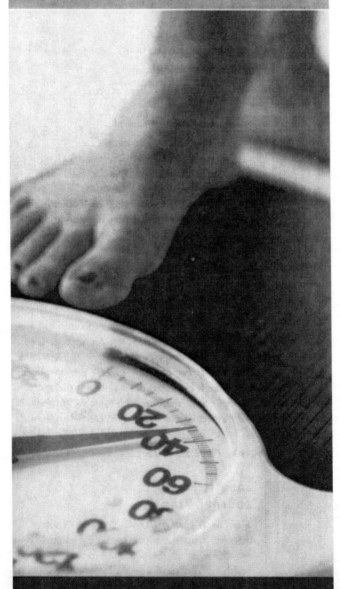

Lose It For Life®
INSTITUTE

Your life doesn't have to be defined by what you weigh.

 No diet, pill or surgery can give you God's tools to address weight loss from an emotional, spiritual and physiological perspective.

Lose It For Life® is an intensive treatment program where you'll discover the root causes of your struggle and address them without pressure, shame or guilt. Let the flame of realistic, gentle lifestyle change be kindled for you!

Steve Arterburn

Founder of New Life Ministries

Stephen Arterburn is the founder and chairman of New Life Ministries and is the host of the nationally syndicated *New Life Live!* radio program. He is also the founder of the Women of Faith conferences and an author of over 50 books, with more than 5 million in print. His most recent releases include the bestsellers *Every Man's Battle* and *Finding Mr. Right*, as well as *Feeding Your Appetites*.

Janelle W. Puff has a degree in Pastoral Counseling from Christian Theological Seminary in Indianapolis, Indiana. She is a licensed clinical social worker, licensed marriage and family therapist, and a member of the American Association of Christian Counselors. Janelle has been a therapist in the mental health field for over 20 years, working with addictions, codependency, marriage and family difficulties, women's issues, and personal growth. She considers this a ministry of God's grace, blending psychology with spiritual principles. Janelle is currently in private practice with Family Counseling Associates, Inc. and lives in Indianapolis with her husband, Larry, and their two daughters.

Misty Arterburn is a full-time writer in the Indianapolis area and a graduate of Ball State University. She leads worship for student and adult ministries and has over five years of knowledge and experience with 12-Step programs and Christian recovery. She is the devoted mother of two sons.